SCHOLASTIC

ALL NEW 100 LITERACY HOURS

YEAR 4

- Differentiated lesson plans
- Photocopiable extracts
- Covers the Early Learning Goals and NLS objectives

Celia Warren, Campbell Perry, Janet Perry, Nikki Gamble

CREDITS

Authors
Celia Warren,
Campbell Perry,
Janet Perry,
Nikki Gamble

Illustrations
Sarah Warburton

Series Designer
Joy Monkhouse

Editor
Kim Vernon

Designers
Andrea Lewis and
Erik Ivens

Assistant Editor
Catherine Gilhooly

Designed using Adobe InDesign

Published by Scholastic Ltd
Villiers House
Clarendon Avenue
Leamington Spa
Warwickshire CV32 5PR

www.scholastic.co.uk

Printed by Bell and Bain Ltd.

3456789 678901234

ACKNOWLEDGEMENTS

The publishers gratefully acknowledge permission to reproduce the following copyright material: **Laura Cecil Literary Agency** on behalf of the Estate of James Reeves for the use of 'Slowly' by James Reeves from *Complete Poems for Children* © 2001, The Estate of James Reeves (2001, Mammoth). **The Countryside Agency** for the use of material from their website http://www.countrysideaccess.gov.uk © 2004, The Countryside Agency All rights reserved. **Faber and Faber** for the use of 'The Coming of the Iron Man' by Ted Hughes from *The Iron Giant* by Ted Hughes ©1968, Ted Hughes (1968, Faber and Faber). **David Higham Associates** for the use of an extract from *Double Act (Playscript)* by Vicky Ireland based on the book *Double Act* by Jacqueline Wilson Playscript © 2004, Vicky Ireland (2004, Corgi Yearling). **Tony Mitton** for the use of 'Carpet' renamed 'Flying carpet' by Tony Mitton from *The Red and White Spotted Handkerchief* by Tony Mitton © 2000, Tony Mitton (2000, David Fickling Books). **Orion Publishing Group Ltd** for the use of an extract 'Snakes and Snails for Lunch' from *Don't Cook Cinderella* by Francesa Simon © 1996, 2005 Francesca Simon (First published in Great Britain in 1996 as *Big Class, Little Class* Orion Children's Books.) **Brian Patten** for the use of 'The Inside of Things' by Brian Patten from *Juggling with Gerbils* by Brian Patten © 2000, Brian Patten (2000, Puffin). **The Penguin Group (UK)** for the use of extracts from *Kasper in the Glitter* by Philip Ridley © 1994, Philip Ridley (1994, Viking). **The Random House Group** for the use of two extracts from *Double Act* by Jacqueline Wilson © 1995, Jacqueline Wilson (1995, Doubleday). **Jane A Russell** for the use of *The Wind* by Jane A Russell © 2005, Jane A Russell (2005, previously unpublished). **Telegraph Group Limited** for the use of 'Proud Penguin Promoted' by Tara Womersley from *The Daily Telegraph* 19th August 2001 © 2001, Telegraph Group Limited (2001, The Daily Telegraph). **3x1** on behalf of Highland Spring Limited for the use of an extract 'Water Cycle' from the website www.highlandspring.co.uk © Highland Spring Limited. **Walker Books Limited** for the use of an extract from *Meet Me by the Steelmen* by Theresa Tomlinson ©1997, Theresa Tomlinson (1997, Walker Books). **ticktock Media Ltd** for the use of an extract from *The Science of Searching for Life in Space* © 2004, ticktock Entertainment Ltd (2004, ticktock Media).

Every effort has been made to trace copyright holders for the works reproduced in this book, and the publishers apologise for any inadvertent omissions.
Due to the nature of the web, we cannot guarantee the content or links of any sites featured. We strongly recommend that teachers check websites before using them in the classroom.

British Library Cataloguing-in-Publication Data
A catalogue record for this book is available from the British Library.

ISBN 0-439-971-683
ISBN 978-0439-97168-3

Contents

ALL NEW 100 LITERACY HOURS: YEAR 4

About the series

The books in the updated *All New 100 Literacy Hours* series offer a set of completely new term-by-term lesson plans, complete with objectives and organisation grids and accompanied, where relevant with photocopiable texts and activity sheets. The series offers a core of material for the teaching of the English curriculum within the structure of the Literacy Hour, but now perfectly matches the recent NLS *Medium-Term Plans*, *Grammar for Writing*, and *Speaking, Listening and Learning* guidelines. The series also builds on current teaching ideas including the provision of activities to match children's preferred learning styles.

Using this book

The units of work

This book provides 100 literacy hours for Year 4 based on the *NLS Medium-Term Plans*, which either form a core scheme of work or can be used to supplement your existing planning. This core should be extended in several ways. For example:

- Repeating the sequence of lessons, but with different texts, for example, Term 1, Unit 1, *Meet Me by the Steelmen* could usefully be followed by a classic text on a ghostly and historical theme, such as Charles Dickens' short story, *The Signalman*.
- Adding additional texts, for example, Term 1, Unit 3, Poetry, is based on poems by James Reeves and Brian Patten. These poems might be well-complemented and extended by looking at poems by poets as diverse as Charles Causley and Ted Hughes.
- Giving extra time for the drafting and redrafting process. This is essential if it is to be done with the thoroughness recommended in *NLS* exemplification, for example, *Improving Writing: Writing Flier 1*.
- It is also well worth allowing more time for final presentation. An example is Term 1, Unit 5, Newspapers and Magazines, where the unit culminates in a class newspaper.

In addition to the above, tried-and-tested resources from previous schemes of work, other publications, or the original *100 Literacy Hours* series, can be used to supplement the new materials.

The lesson plans

The lesson plans should be seen as a source of ideas, not as a straitjacket, and should therefore be used flexibly. Most lessons plans can easily be adapted for rotational use by rotating the independent and guided activities. The number of guided activities that are possible in one week will depend on the number of available adults. When planning rotation, it is important to ensure that all children experience the key activities throughout the week. If following the linear model, guided activities will usually need to involve a guided version of the independent activity, otherwise children may miss out on key experiences.

Organisation of teaching units

Each term is divided into teaching units comprising between five and ten hours. Each of the units cluster the NLS text-, sentence- and word-level objectives. The units are organised as follows:

Unit overview

Introduction
Overview of each unit including ideas for extending units.

Organisation grid
Outlines the key activities for each lesson.

Key assessment opportunities
A bulleted list of key assessment opportunities. These will help you to plan assessment opportunities throughout each unit.

Unit lesson plans

Each unit of lesson plans is written with the following headings:

Objectives
NLS objectives including Speaking and listening emphases.

What you need
Provides a list of resources required for each lesson.

Shared work
Sets out the shared text-, sentence- and word-level work in each lesson. Some of these objectives are taught discretely, while others are integrated into the theme of the unit as the NLS recommends.

Guided work and Independent work
Every unit contains at least two suggestions for guided work to be used if the lessons plans are reorganised on a rotational basis. The lessons also include ideas for independent group, paired or individual activities. In some units, you may wish to re-organise these, along with the suggestions for guided work, on a rotational basis, for example, when a group set of books is being shared around the class.

Plenary
Sets out what to do in the whole-class plenary session.

Differentiation
Ideas for supporting more or less able children including ideas for peer and other adult support.

Links to the NLS Medium-term plans

The units provide clear links to the requirements of the NLS *Medium-Term Plans*. Genres are matched exactly with appropriate texts for the age group and the range of objectives covered, as shown on the grid for each term. Some of the word- and sentence-level objectives identified in the *Medium-Term Plans* have been relocated from the specified units to meet the needs of specific texts and the running order of the selected units.

Differentiation

In every lesson plan, suggestions for supporting the less able and stretching the more able are given. However, it is important to use these advisedly as a child may be 'less able' in some aspects of literacy, but 'more able' in others. These suggestions should be applied when appropriate to the individual child and not be automatically given to a predetermined group. Other important considerations are children's different learning styles, and the concept of 'multiple intelligences'. Children also need to experience working individually, in pairs, and in a range of larger groups, organised in different ways to meet different educational objectives. The number of groups will depend on class size, spread of ability and learning style. Try to ensure a balance of gender and personality type in each group, and don't hesitate to separate children who cannot work well together.

Assessment

Each unit includes a list of bullet points to help with the children's ongoing assessment. It is important to note that, these are not intended to replace National Curriculum assessment, but represent the 'bottom line' that all the children should have achieved by the end of the unit. If a number of children have failed to achieve satisfactory standards in any of the bulleted areas, then the unit may need to be revisited (with different resources).

Using the photocopiable resources

Where there is instruction to copy material from copyright texts, it is important that you ensure this is done within the limits of the copying licence of your school. If the children are using their own exercise books or paper for their answers, then all of the photocopiable resources are available for reuse.

Usually, the best way to share a resource with the class is to make a display version for an overhead projector or data projector. However, try to avoid this becoming routine. An effective alternative is to sit with the children in a circle and work together with a hard copy of the text, so that, where possible the children can engage with actual books.

Interactive whiteboard use

Permission is granted for those pages marked as photocopiable to be used in this way. Where third party material is used, permission for interactive whiteboard use must be obtained from the copyright holder or their licensor. This information can be found at the front of the book in the acknowledgements section.

Annotations

The methodology of analysing texts by annotation is used in this book. Annotations to texts are given in one margin only, without lines pointing to the textual features they describe. In this manner, the resource can be used both as an exemplar of annotations and as a blank resource on its own.

- To make blank resources, cover or fold back the annotations when photocopying. The annotations can be used in several ways:
- Write them 'live' on an enlarged version of the blank resource, adding lines from notes to text as appropriate, to demonstrate how to annotate a text.
- Read a text with the annotations covered, discuss key points, then reveal the annotations.
- Annotate the first part of a text for demonstration purposes then ask the children to complete the annotations for the rest of the text in the independent session.
- In an independent reading session, give the children a jumbled up version of the annotations and ask them to link them to the appropriate text features.
- In a plenary session, display the text and notes together at the same time and ask the children to add lines from notes to text as each point is raised in discussion.

Speaking and listening

When speaking and listening is one of the main focuses of the lessons, links are made to the Primary National Strategy's *Speaking, Listening and Learning* (DfES, 2003), and to the speaking and listening emphases within the *Medium-Term Planner*. These links are also highlighted in the objectives grid through the use of a logo .

Children will use speaking and listening as a process skill in every lesson. To encourage this, particular emphasis is given to children working with 'talk partners'. When a larger group is needed, 'talk partners' can join into fours. Groups of this size are ideal for discussion and collaborative work as they provide a range of opinion and yet are not too large to make full participation difficult. It is important to vary group organisation so that children experience working with different partners with different approaches or abilities.

Creativity

Recent reports have emphasised the importance of creativity, and creativity is embedded within many of the lessons this book. Creativity can also be encouraged by using some of the following ideas:

- Children as Real Writers - encourage children to see themselves as real writers writing for real purposes. This means giving them a strong sense of audience and purpose, using redrafting techniques and finding a way of 'publishing' completed work.
- Writing Journals - encourage the children to write something in their journal every day. This can be anything they like - diary entry, story, poem, exploration of a problem, and so on. This is the one place where grammar, and punctuation do not matter. The aim is to develop writing fluency, such as, a free flow between thought and written page.
- First-Hand Experiences - many NLS writing tasks are responses to texts. Balance this by using stimulating 'real-life' starting points such as visits, visitors, artefacts, and so on.
- Experimentation - encourage the children to play with ideas, and explore alternatives. Positively encourage them to suggest alternative tasks.
- Writing Materials - provide inspiring media such as paper in various colours and sizes; a variety of pens and pencils (for example, felt-tipped pens, calligraphic pens); rulers; scissors; glue; DTP and presentation software; a clip art library; a colour printer.

Learning styles

Researchers have identified three different learning styles: auditory, kinaesthetic and visual. Most children will use a mixture of all three styles, but in some children, one style will predominate. Many lessons in this book offer specific opportunities for different learning styles.

Media and ICT

There have been major advances in media and ICT. We need to give more emphasis to media education and ICT in the primary classroom. This can be done by showing film versions of books and documentaries on non-fiction topics, and by ensuring that, every time writing takes place, at least one group is writing on a word-processor and that children take it in turns to do their research via the internet.

TERM 1

Medium-term plan/ *All New 100 Literacy Hours* unit	Text level	Sentence level	Word level	Number of hours	Text(s)	Links to GfW, S&L	Outcome
Narrative: plot	T2 T9 T3 T10 T4 T15	S1 S4 S2 S3	W4 W5 W6	5	***Meet Me by the Steelmen*** by Theresa Tomlinson	**GfW:** 20-23 **S&L:** 37	A whole-class story
Narrative: character and setting	T1 T11 T2 T12	S2 S3	W11 W15	5	***Double Act*** by Jacqueline Wilson	**GfW:** 22 **S&L:** 37	Invention/description of characters/ settings
Poetry	T7 T8 T14	S2 S3 S4 S5	W7 W11 W12	5	'Slowly' by James Reeves; 'The Inside of Things' by Brian Patten	**GfW:** 21 **S&L:** 37	Poem based on shared texts; children's original poems
Plays	T5 T6 T13	S2 S4		5	***Double Act (Playscript)*** by Vicky Ireland; 'Snakes and Snails for Lunch' from ***Don't Cook Cinderella*** by Francesca Simon	**GfW:** 21 **S&L:** 38, 40	Extended scenes for a play/performance of a play
Newspapers/Magazines	T16 T20 T17 T21 T18 T23 T19 T24	S2 S5	W3 W12 W4 W7 W11	10	Newspaper articles ; 'Fido and the doggie dentures' by Celia Warrren	**GfW:** 24 **S&L:** 39	News stories/advertisements
Instructions	T22 T23 T25 T26	S1 S2	W10 W11	5	'The Countryside Code' by The Countryside Agency	**GfW:** 20 **S&L:** 39	Sets of instructions
Reports	T17 T26 T18 T27 T19	S1 S2 S4	W3 W9 W11	5	Texts on the wind and origami	**GfW:** 21 **S&L:** 37	Written reports

TERM 2

Medium-term plan/ *All New 100 Literacy Hours* unit	Text level	Sentence level	Word level	Number of hours	Text(s)	Links to GfW, S&L	Outcome
Narrative setting	T1 T4 T2 T10 T3 T13	S1	W1 W4	5	***Kasper in the Glitter*** by Philip Ridley; 'I asked the little boy who cannot see', Anon; ***The Iron Giant*** by Ted Hughes	**GfW:** 26 **S&L:** 41, 44	Comparison of texts; writing on setting, character, event
Audience	T8 T9 T12	S2	W2 W9	5		**GfW:** 27 **S&L:** 41	A writer's brief; book chapters
Poetry	T4 T11 T5 T13 T6 T7	S1	W6 W11	5	'Flying carpet' by Tony Mitton; 'The Splendour Falls' by Alfred Lord Tennyson	**GfW:** 26 **S&L:** 41, 43	Adaptations of shared poems; oral presentation of a poem; presentation of poems using presentation software
Notes and information texts	T14 T18 T15 T21 T16 T22 T17 T23	S3 S4	W15	10	Astronomy text	**GfW:** 28	Wall chart including diagrams, using research skills including a research frame
Explanation texts	T19 T20 T24 T25	S4	W4	5	Texts on the classical guitar and the water cycle	**GfW:** 29 **S&L:** 41, 43	A textual explanation of a process, based on a diagrammatic explanation

Medium-term plan/ *All New 100 Literacy Hours* unit	Text level	Sentence level	Word level	Number of hours	Text(s)	Links to GfW, S&L	Outcome
Poetry	T4 T9 T5 T10 T6 T14 T7 T15	S1	W3 W4	5	'It's a dog's life', 'Reddy Neddy?', 'If Stan was a man', 'Clapping rhyme', 'Skipping rhyme', 'Bobdog', 'Love at First Sight!', 'I am Cat' and 'Face' by Campbell Perry	**GfW:** 30 **S&L:** 46	Extension of shared poems; children's own poems; reviews of poems
Issues and dilemmas 1	T1 T11 T3 T20 T10 T24	S1 S2	W4	5	'Amul and the drum' re-told by Campbell Perry	**GfW:** 31 **S&L:** 44, 47	Children's stories containing dilemmas
Issues and dilemmas 2	T8 T20 T9 T24 T12	S2 S3		5	'The Dreamweaver's child' re-told by Campbell Perry	**GfW:** 31 **S&L:** 44, 47	Reviews of stories; improvisation of shared text; alternative endings
Narrative reading and writing	T1 T11 T2 T12 T3 T13	S2 S3 S4	W1 W10 W2 W12 W3 W13 W6 W14 W8	10	'The twelve stones', 'The knight's ten-thousand jewels' re-told by Celia Warren	**GfW:** 32 **S&L:** 44	Children's own stories; extension of shared texts
Note-taking and discussion	T16 T23 T17 T20 T21	S4		5	Texts on fox hunting, litter louts	**GfW:** 32 **S&L:** 46	School uniform debate, children's for and against texts
Persuasion	T18 T19 T25	S3 S4	W12 W15	5	Scam email text, mobile phone advertisement	**GfW:** 31	Persuasive letters, advertisements, jingles

Narrative: plot

Unit one is primarily concerned with plot development and the pacing/passage of time in narrative, and so character and setting are also considered in relation to the plot. The chosen novel is contemporary with a historical component. Its real-life setting is Sheffield's *Meadow Hall* shopping mall, built on the site of a former steelworks. Try to display steel cutlery marked *Made in Sheffield* and explain the importance of the industry in its heyday. The five hour-long plans should be spread over a two-week period, allowing time to read and study the whole book, as well as plan and write a story. This unit also covers aspects of Units 20 - 23 of *Grammar for Writing*.

Hour	Shared text-level work	Shared sentence-/ word-level work	Guided work	Independent work	Plenary
1 People, place and plot	Reading the first chapter of the novel. Discuss narrative order and characteristics of main characters.	Identifying changes in tense.	Practising new spellings.	Preparing summary of main plot and characters.	Discussion of plot and character.
2 Telling stories	Exploring chronology in narrative, looking for time jumps.	Identifying adverbs. Re-reading work checking tenses and coherence.	Telling stories and changing tenses.	Using strong verbs in own writing. Check for consistency in tenses.	Discussing and employing use of past and present tenses.
3 Chapter by chapter	Brainstorming story ideas. Identifying stages of telling.	Investigating homophones.	Using chapter titles to pace narrative.	Writing opening paragraphs of own story.	Review opening sentences. Revise homophones.
4 Detailed paragraphs	Investigating narrative order. Exploring the position, degree and use of detail.	Spelling words with double consonant.	Writing in paragraphs.	Revising spellings. Using adverbs and strong verbs.	Practise oral spellings of words with double consonants. Recall details from text.
5 Loose ends and resolutions	Looking at chronology of novel.	Revising purpose and structure of tenses and adverbs.	Developing and concluding own stories using paragraphs.	Manipulating tenses in writing. Identifying adverbs.	Listen to and comment on children's writing. Reinforce adverbs.

Key assessment opportunities

- Do the children break up their own story writing into meaningful paragraphs?
- Are they using strong verbs to vivid effect?
- Can they choose and position an appropriate adverb in the correct position within a sentence?
- Can they switch between past and present tenses, recognising the terms?
- Are they able to draw quotes from a text to support opinions about the narrative?

Objectives

NLS

T2: To identify characteristics of main characters and justify opinions from text.
T3: To explore narrative order and stages in the plot.
S2: To recognise and identify change in tense and its narrative purpose.
W4, W5: To practise new spellings and words with double consonants.

What you need

- Copies of class novel *Meet Me by the Steelmen* by Theresa Tomlinson
- photocopiable pages 17 and 18.

People, place and plot

Shared text-level work

- Provide historical background to the real-life story setting (see Introduction).
- Read the opening paragraph. Why does the author use the personal pronoun, *they*, before we know *who*?
- Continue the first chapter and sum up the plot so far. Make notes from the children's responses and compare with those on photocopiable page 17. Discuss the level of importance of details, for example, the musical band adds atmosphere and provides a reason for Jenny to leave Stevie alone. It does not in itself pertain to the plot.
- Look at the contents page. Discuss the value of chapter titles: plot reminders; appetite-whetters; aids to relocating key events.

Shared sentence- and word-level work

- Examine the presentation of text – mostly past tense, first person. Is the narrator the most central character? Support opinions by close reference to the text. What effect is achieved by using the first person?
- Where and why does the narrative dip into the present tense. Who is the common subject? For example, on page eight: *He's weird, my brother*. Can the children find more examples?
- Write the word *Sheffield* and ask the children to find smaller words within it. Write *she* and *field* close enough to just leave space for the missing *f*. Read them as *she-field*, to hear the long *e*. Explain how doubling the consonant shortens the vowel. What else is needed to write the name correctly? (Capital *S*.)

Guided and independent work

- Ask the children to read on, over a number of lessons. On photocopiable page 17, make concise notes to sum up each chapter's main events and plot development.
- Using photocopiable page 18, ask the children to describe characters in the present tense. Support statements with quotations from the text. Locate the example on the worksheet, and read the full quotation. Explain how to quote opening and closing words, using an ellipsis to indicate omitted text.
- Practise spelling *field* and *Sheffield* through the *Look>Say>Cover>Write>Check* strategy.
- Search the text for other double consonant words, including proper nouns.

Plenary

- Invite the children to read their chapter summaries. Which notes are vital to the plot and which are subsidiary details?
- Listen to the character descriptions. Are they written in the present tense? Do their quotations support their conclusions?

Differentiation

Less able

- Ask an adult helper to read aloud and act as scribe.

More able

- Based on plot development, invent alternative chapter titles.
- Add *Frank* to the table of characters. Write about him in present tense.

Telling stories

Objectives

NLS

T3: To explore chronology in narrative, noticing how time jumps are achieved and how detail levels vary.
S1, S2, S3: To re-read own work to check for coherence, with special attention to use of tenses and powerful verbs.
S4: To identify adverbs.

S&L

37 Speaking: To speak audibly and listen actively to one another.

What you need

- Enlarged copy of photocopiable page 19
- highlighter pen
- children's thesauruses.

Shared text-level work

- Read the extract on photocopiable page 19 with the children following the text.
- Point out that, here, the use of ellipsis indicates *a passage of time*.
- Choose two children to read aloud the direct speech in role, demonstrating the pauses.
- Ask the children to identify time expressions or devices that denote an interval. Highlight these. Which suggests the longest interval? How do three stars between paragraphs compare to three dots between words?
- Compare the lengthy description of Ethel's arrival with the line showing the passage of time (*A week went by...*). Examine levels of detail in the telling.
- Identify verbs in the passage. Which are strongest, especially in relating movement or stance? (Jenny) *crept, frowned*, (Ethel) *leaning, clutched*, (scent) *drifted*.
- Identify adverbs – *really, sleepily* – draw attention to the root word, *real* + *ly*; note how the *y* in *sleepy* changes to *i*.
- Tell the children the following story or a similar personal experience:

> Recently, I took my elderly neighbour, Mabel, shopping for a loaf of bread. So many bright things caught her eye in the precinct that she popped into all sorts of extravagant shops. After a while, spent looking at fancy goods, she dithered over which buttons to buy for her cardigan. Eventually, I drove her home – only to discover, that in her excitement, Mabel had completely forgotten to buy bread.

- Point out that your story is in the past tense – list sample verbs. Ask individuals to make a statement about Mabel in the present tense.

Guided and independent work

- Ask the children to relate a story to a partner; an event that they experienced centring on a family member or close friend. Explain that the listener should be able to make some comment about the character based on the events.
- Ask them to write their account in the past tense and to include a present tense character comment in mid-narrative. Encourage the use of time expressions.
- Remind the children to check their punctuation and tense. Use thesauruses to strengthen verbs.

Plenary

- Make comments on the children's writing that, themselves, demonstrate change of tense: *Mel wrote that well. She is a careful worker.*
- Invite comments from the children. In their opinion was any part too detailed or too concise?

Differentiation

Less able

- Act as scribe as the children tell their stories. Help them to discern how a character's reaction to events points to their character.

More able

- Suggest the children start a collection of similar accounts. Think up a suitable title, for example *Family fun and fables.*

Chapter by chapter

Objectives

NLS

T9: To use different ways of planning stories – brainstorming, notes, diagrams.

T10: To plan a story identifying the stages of its telling.

W6: To distinguish spellings and meanings of common homophones.

S&L

37 Speaking: To make structured, extended contributions, speaking audibly with explicit meaning, listening actively.

What you need

- Class copies of the novel *Meet Me by the Steelmen*
- whiteboards and pens
- planning paper.

Shared text-level work

- Write and read aloud the title of the novel. Ask the children why the author chose it: for meaning – the larger than life sculpture is an obvious meeting place; for memorable sound: alliteration and repetition of the long *ee* sound.
- Rewrite the title substituting *Meat* and *Steal* in place of their homophones. Discuss the nonsensical change of meaning.
- Following on from previous work on chapter titles, ask the children to plot a story that takes place in a shopping centre.
- Re-read the opening paragraph of *Meet Me by the Steelmen*. Remind the children how the pronoun *they* is used before we know who *they* are. How does this encourage us to read on?
- Write the following chapter titles, leaving space for notes:

  Meet me in the Precinct
  Something's Not Right
  Lost!
  The Last Bus Home.

Using these as springboards, brainstorm ideas to plot a story. If possible, use local historical features, adapting chapter titles.

- Collect ideas for two to three main characters. Why, where and when are they meeting?
- What is wrong? How do they find out? How does it affect them?
- Who/what is lost? How are they involved? Who will solve the problem?
- Consider the final chapter title that concludes their story. Do the characters miss the bus? What are the implications? Do they meet someone on the bus home who solves the mystery? Is the bus late or is the journey unusual?
- Ensure that the children listen to each other's ideas. Provide paper for individual notes or plot variations for later use.

Shared word- and sentence-level work

- Demonstrate using *meat* and *steal* in sentences that do make sense.
- Invite suggestions for further ee/ea homophonic words: *see/sea*; *tea/tee*; *been/bean*; *week/weak*, *cheep/cheap*, listing them side by side.

Guided and independent work

- Challenge children to put paired homophones into sentences that show their meaning.
- Use the chapter titles as headings for individual story-planning notes.
- Ask the children to begin writing the whole-class story. Draft an opening paragraph that will draw in the reader. Allow individuals to decide to write in the first or third person. Use the past tense.

Plenary

- Review children's opening paragraphs. Check for consistency of tense. Could any opening sentences be improved? Invite children to explain their suggestions.
- Listen to some homophone sentences. Are the meanings clear?

Differentiation

Less able

- Produce a cloze procedure of sentences for homophones to be inserted. Supply dictionaries.

More able

- Encourage the children to complete the first chapter of their story, using paragraphs.

Detailed paragraphs

Objectives
NLS
T4: To explore narrative order; identify and map out the main stages of the story: introduction - build-up - climax - resolution.
T15: To use paragraphs in story writing to organise and sequence the narrative.
W5: To spell two-syllable words containing double consonants.

What you need
- Photocopiable pages 19 and 20
- story planning notes from novel chapter headings and the children's own stories.

Shared text-level work

- Remind the children of the chapter headings of *Meet Me by the Steelmen*. Tell them to decide how these might be grouped to show four stages to the story plot: *introduction, build-up, climax(es), resolution*.
- *Introduction* – at the end of which we should know the setting and all main characters and the opening situation. All the main characters have been introduced by the end of Chapter 2, *The Steelman's Pot*. Even the woman who looks after the steelwork cats has been mentioned by Chapter 2, although readers do not encounter her again, until within a page of the last chapter.
- Discuss which chapters would fit into the remaining three categories. Is there one or more resolution?

Shared sentence-level work

- Re-read the last paragraph from the extract from Chapter 3, *What's Snap?* What does the detail of Ethel's outfit tell us about how important the trip to Meadow Hall is to her? How does this influence the reader's view of the trip?
- How important is detail in the build-up and other stages in the story?
- Ask the children to search the text for further details that have relevance to the whole story. Examine how these keep the reader's interest and make the story realistic and convincing.
- Why are the details about the steelmen's appearance particularly important to the plot?

Guided and independent work

- Remind the children that in Hour 3 they made notes for their own whole-class story. Ask them to return to these and decide which chapter(s) of their accounts of the class-story (allowing for individual variations) will cover the four stages.
- Ask the children to draft a paragraph for inclusion in the build-up of the story. Explain that extra detail at this stage can draw the reader in to feel involved. It can mean that readers take more notice of what is happening in the story at this stage.
- Emphasise the importance of detail in the children's writing. Encourage them to use strong verbs and occasional adverbs.
- Remind the children how in Hour 1 they practised the spelling of *Sheffield*. Point out that there are many words with a double consonant in the middle. Use photocopiable page 20 to practise these spellings.

Plenary

- Invite the children to spell dictated double-consonant words orally.
- Ask the children if they can recall details from any scenes in the book. Why do they feel they remembered them? Why did the author include them?

Differentiation

Less able
- Provide large flash cards of double-consonant words for children to copy.
- Make individual copies of the text extract on photocopiable page 19. Ask the children to underline, read and spell aloud any words containing a double consonant.

More able
- Invite the children to write further episodes for their own story, arranging then in order.

Loose ends and resolutions

Objectives

NLS
T4: To look at the chronology of novels, especially the resolution.
T15: To use paragraphs in story writing to organise and sequence the narrative.
S2: To revise understanding and purpose and structure of tenses.
S4: To identify and use adverbs.

What you need

- Photocopiable page 19
- copies of class novel
- children's own story notes and drafts from previous hours.

Shared text-level work

- Look closely at the newspaper report in Chapter 3. Why does it begin with an ellipsis? Can children suggest what the missing words might have been? (For example: *Police are investigating... Everyone is puzzled by...* and so on) In what tense is the report written? How does it differ from the remaining narrative?
- Read the last two chapters of the novel. How would Frank feel at hearing Stevie's closing words? Is this a satisfying end to the story for all the characters? Are all loose ends tied up? Discuss why, with reference to the text to support opinions.
- What values does the story promote? Back up opinions with text references and quotations.
- Remind the children of the plot of their own class story and read some selected passages. Review the planning notes for how their story will continue. How will they tie in loose ends? How will their characters feel at the end? Will any have changed their opinions, feelings or values?
- Look again, briefly, at photocopiable page 19. Draw attention to the use and purpose of paragraphs. Remind the children of the use of time-phrases at the onset of the last two paragraphs of the extract.

Shared sentence-level work

- Can the children identify the adverbs on pages 62–63 of the novel? (They include: *solemnly, terribly, steadily*).
- Encourage the children to add adverbs to their texts, in order to qualify verbs, reflecting character and action.

Guided and independent work

- Ask the children to find adverbs in the novel. Write the sentence in which they occur, underlining the adverb. Rewrite the sentence, changing it to the present tense – *Stevie nods solemnly*, and so on.
- Ask children to finish writing their own stories, making sure they tie in loose ends and have a satisfying ending. Remind them to ensure that the reader knows how the main characters feel – have they or their lives changed in any way?
- Remind the children to make use of paragraphs within their story. Re-read and reorder paragraphs as appropriate.
- Ask the children to write a newspaper report about an event within their class story, written in the present tense. Can this be usefully included in the finished narrative?

Differentiation

Less able
- Use sticky notes to mark adverbs for the children to locate in the text.

More able
- Ask the children to substitute alternative adverbs in the copied sentences.

Plenary

- Listen to some of the children's story endings. Invite comments on which work well and why.
- Play an adverbs game orally. Taking turns around the class, find adverbs to qualify the author's writing ability, as displayed in the class novel; each child is to speak a full sentence, inserting an adverb: *The author, Theresa Tomlinson, writes admirably; beautifully, concisely, descriptively*, and so on.

Meet Me by the Steelmen

by Theresa Tomlinson

Chapter summaries

Chapter	Summary of plot development
The Statues	Meadow Hall: Statues of steelmen. Mum, Jenny + little bro. Stevie looking round. Band, crowds, policemen. Apparent break-in at Yorkshire Pudd. shop – hole in metal shutter. Stevie thinks he sees one statue move.
The Steelman's Pot	
What's Snap?	
Another One Hooked!	
A Steelman's Picnic	
Oven Bottom Cakes	
Heat and Dirt	
Just Like Cokey	
Can We Get Home?	
Bessie Bessemer's Children	

Characters' characteristics

■ Use the present tense to write short sentences about each character's personality, just as Jenny sometimes does when describing Stevie.

He really understands
a lot for a little kid.

Illustration © Anthony Lewis

■ Support your sentences with direct quotations. If your quotation is more than one sentence, or a paragraph, show the *beginning and end words* from the passage, with an ellipsis *(...)* showing the position of words you have left out.

Character	My comments	Page reference	Quotation
Jenny	Jenny can act on impulse but is generally reliable. She trusts her brother.	10	"I turned and looked at Stevie ... Don't move!"
Ethel			
Stevie			
Mother			

What's Snap?

"What's snap?" said Stevie. "Is it food?"

He does ask some crazy questions, just when you're least expecting them.

I clicked my fingers in his face. "That's snap!" I told him, and we all laughed.

* * *

Later that night I crept up to bed trying not to wake Stevie. I needn't have bothered. He called me into his room.

"Jenny ... Jenny. Come here! What's snap really? Tell me!"

I frowned and sat down on his bed. "What do you mean?" I asked.

"The big man," said Stevie, "the one that's got great long scissors in his hand ... he spoke to me. He said, "Where's our snap?"

"Spoke?" I said, "Spoke and pulled faces?"

I was very puzzled and a little scared.

Stevie was really imagining strange things. I just shook my head.

A week went by and then the following Monday morning we heard a sharp knock on our door. It was very early, before we'd even got out of bed. I went sleepily downstairs to answer it, hoping it meant the postman must have a parcel for us. Stevie had got there before me. He always got out of bed at the crack of dawn and went down to watch the telly. He opened the door, still wearing his pyjamas. It was not the postman, it was Ethel, leaning on her walking stick and all dressed up in a smart black suit. She clutched a cream leather handbag and wore a soft cream hat with a sparkly brooch pinned on to it. A faint scent of violets drifted in through our door.

From "Meet Me by the Steelmen" by Theresa Tomlinson (1997, Walker Books Ltd).

Seeing double

- All these words have a double-letter in the middle.
- Read and spell each word aloud.
- Cover – write – check each spelling.
- Select each word to fit into a sentence below.
- Read each sentence to check it makes sense.

puzzle	giggle	struggle	bottle	middle
bottom	Sheffield	hobble	kitten	supper

- All these mi**ss**ing words have a double le**tt**er in the middle.

She lived in a house at the ____________ of our street.

Cokey was a tiny grey and white ____________ .

The ____________ was filled with lemon barley water.

Meadow Hall shopping centre is in ____________ .

I heard someone ____________ behind me.

For ____________ they ate stew and dumplings.

It was a ____________ to carry everything.

Ethel cannot walk well she can only ____________ .

No-one knew what had happened. It was a complete ____________ .

- Test a friend to see if you and they can spell these words without looking.

UNIT 2

Narrative: character and setting

Both novels chosen for Units 1 and 2 involve change - changing times, changing relationships and changing feelings. Both are written in the first person in a domestic setting. This unit, for which five hours are suggested, covers a two-week period, allowing time to complete the reading of both stories. Hour 1 follows up on Unit 1's *Meet Me by the Steelmen*. Others introduce and work with Jacqueline Wilson's short novel, *Double Act*, which has scope for looking at other genres of writing, including letters. This unit also covers aspects of *Grammar for Writing* unit 22.

Hour	Shared text-level work	Shared sentence-/ word-level work	Guided work	Independent work	Plenary
1 Love 'em or loathe 'em	Investigating how characters are built up through small details.	Using verbs to create a vivid image rather than adjectives.	Creating a character.	Using strong verbs.	Checking how vividly narrative conveys a picture and evokes feelings.
2 Double Act	Looking at how settings and characteristics are conveyed.	Examining how tense relates to structure and purpose.	Identify characteristics by close reference to text.	Recognising tense changes and the rationale behind them.	Making deductions to reinforce textual clues about character.
3 First person accounts	Supporting own views by relocating textual justification.	Looking at powerful verbs that strengthen images.	Writing independently, linking own experience to stories.	Using verbs evocatively and imaginatively.	Drawing attention to powerful verbs and their effect.
4 Fleshing out characters	Observing how readers respond to detailed characters.	Testing if words are verbs by changing tenses.	Developing further characters.	Making characters interact through some form of communication.	Discuss written devices used and whether successful.
5 Feeling changes, changing feelings	Focusing on how character detail evokes sympathy in the reader.	Shared reading of textual extract with close attention to verbs.	Using vivid verbs within description to reflect feelings of characters and evoke reader sympathy.	Using physical description to reinforce character's feelings.	Assessing effectiveness of verbs in description to evoke sympathy.

Key assessment opportunities

- Are the children able to support their views by direct appropriate reference to the text?
- Can they use detail to build up a character's personality without using simple adjectives to describe them?
- Can they discern characteristics from close study of descriptive details and characters' reactions to their situations?
- Are they confident in recognising and handling verbs?

Love 'em or loathe 'em

Objectives

NLS

T1: To investigate how characters are built up from small details.

T11: To write character sketches, focusing on small details to evoke sympathy or dislike.

S3: To use powerful verbs.

What you need

- Photocopiable extract from *Meet Me by the Steelmen* on photocopiable page 19
- a collection of personal objects that relate to different genders/age-groups.

Shared text-level work

- Return to the extract from Unit 1 (photocopiable page 19). Tell the children that someone who read this extract has made these comments about the character, Jenny: *She has a sense of humour. She is a good listener. She is open-minded.* Ask the children if they agree and can support their opinions with reference to the text.
- Reinforce that these aspects of Jenny's character are not explicit; we infer them from the character's actions, manner and behaviour.
- Remind the children of verbs used in the text that create a picture, implying an adjective, such as *I frowned* – meaning that Jenny was *puzzled* and concerned.
- Do the children like Jenny? Why? Do they think the author intended the readers to like her? How did she succeed?

Shared sentence-level work

- Arrange the collected items and ask the children to whom they might belong. Together, invent a character, giving him or her an age and a name.
- List adjectives to describe the person, prompting the children with questions, such as, *Does this belong to a quiet or talkative person? How old are they? Are they courteous or off-hand or rude?*
- Having collected a few adjectives, decide on a location: *Where is this person? What are they doing today?*
- Together, construct a sentence that tells us something about the character, based on an adjective, but using strong verbs. Start by choosing a couple of items: a shirt button, an empty pencil case. For example, *Jack: careless, untidy; setting: school classroom: Jack's pencils were spread across the table, their empty case collapsed on the floor. He crayoned madly, not noticing that one elbow obscured half the page that Sam was trying to read.*

Guided and independent work

- Ask the children to pick a new object and decide whose it is. Why is the object important to that character? Ask them to choose a setting and an adjective or two to describe the character, as in the shared sentence-level activity.
- Ask the children to write a sentence about their character, showing but not telling what the adjectives are. Encourage them to use strong verbs that convey a vivid picture, such as *collapsed* and *obscured*.
- Challenge them to make the class like or dislike their character through their writing.

Plenary

- Ask the children to read their sentences for others to guess the adjectives describing the characters that their sentences were trying to convey. How did they manage to influence the listeners' feelings towards their characters?

Differentiation

Less able

- Ask the children to copy the shared sentence-level text and expand on the character with follow-up sentences.

More able

- Challenge the children to create a second character and make them interact with the first in such a way as to show their personality traits.

Double Act

Objectives

NLS

T1: To investigate how settings and characters are built up from small details.
T2: To identify the main characteristics of the key characters, drawing on the text to justify views and using this information to predict actions.
S2: To develop awareness of how tense relates to purpose and structure of text.
W11: To define familiar vocabulary in own words.

What you need

- Photocopiable page 27
- copies of the novel *Double Act.*

Shared text-level work

- Explain that the extract opens the short novel, *Double Act*, by Jacqueline Wilson. Later in the chapter, it is revealed that twins, Ruby and Garnet, are keeping an account of their life.
- Establish who is speaking first. Whose words are in italics? Ask what *identical* means. Beyond appearance, are the twins alike? Ask the children to support their opinions with reference to the text.
- Ask who else is introduced? What do we learn about them and the setting?
- Can the children identify the three locations mentioned in this extract? Which most involve the twins?
- Read quotations from further on in the story. Can the children deduce which twin is speaking?

  Of course we want to be actresses. (Ruby)
  You haven't written down your *secrets. You've written down mine.* (Garnet)
  I hate changes. I want every day to be the same. (Garnet)
  I don't know why you're so shy. I *never feel shy.* (Ruby)
- Ask the children to anticipate whether Ruby will continue to dominate Garnet. Do we expect the characters' experiences to change them?

Shared word- and sentence-level work

- Write the word: *accounts.* Consider its meanings. Can the children explain for what sort of accounts the blank book was originally intended?
- Establish the tense of the extract – this is how life is *now* for the twins and is setting the scene for the reader.
- As the story continues, more is revealed about the twins' earlier life. Ask what tense the children would expect for that purpose?

Guided and independent work

- Based on the extract, ask the children to sketch the twins looking identical. Write these adjectives and ask the children to allocate them to each twin: *greedy, quiet, bossy, yielding, untidy, shy.*
- Ask them to write a direct quotation in support of each adjective.
- Ask the children to write one or two adjectives that describe Dad, with quotations to back them up.
- Encourage the children to read to the end of chapter one and write the first sentence they find written in the past tense, explaining why the tense has changed.

Differentiation

Less able

- Guide the children to work in pairs. Prompt them to make deductions from textual quotes.

More able

- Ask the children to write a few quotations about Gran using adjectives to describe her personality.

Plenary

- Return to the text and re-read a few sentences reinforcing how the author *shows* us aspects of the characters and leaves us to *deduce* what this means they are like.
- Ask questions such as *Is Dad a morning person? Is he lazy/hard-working?* How do we know?

First person accounts

Objectives

NLS

T2: To identify the main characteristics of the key characters, drawing on the text to justify views.

T12: To write independently, linking own experience to situations in stories.

S3: To identify and use powerful verbs.

W15: To use joined handwriting.

S&L

37 Speaking: To make structured comments reflecting own views supported by textual evidence.

What you need

- Photocopiable page 27
- copies of *Double Act*, one between two children.

Shared text-level work

- Return to the shared text from Hour 2. Ask the children what effect the journal-style has on revealing information about the characters? Is it more direct than in descriptive narrative?
- Can they determine if Garnet agrees with all Ruby's representations? Ask, how reliable and accurate is a *first person* account?
- Garnet's contributions are very limited. Can we tell if her comments are more or less reliable than Ruby's, even from so few words? Discuss the importance of context.
- Ask the children to continue reading the story aloud, in turn, around the class. Have stronger readers read Ruby's accounts and less confident readers, Garnet's, while others follow the text.
- Discuss the twins' opinion of Rose. Compare Gran's opinion. Ask the children to find evidence from the text to support their views.

Shared sentence-level work

- Look closely at the use of expressive verbs in the extract's final paragraph.
- Ask the children to describe how *charge* differs from *run.* To demonstrate *hunch up,* ask why Jacqueline Wilson did not simply write *Garnet will read for hours*? What does this stronger expression reveal about Garnet's *attitude*? Ask them what *shoves on his clothes and then dashes off* reveals about Dad.

Guided and independent work

- Arrange the children in pairs. Ask each to write a first-person present-tense paragraph about their partner. Explain that they should adopt Ruby's confident style. Remind the children to use imaginative, evocative verbs and to use joined-up handwriting.
- After ten minutes, ask partners to swap and read each other's account. Invite each to write one short statement, adopting Garnet's put-upon style, that refutes or qualifies something that their partner says, such as, *I do like chips, but not every day* or *Actually, I AM good at maths!*
- Ask the children to imagine that they are in the story, as the Barker Twins' triplet, choosing an appropriate name, such as *Topaz* or *Amethyst.* In role, write a few paragraphs for the journal. For context, either use an event from the story or invent a new one. Remind the children to ensure that the reader learns something about their character, and about their feelings towards at least one main character.

Plenary

- Ask the children to read some of their accounts. What do others learn of their personality and tastes? Draw attention to the use of powerful verbs, showing something beyond the superficial action, as in *hunches up* and *shoves on.*

Differentiation

Less able

- Discuss their new character with the children, inviting them to talk in role as a writing springboard.

More able

- Challenge the children to dramatise an episode to present to the class.

Fleshing out characters

Objectives

NLS

T1: To identify how the reader responds to detailed characters and settings.

T11: To write character sketches, focusing on small details to evoke sympathy or dislike.

S2: To understand that one test as to whether a word is a verb is whether or not the tense can be changed.

What you need

- Photocopiable pages 19 (from Unit 1) and 27.

Shared text- and sentence-level work

- Following on from Hour 3, ask the children to share some of their opening sentences. Write good examples on the board, highlighting effective verbs.
- Return to the shared texts from *Meet Me by the Steelmen* and *Double Act*. Ask the children to recall the settings of each scene: both domestic; both involving siblings' interaction. Ask which is primarily scene-setting and which carries the plot forward.
- Find examples from each text, examining how each involves conversation - one explicitly, and the other through recorded dialogue. Discuss how conversation reveals something about the characters' relationship.

Shared word-level work

- Identify the direct-speech tag words in the *What's Snap?* extract: *said, told, called, asked.* Ask the children what sort of words these are. Experiment changing tense to establish that they are verbs.
- Show how direct speech may have no tag word, when the action clarifies who is speaking, such as: *He called me into his room. "Jenny ..."*
- Ask the children to remind you what device shows who is the narrator in *Double Act* (alternating regular font/italics).
- Discuss how the characters' conversation can tell us about their personalities, making us warm or cool towards them. Do we feel sorry for any of the characters in these extracts? For example, do we sympathise with Stevie's need to be believed? With Jenny's sense of responsibility as the older child? With Ruby's need to speak for herself and her twin? For Garnet's need to express her differences?
- Explain the importance, when writing, to make the reader dislike aspects of a character, of the character always having some likeable qualities that the reader can relate to - some saving graces.

Guided and independent work

- Following on from the work on characters in Hour 1, ask the children to develop a second character to interact with their first. Ensure that they understand that the second character must somehow contrast with the first.
- Ask the children to plan a situation for their characters, using the shared texts for inspiration: one trying to convince the other of something unbelievable; one bossing the other.
- Within their setting, ask the children to place their characters in a conversational scenario. They may use direct speech, alternating journal-writing, a phone conversation, emails, chatting over a fence, passing notes in class - anything where the characters interact, where their mutual response helps the reader learn more about them.

Differentiation

Less able

- Help the children to invent a second character through speaking in role with them.

More able

- Ask the children to begin to develop a story plot, carried mainly by character interaction.

Plenary

- Listen to some of the children's writing. Discuss how effectively they have developed their characters and what devices they have used.

Feeling changes, changing feelings

Objectives

NLS
T1: To investigate how characters are built up from small details, and the reader's response.
T11: To write character sketches, focusing on small details to evoke sympathy.
S3: To identify and use powerful verbs.

S&L
37 Speaking: To describe and discuss characters including reference to small details in the text.

What you need

- Copies of the novel, *Double Act*
- photocopiable page 28.

Shared text- and sentence-level work

- Discuss how circumstances cause characters to change and develop. *Double Act* is more than a story about being a twin, it is about feelings – especially feelings related to coping with change.
- Draw a time-line showing the twins' life. Ask the children to pinpoint major changes in the twins' lives: *birth; mother's death; starting school; Rose's arrival; moving house/changing school* ... Continue, making the timeline fork where the twins split – where they learn that Garnet will go to the boarding school without Ruby, that is, *before* she actually goes.
- Together, look closely at Chapter 12. Ask why this chapter is written wholly in italics. Compare with the amount of italics in earlier chapters. What is the significance of this change? How does it reflect the twins' changes?
- On page 158, Garnet writes: *But we're not us any more and we can't ever be. We'll be split up even if we stay together.* Ask the children to discuss whether they believe Garnet's comment is correct, drawing on textual evidence.
- How do Garnet's and Ruby's feelings towards Rose alter? Do they change gradually? In tandem? Ask the children how they feel about each character.
- Look for specific textual evidence as to why they feel as they do.

Shared sentence-level work

- Read the description of Rose's meal in Chapter 12. Encourage the children to make connections between the characters' feelings at that stage in the story and the sadness of Rose's meal; how the latter mirrors the former.
- Ask the children to identify the verbs. Look for personification – can food *sulk*?

Guided and independent work

- Use photocopiable page 28 to reinforce how the detailed description of the meal reflects the characters and their feelings.
- Ask the children to invent a character. Write a descriptive paragraph of their character feeling happy and another of the same person feeling sad. Encourage them to use physical descriptions to reflect the character's feelings, such as the clothes they wear; how their hair is done; what they are eating; what shops they visit and what they buy, and so on. Remind them to focus on small details, such as buttons done up wrongly; mismatched socks.

Differentiation

Less able
- Ask the children to draw their character and describe him/her verbally.

More able
- Encourage the children to place their character in a situation, expanding on their feelings, and using close detail.

Plenary

- Listen to the children's descriptions, highlighting the effective use of verbs. From their writing, can others tell how the character is feeling? How can they tell? Ask them to support their responses.

Double Act

We're twins. I'm Ruby. She's Garnet.

We're identical. There's very few people who can tell us apart. Well, until we start talking. I tend to go on and on. Garnet is much quieter.

That's because I can't get a word in edgeways.

We are exactly the same height and weight. I eat a bit more than Garnet. I love sweets, and I like salty things too. I once ate thirteen packets of crisps in one day. All salt-and-vinegar flavour. I love lots of salt and vinegar on chips too. Chips are my special weakness. I go munch munch munch gulp and they're gone. So then I have to snaffle some of Garnet's. She doesn't mind.

Yes I do.

I don't get fatter because I charge around more. I hate sitting still. Garnet will hunch up over a book for hours, but I get the fidgets. We're both quite good at running, Garnet and me. At our last sports day at school we beat everyone, even the boys. We came first. Well, I did actually. Garnet came second. But that's not surprising, seeing as I'm the eldest. We're both ten. But I'm twenty minutes older. I was the bossy baby who pushed out first. Garnet came second.

We live with our dad and our gran.

Dad can't tell us apart in the morning at breakfast, but then his eyes aren't always open properly. He just swallows black coffee as he shoves on his clothes and then dashes off for his train. Dad works in an office in London and he hates it. He's always tired out when he gets home. But he can tell us apart by then. It's easier in the evening. My plaits are generally coming undone and my T-shirt's probably stained. Garnet stays as neat as a new pin.

From "Double Act" by Jacqueline Wilson (1995, Doubleday).

Meal that Mirrors Feelings

- Garnet's description of the meal that Rose cooked (chapter 12):

Rose tried ever so hard to cook a proper Sunday lunch for everyone, but somehow the beef got burnt and the Yorkshire pudding sulked and the potatoes wouldn't roast and the beans went stringy and the gravy had lumps, Dad still ate up every scrap on his plate and said it was super and even asked for seconds.

From "Double Act" by Jacqueline Wilson (1995, Doubleday).

1. Which verb personifies which part of the meal?

Verb: ____________ describing the ____________

2. How does the meal reflect each character's feelings at that point in the story?

3. Why was Rose trying so hard to make a proper roast lunch?

4. Why was Dad so enthusiastic about it despite its poor quality?

____

____

____

____

5. Imagine Garnet's return home at the end of her first term at boarding school to a successful **Welcome Home** lunch cooked by Rose. Describe the meal in as much detail as above. Use strong verbs and some personification.

____

____

____

Poetry

The focus of this term's poetry unit is shared themes and styles, and poems based on personal response and experience. Research of a modern living poet (Brian Patten) and an older poet, James Reeves, gives children the opportunity to gain confidence in using an index and alphabetical sequence. Writing their own poems hones their skill in using powerful and expressive verbs. Links with *Grammar for Writing* Unit 21, revising work on verbs and changing verb tenses is incorporated into Hours 1, 2 and 5.

Hour	Shared text-level work	Shared word-/ sentence-level work	Guided work	Independent work	Plenary
1 Slowly and loudly	Writing poems linked to reading.	Comparing tenses and recognising function of adverbs.	Turning adjectives into adverbs.	Using a writing frame to draft a poem.	Identify verbs and adverbs.
2 Inside out	Comparing poems on similar themes and use of verbs.	Examining purpose and structure of tenses.	Finding examples from text to support personal response to poems.	Writing comparison of poems; substituting verbs.	Examine suitability of synonyms, looking at mood and effect of substitutions.
3 What's inside?	Writing lines and phrases based on poems read to develop into own poem.	Using powerful verbs to evoke emotion; commas for demarcation.	Using verbs to create abstract metaphors after shared poem's model.	Drafting own writing with correct use of commas.	Reading aloud, with pauses at commas to demonstrate position and purpose.
4 Collecting flowers	Finding out more about popular poets and making personal choice of their work.	Using third and fourth letters to sort and sequence alphabetically.	Exploring anthologies and collections for research.	Using the internet to research a living poet's biography.	Justifying choices of favourite poems by reference to text, structure and style.
5 Empowering verbs	Experimenting with altering and expanding phrases.	Using regular verb endings *ed* and *ing* with confidence.	Experiment with new phrases assessing the effect of changing verbs.	Using powerful verbs creatively in free poetry writing with more open structure.	Sharing and discussing evocative use of powerful and expressive verbs.

Key assessment opportunities

- Do the children recognise verbs and are they able to find suitable alternatives?
- Can the children consistently spell past/present participles of regular verbs?
- Can they demonstrate how altering the verb changes tense?
- Can the children discuss a poem's strengths, and compare poems, drawing on direct quotations to support their opinions?
- Are they able to match their own writing to reflect the styles of poems read?

Slowly and loudly

Objectives

NLS

T14: To write poems based on personal experience, linked to poems read.
S2: To understand and compare effects of writing in different tenses.
S4: To understand the function of adverbs, linking them with verbs they modify.

What you need

- Photocopiable page 35 (enlarged copy)
- writing frame based on the shared poem 'Slowly' by James Reeves (see Guided Work).

Shared text-level work

- Display only James Reeves' poem 'Slowly' and read it together. Invite comments on subject, pattern and rhyme scheme.
- Consider how long each activity would take. If it is a sunny day, watch the progress of a real shadow.
- What do the poem's slow activities say about the observer? Is he or she catching glimpses or watching carefully?
- Compare the old man's movements with the wider, slower events. Ask how these bigger pictures emphasise his age. Question the use of possessives, his (*mile*). Are these used to describe personal obstacles? Is the slow contact creating ownership?
- Which of the five senses do they think the poet has drawn on? Which image, if any, could the observer hear?
- Ask what sounds they might hear in the same landscape.
- Note how each line presents a separate real-life image, almost like photographs, to make the reader look in an uncomplicated but careful way.
- Which line tells us about the era of the poem?

Shared word- and sentence-level work

- Establish which tense the poem is written in. Experiment changing the tense of some verbs (*has crept*; *will creep*). Which is most immediate sounding? Which most strongly involves the reader?
- Highlight the stem of the word *slowly, slow* and *slowest*. Establish that the *ly* suffix creates an adverb. Find each respective modified verb.
- Draw attention to how the long vowel-sounds in *tide, creeps, old, mounts*, and so on slow the pace of the poem. Ask individuals to read lines aloud to demonstrate.

Guided and independent work

- Write the following adjectives: *slow, swift, smooth, rough, deep, shy, brave, bold, quiet, loud, kind, cold*. Ask the children to turn each one into an adverb.
- Encourage the children to use each adverb to open a descriptive sentence. Remind them to begin with a capital letter, using the format of the first four poem lines as a model.
- Create a writing frame based on the shared poem, substituting *loudly/loud, loudest* for *slowly/slow* with blank lines for the remaining omitted words. Explain that the children should use their experience of sounds and listening to write the poem within the frame. Stress that, at this draft stage, sense is more important than rhyme.

Plenary

- Ask the children to nominate favourite lines from the shared poem and from their own drafts and explain the merits of both.
- Ask the children to identify verbs and adverbs in each line of the shared poem.

Differentiation

Less able

- Support imagination by taping different kinds and volumes of sounds.

More able

- Challenge children to create a rhyming couplet from another of their adverb sentences.

Inside out

Objectives

NLS

T7: To compare poems on similar themes, especially form and language, discussing personal responses and preferences.
S2: To develop awareness of how tense relates to purpose and structure of text.
S3: To identify powerful verbs and their effect.

S&L

37 Speaking: To compare and contrast poems through discussion.

What you need

- Photocopiable page 35 (enlarged copy).

Shared text-level work

- Display both poems. Invite a confident reader to reread 'Slowly', others chorusing the word *slowly*.
- Introduce 'The Inside of Things' and ask the children to follow the poem as you read.
- Ask what they notice about subject matter, structure, viewpoint, tense. Point out how, in the second stanza, the lines that begin *Inside...* have no comma as the sentence continues into the next line - enjambement.
- Invite the children's reactions to the things inside. Are they tangible? Compare the imagery (metaphor) in this poem to the images (pictures) in the first poem. Is there really a clock inside the dandelion?
- Ask the children to make a fist? What does it feel like? Could an army fit inside? What did the poet mean by this?
- Offer the children an open palm. How does it differ? Examine the feelings the two images suggest.
- Contrast close-up and broader images. Are some threatening? What are the implications of an avalanche?
- Why is a clock the first image of the poem? Compare the real clock in 'Slowly'. Where might it be - on a church tower?

Shared word- and sentence-level work

- Identify powerful verbs and how they create tension and anticipation: *awaits, trembles, plots*. Compare verbs from the first poem: *creeps, mounts, spreads*. Which poem sounds menacing? With which word does this begin?
- Consider how everything is held in suspense in the second poem. Could this effect be achieved in another tense? Experiment changing tenses to reinforce the need for the present tense.
- Which is the more peaceful poem and why? Compare the short vowel sounds in the second poem (*clock, egg, fist, kiss, get, run*) with the longer, slower vowels of the first.
- Open a class discussion as to which poem individuals prefer and why.

Guided and independent work

- List the following emotions: *peace, anticipation, longing, excitement, fear, calm, patience, anger*. Ask the children to find and copy a line from either poem that, respectively, produces these feelings, and quote them alongside.
- Ask the children to write a short comparison of the poems, explaining their preference. Remind them to mention how the poems make them feel and quote a line or two that caused their emotional response.
- Ask the children to choose one of the poems in which to substitute alternative verbs throughout, such as *slides up the sand*, while preserving place and mood.

Differentiation

Less able/More able

- In mixed-ability groups, ask children in collaboration to illustrate the poem 'Slowly', using the components of successive lines and moving progressively closer to the observer, starting with the distant coastline.

Plenary

- Listen to some favourite replacement lines. Have the children chosen appropriate synonyms to retain mood and sense?

What's inside?

Objectives

NLS

T14: To write poems linked to poems read.
S3: To use powerful verbs to evoke strong feelings.
S5: To practise using commas to mark grammatical boundaries within sentences.

What you need

- A selection of hollow objects, such as a coconut shell, sea shell, football, cup, supermarket bag, boot, flower-pot, ice-cube tray, recorder, matchbox
- thesauruses
- photocopiable page 35 (the poem 'The Inside of Things') and small sticky paper-strips.

Shared text- level work

- Ask a pair of able readers to re-read 'The Inside of Things', to the class alternating voices.
- Ask the children to identify and underline the first noun in each line. Ask what the nouns have in common - look for recognition of their diminutive size.
- Show how each noun has potential for bigger things. What infinite thing does the clock suggest - time?

Shared sentence-level work

- Cover each verb with sticky strips - for example, *Inside a fist an army...* (cover-up *awaits)*, also covering lines two and four of the second stanza.
- Read these verb-free lines together, establishing that they are now phrases not sentences.
- Re-read the poem, inserting different verbs in the present tense. Experiment with the position of the verb - for example, *Inside the egg a chicken fusses.*
- Hold open a plain-covered book, cover outwards, not revealing the content. Write, *Inside the book...* and invite suggestions for nouns describing things inside the book - developing ideas from concrete to abstract: *words, pictures, poems, a story, thoughts, a world, adventure...,* encouraging the children to think about the type of feelings that the content might promote.
- Select a noun and ask for verbs to turn the phrase into a sentence, such as: *Inside the book lies an adventure... ; Inside the book an adventure beckons/ lurks/waits/threatens.*
- Write and read experimental lines and discuss their effects and the feelings they evoke.
- Point out the use of a comma, semi-colon or full-stop before each new *Inside...* .

Guided and independent work

- Ask the children to write lines of *Inside the book is...* .
- Encourage them to develop these simple lines by using powerful, evocative verbs. Use thesauruses to help.
- Reveal the collection of hollow objects. Challenge the children to draft a poem where each line begins *Inside...* and makes the reader feel a sense of excitement or anticipation, such as *Inside the football a winning kick bounces in the goal.*
- Remind them to check their draft poem and insert commas at the end of each line unless it uses enjambement.
- Provide an unpunctuated copy of both the shared poems, asking the children to insert commas correctly.

Plenary

Invite the children to read their own poems aloud with a partner. Do the commas help them know whose turn it is to read?

Differentiation

Less able

- Ask an adult to scribe the children's suggestions, for them to copy-write.

More able

- Encourage the children to extend their ideas, such as *Inside the recorder is a song without words, waiting for children to dance.* Ask them to look up and compare the poem, 'Amulet' by Ted Hughes.

Collecting flowers

Objectives

NLS
T8: To find out more about popular poets and further poems.
W12: To use third and fourth place letters to locate and sequence names in alphabetical order.

What you need
- Photocopiable page 36
- a selection of poetry anthologies such as *Sensational* by Roger McGough and *Read Me and Laugh* by Gaby Morgan; poetry collections such as *Juggling with Gerbils* by Brian Patten and *Complete Poems for Children* by James Reeves
- word cards of poets' surnames (see *Shared text-level work*).

Shared text-level work

- Write the names James Reeves and Brian Patten on the board. Ask if the children recognise them. Establish who wrote which of the shared poems.
- In brackets underneath, write their respective dates: (1909–1978) and (1946–). Discuss why there is only one date under Patten's name. Ask how old Reeves was when he died. How old is Patten now?
- Explain that, later, they will be looking for more poems by these poets and for information about the living poet's biography.

Shared word-level work

- Reveal a pile of anthologies and collections. Explain the difference between an anthology to which many contribute and a collection by a single author. Discuss whose name will appear on the covers of each.
- Choose an anthology containing work by both chosen poets and explain how to use the alphabetical index. Remind the children that poets are arranged by surname, sometimes with a separate 'Index of Poets'.
- Write the following poets' names: Reeves, Moses, Bloom, Harmer, Mole, Patten, Harvey, Cotton, Warren, Magee, MacCaig, Mayer, Ward, Rice, Cope, Cooper on cards and ask children to help to sort them alphabetically.
- Explain that these are poets' surnames. Begin by putting names with common initial letters into respective sequential piles and then rearrange according to subsequent letter-sequences, demonstrating how to do this.
- Show some examples of anthologies. Explain that anthology means a collection of flowers – a metaphor for poems.
- Demonstrate how to use an index. Show how acknowledgements pages also reveal if any particular poet is represented.

Guided and independent work

- Ask the children to find further poems by James Reeves. Encourage them to work in pairs or groups, and to read poems aloud to one another, as poetry is an aural art.
- Ask them to use books and the internet to find out more about Brian Patten and to write a brief biography.
- Invite the children to re-sort the poets' surnames and list them alphabetically, including their own surname correctly positioned. Challenge them to add poets' first names, separated by a comma.
- Using photocopiable page 36, ask the children to transcribe their chosen James Reeves' poems (or second favourite if they like the shared poem best) and to answer the questions.
- Remind them what each poetic term means, especially the more difficult French word, enjambement.

Plenary

- Invite the children to read aloud their chosen poems and explain why they like them.
- Hear some biographical facts about Brian Patten.

Differentiation

Less able
- Provide desktop alphabets and arrange mixed-ability pairs.

More able
- Challenge the children to discover who formed the Mersey Poets. Why were they so named?

Empowering verbs

Objectives

NLS

T14: To list brief phrases and words, experiment by trimming or extending sentences; experiment with powerful or expressive verbs.
S3: To identify the use of powerful verbs.
W7: To spell regular verb endings *ed* and *ing*.
W11: To define familiar vocabulary in their own words, using alternative phrases or expressions.

What you need

- Poems by the selected poets, Reeves and Patten
- a list of quotations (see *Shared* and *Guided* work)
- photocopiable page 35.

Shared text-level work

- Return to the shared poems, obscuring the verbs: *creeps, mounts, spreads, trembles, plots.* Ask the children if they can [a] remember the missing verbs and [b] substitute an equally expressive verb.
- Display quotations from other poems, explaining that they are out of context, having been chosen for the strength of the verbs:

Reeves:
...grey smoke tumbling from the chimney-pot ('Grey')
...I heard the grey leaves weep and whisper round my bed ('Boating')

Patten:
...I was dumped here long ago ('The Earthling')
...stars poured down ('The Earthling')
...the gurgling of water over stones ('The Mud Mother')
...Kingfishers, disguised as rainbows ('The River's Story')
...left me cowering in monstrous shadows ('The River's Story')

- Highlight the *ed* and *ing* endings of the verbs.
- Consider which verbs are powerful, creating strong, expressive images (unusual or metaphoric). For example, compare *poured* (a drink) and *stars poured down*. When might smoke *tumble*? Can leaves *weep* and *whisper*?

Shared word- and sentence-level work

- Invite the children to substitute verbs in the quotations above.
- Try using the original verbs with new nouns, such as *Poplar trees, disguised as statues*.

Guided and independent work

- Challenge the children to write poetic phrases. Use some of the quotations above as springboards for fresh contexts:

__________ tumbling from __________ poured down.
I was __________ here long ago.
__________, disguised as __________.
__________ burning on __________.

- Encourage the children to take one of their new lines and extend it into a poem about something they have seen or experienced.
- Ask them to invent a completely new phrase, using a powerful verb.
- Challenge the children to create a title for a poem, or offer a choice. Allow their imaginations free rein to create a poem.
- Ask the children to look for the quoted poems in anthologies to read the lines in context. Find examples of strong, expressive verbs.

Differentiation

Less able

- Write the quotations as a cloze procedure for the children to replace verbs.

More able

- Ask the children to re-read and improve their poems, reading them aloud to hear the sound and rhythm.

Plenary

- Share examples of the effective use of verbs in new contexts and new verbs in original contexts. Discuss the effects of powerful verbs.

Slowly

Slowly the tide creeps up the sand,
Slowly the shadows cross the land.
Slowly the cart-horse pulls his mile,
Slowly the old man mounts the stile.

Slowly the hands move round the clock,
Slowly the dew dries on the dock.
Slow is the snail – but slowest of all
The green moss spreads on the old brick wall.

James Reeves

distant viewpoint grows ever closer
aabb rhyming couplets
possessive pronoun

present tense verbs
long vowel sounds' slowing effect

First words of lines repeated in both poems

The Inside of Things

Inside the dandelion seed is a clock,
Inside the egg is a chicken farm;
Inside a fist an army awaits,
Inside a kiss is an open palm.

Inside a snowflake an avalanche
Trembles and waits to get free;
Inside a raindrop a river plots
The best way to run to the sea.

Brian Patten

abcb rhyming quatrains

metaphors – compare imagery with real life literal images in previous poem
enjambement

Collecting Flowers

- I have found more poems by James Reeves (1909–1978). This is my favourite:

- I found it in a book entitled

____

- I like it because ______________________________

____

____

____

- In this poem James Reeves uses (place a ✓ or a × in each box):

1. Rhyme	2. Alliteration	3. Assonance	4. Repetition	5. Simile	6. Metaphor	7. Enjambement

- Now write the **numbers** above next to **underlined examples** in the poem you have copied.

UNIT 4

Plays

In this unit, the children read and analyse the features of playscripts, extend a scene and perform it in small groups. Prior to working on plays, the children should have some experience of read-along plays and of watching plays on television or at the theatre. This unit is based on the play adaptation of Jacqueline Wilson's *Double Act* but the teaching suggestions can be adapted to any other play if required. A Channel 4 televised version of *Double Act* is available. The children will develop their knowledge of the key features of a script and the work in this unit also relates to *Grammar for Writing* Units 21 and 23.

Hour	Shared text-level work	Shared word/ sentence-level work	Guided work	Independent work	Plenary
1 What is a playscript?	Preparing and reading a play, discussing key features of plays.	Looking at conventions of scriptwriting and punctuation.	Predicting what might happen next in the story and starting work on extending the scene.	Starting work on extending the scene.	Comparing and discussing the children's extended scenes.
2 Characters in plays	Analysing what can be learnt about character from dialogue.	Comparing dialogue in script and in narrative.	Rewriting dialogue in narrative as a playscript.	Writing extended scenes.	Reviewing scenes. Use children's writing to illustrate good character development.
3 Action in plays	Analysing how action and words combine to make the drama.	Looking at adverbs in stage directions.	Including adverbs in scenes.	Editing extended scenes.	Looking at openings and endings of scenes.
4 Preparing a performance	Preparing for performance: vocal warm-up and effective speaking prompts.	Using the present tense in stage directions.	Preparing voice-only performance.	Finishing extended scenes.	Discussing the criteria for evaluation: what makes a good performance?
5 Rehearsing and performing	Rehearsing, performing and evaluation of scenes.	Playing 'Yesterday/today' to practise changing tenses.	Performance of scenes.	Writing evaluations of plays.	Sharing self-evaluations. Review what we have learned.

Key assessment opportunities

- Written scenes: can the children use the conventions of setting out a script?
- Can the children perform play scenes using evaluation criteria?

What is a playscript?

Objectives

NLS

T5: To prepare, read and perform playscripts; compare organisation of scripts with stories – how are settings indicated, story lines made clear?

T6: To chart the build-up of a play scene e.g. how scenes start, how dialogue is expressed, and how scenes are concluded.

T13: To write playscripts using known stories as a basis.

What you need:

- Channel 4 production of *Double Act*, Episode 1
- a collection of playscripts including 'read aloud' scripts and scripts of plays written for children such as Philip Ridley *Krindlekrax*; Jacqueline Wilson *Double Act*; Kaye Umansky *Cruel Times: A Victorian Play*; Geraldine McCaughrean *The Greeks on Stage* and *Britannia On Stage;* Julia Donaldson *Bombs and Blackberries*
- photocopiable page 43.

Shared text-level work

- View the opening of *Double Act* (or alternative) together. How do the actors know what to do and say?
- Explain that plays are texts written for performance – different kinds of plays are written for television, film, theatre, radio.
- Consider the reasons that a playscript might be written down, for example, so that it can be performed on more than one occasion; to help actors remember lines; to give production teams cues for lighting.
- Revise the conventions of scriptwriting from Year 3 Term 1. List suggestions on the whiteboard. For example:

- A character list
- Divided into acts or scenes (an act is a bigger section than a scene)
- Set notes – often a brief mention of setting, time and place
- Stage directions (actions and speech might be written in brackets or italics)
- Directions to tell actors when to enter and exit
- No speech marks
- Every speech starts on a new line
- Character's name shows who is speaking.

- Read the opening of *Double Act* (photocopiable page 43). Ask the children, in pairs, to practise reading the extract with appropriate expression.

Shared sentence-level work

- Continue writing with Garnet's next piece of dialogue. A line that shows the contrast in Ruby and Garnet's characters would be appropriate. (For example, *But I like having lots of books in the house.*) As you write, reinforce the conventions of script writing, for example, *First we write the name of the character who is speaking followed by a colon...* Take suggestions for the next line and write them down.
- Prompt the children to consider correct punctuation. Reinforce that only the actual words spoken are written after the character's name.

Guided and independent work

- Ask the children to re-read the extract in pairs. Predict and discuss what might happen next. Share ideas in groups of four. Ask the children to explain why they think the scene would develop in a particular way.
- Ask them to improvise, in pairs, what might happen next. When they have decided how they think the scene would progress, ask them to write down the extended scene using the conventions for playwriting.

Plenary

- Invite the children to share their work in progress. They should ask questions about the ways they have extended the scene. Encourage them to refer to the text when asking/answering questions.
- Ask the children to reflect on how the improvisation helped them to write their scenes.

Differentiation

Less able

- Carefully select pairs to support those children requiring additional help with writing.

More able

- More able children might prefer to develop their own plays rather than work on an extended scene.

Characters in plays

Objectives

NLS

T5: To prepare, read and perform playscripts; compare the organisation of scripts with stories – how are settings indicated, story lines made clear?

T6: To chart the build-up of a play scene e.g. how scenes start, how dialogue is expressed, and how scenes are concluded.

T13: To write playscripts using known stories as a basis.

S&L

38 Listening: To compare the different contributions of music, words and images in short extracts from TV programmes.

What you need

- Photocopiable page 43, and pages 44 and 46 (enlarged).
- prepared musical extracts for selection. Include some that do not suit the scene, and a few that do, in order to generate discussion about matching music to mood and character.

Differentiation

Less able

- The children continue to be supported by working in teacher-selected pairs. An adult might scribe for children requiring extra support with writing. They can also use an audio tape for recording and editing their work.

More able

- These children can continue working on their own scenes.

Shared text-level work

- With the class re-read the opening page (photocopiable page 43). Ask them what we learn about Ruby from this opening extract.
- Using a prepared enlarged version of the grid 'Introducing characters' on photocopiable page 46, add the pupils' suggestions to the columns.

Ruby

Speech	Appearance	Actions	Likes/Dislikes
Fiery, bossy. Does most of the talking. Makes a lot out of being the eldest twin.	Untidy – plaits come undone, T-shirt usually stained.	Very active. Runs around. Talkative.	Likes sweets, crisps and chips. Hates sitting still.

- Why do they think the writer suggests that Ruby and Garnet enter from opposite sides? Experiment by having them enter together, and then from opposite sides.
- Play some examples of music extracts to the children. Ask them to justify their choices of music for the scene by referring to the text.

Shared sentence-level work

- Review the presentation of dialogue in a script from the previous lesson.
- Use an enlarged copy of *Snakes and Snails for Lunch* (photocopiable page 44). Using a marker pen, highlight the conventions for presenting dialogue in a narrative text:

> - Punctuation: opening and closing speech marks, commas before closing speech marks when speech is tagged
> - Tags including speech verbs, for example, *snarled troll*

- Show how the dialogue would be written differently if it were a play:
  Dinner Lady: What are you doing?
  Troll: (grumpily) Nothing.
- Continue writing the dialogue, taking suggestions on what it should look like.

Guided and independent work

- In pairs, ask the children to complete a character introduction grid for Garnet, using the one prepared in shared reading as a model.
- The children continue to write their extended scenes. Encourage them to think about the characters and to review their work, focusing on the development of characters in the scene. Ask them to show the character through dialogue and stage directions.

Plenary

- Ask the children to consider what makes a good scene opening – is it attention grabbing, does it provide necessary information? How does the opening of *Double Act* grab the audience's attention?

Action in plays

Objectives

NLS

T5: To prepare, read and perform playscripts; compare organisation of scripts with stories – how are settings indicated, story lines made clear?
T13: To write playscripts using known stories as a basis.
S4: To identify adverbs: collecting and classifying examples of adverbs e.g. for speed: *swiftly, rapidly, sluggishly*; for light: *brilliantly, dimly.*

What you need

- An enlarged photocopiable of scene 1 from *Double Act* (page 43)
- photocopiable page 45
- a set of adverb cards (teacher- or pupil-made).

Shared sentence-level work

- Play 'In the manner of......' A volunteer selects an adverb card and keeps it hidden. Suggest a simple action (for example, *eating*), which the volunteer has to mime in the manner of the selected adverb, for the others to guess. After a few rounds, ask what type of word is written on the card. Introduce the term *adverb* and explain that adverbs often answer the question *How?*
- Demonstrate adverbs by writing illustrative sentences. For example, *Natasha was dancing happily*. Highlight the adverb. Ask, *How was Natasha dancing?*
- Model examples of adverbs, taking suggestions from the children.
- Explain that adverbs can be used to describe manner of speech. List suggestions on the whiteboard. Add new words throughout the week.
- Use examples from class work to illustrate good use of adverbs.

Shared text-level work

- Review work on dialogue from Hour 2. Explain that how a character speaks gives an insight into their thoughts and feelings.
- On the whiteboard, write from the dialogue:

> **RUBY:** We're twins. I'm Ruby. She's Garnet. Not many people can tell us apart. Well, until we start talking. I tend to go on and on; Garnet is much quieter.
> **GARNET:** That's because I can't get a word in edgeways.
> **RUBY:** I eat a bit more than her but I don't get fatter because I charge around more. I hate sitting still. I'm the oldest by twenty minutes – the bossy baby who pushed out first.

- Ask how these lines might be spoken. Invite them to read Garnet's line in an irritated tone, or laughing, or whispered. Which fits best?
- Ask the children to add adverbs to the dialogue.
- In pairs, the children re-read the opening scene, experimenting with different ways that lines can be read.

Differentiation

Less able

- For children requiring more support, provide them with the 'Adverbs and action cards on' photocopiable page 45. They have to match each adverb with the situation on each action card.

More able

- Encourage the use of thesauruses and dictionaries to extend vocabulary. New words should be used in these children's written work.

Guided and independent work

- The children continue writing their extended scenes. Encourage them to review work by reading aloud and checking for appropriate adverbs to describe speech and actions.
- Make posters showing different speech adverbs. Display these as prompts for writing. Encourage use of a thesaurus to find similar words.

Plenary

- Ask the children to explain any changes they have made to their scripts as a result of thinking more about adverbs.
- Note that it is not necessary to have stage directions with each line of dialogue. Actors will interpret lines as well.
- Prompt the children to think about ending scenes. Invite suggestions.
- Note that there has to be a definite end, but this is the end of a *scene* (not the *play*). The audience should want to know what will happen next.

Preparing a performance

Objectives

NLS

T5: To prepare, read and perform playscripts; compare organisation of scripts with stories – how are settings indicated, story lines made clear?

S2: To revise work on verbs from Year 1 Term 3 and to investigate verb tenses: (past, present and future).

What you need

- The children's completed scenes
- photocopiable page 43 (enlarged).

Shared word-and sentence-level work

- Using an enlarged copy of the opening scene of *Double Act*, highlight the setting.
- Note that a play is performed in front of an audience, as though it is happening 'now', so directions are always written in the present tense.
- In narrative, the action would usually be written in the past tense: for example, *Ruby and Garnet were dressed the same.*
- Write the following sentence on the whiteboard:

Gran walks with difficulty because of her arthritis.

- Can we write this in the past tense? Write suggestions on the board. Which words have changed? Note that it is the verb that indicates whether something is happening now (the present) or has already happened (past).

Shared text-level work

- Explain that plays are written to be performed. Draw on the children's experiences of plays. Ask what makes a play enjoyable? For example, *actors memorise lines – they don't have scripts when they are performing; they speak expressively; they use gestures and movement.*
- Ask the children to consider how to speak expressively. How can they make their voices sound interesting by varying:
  - volume (loud/soft)
  - pace (fast/slow)
  - pitch (high/low)
  - emphasis (emphasis on different words)
  - pause (silences are as important in speech)?
- Play games to warm-up the children's voices and to develop understanding of volume, pace and so on.
- Using *Double Act*, demonstrate ways that a playscript can be marked to show how the lines are spoken.
- Agree a simple marking code with the children.

Guided and independent work

- The children continue with their extended scenes. Ask them to give attention to their scene ending. Does it have a definite end? Does it leave the audience wanting to know what will happen? Are stage directions written in the present tense?
- When the scenes are finished, ask them to re-read their work in pairs and mark them up for an expressive oral reading.

Plenary

- Explain that the scenes will be performed and evaluated in the next lesson.
- Ask the children to reflect on *what makes a good performance.* Then, negotiate and write criteria for evaluating performances.

Differentiation

Less able

- Expressive reading is aided as children are reading their own writing and are familiar with the words. Rather than working on text marking, use adult support during preparation for performance. Talking at this stage reinforces teaching points covered previously.

More able

- In addition to marking the text for expressive reading, able children might also consider staging the scene and can be encouraged to memorise their lines.

Rehearsing and performing

Objectives

NLS

T6: To chart the build-up of a play scene e.g. how scenes start, how dialogue is expressed, and how scenes are concluded.

S & L

40 Drama: To comment constructively on plays and performance, discussing effects and how they are achieved.

What you need

- Prepared stage directions, including incorrect examples in the past tense
- criteria for evaluating a performance (from previous lesson)
- teacher-made verb cards and 'Yesterday/ Today' cards.

Shared word- and sentence-level work

- Play the game 'Yesterday/Today': group the class in a circle and place the pack of verb cards in the centre. Ask a volunteer to select a verb card from the pile. The child mimes the action and the rest of the class guess what they are doing.
- In turns show the 'Yesterday/Today' cards. Work orally to create sentences about the present and the past. For example, *Today, Sam is asleep. Yesterday, Sam slept.* After a few examples, ask the children to work in pairs, using dry-wipe boards for writing sentences.
- On the whiteboard, display the set of prepared stage directions. In pairs, ask the children to identify the odd ones out. Why are they written incorrectly? Highlight the incorrect examples and draw attention to the verb.

Shared text-level work

- Explain that this lesson is devoted to the rehearsal, performance and evaluation of the children's extended scenes.
- Briefly recap on the main points from the previous lesson, drawing attention to the negotiated criteria for evaluating a good performance. Explain the format for the lesson:
  - rehearsal
  - performance in small groups (two to three pairs in a group)
  - feedback to each other.
- Set ground rules for feedback. If children have little experience of response partners, they will need specific guidance, so insist that only positive feedback is given. Children need to learn how to be critical friends and this is best done in the plenary session with the guidance and supervision of the teacher.

Guided and independent work

- Allow the children a set-time (10–15 minutes) to rehearse their scenes.
- Organise the class into small groups made up of two to three pairs. Each pair performs their scene. The other children use the criteria for performance to provide positive feedback in the form of notes.
- When each pair has performed their scene the groups provide feedback to each other.

Plenary

- Together, review this unit of work by asking the key questions below:

> - What have we learned about writing plays?
> - What have we learned about performing plays?
> - What have we learned about evaluating each other's work?
> - Is there anything we would do differently next time?

Differentiation

Less able

- Differentiation in this lesson is by outcome.

More able

- Differentiation in this lesson is by outcome.

Double Act

CHARACTERS

RUBY BARKER	*The elder twin by twenty minutes. She feels this makes her the boss. She's definitely bossy – a fiery, funny, ultra-determined girl who is desperate to be an actress.*
GARNET BARKER	*The younger twin. She nearly always does what Ruby says. She's sweet, shy and living in Ruby's shadow.*

ACT ONE

The twins' home.

(Music. Enter RUBY *and* GARNET *from opposite sides. They are dressed the same and both have their hair in plaits. They do a short, fun 'twin' dance sequence: they dance the same steps and mirror each other's actions.)*

RUBY: (*to audience*): We're twins. I'm Ruby. She's Garnet. Not many people can tell us apart. Well, until we start talking. I tend to go on and on; Garnet is much quieter.

GARNET: That's because I can't get a word in edgeways.

RUBY: I eat a bit more than her but I don't get fatter because I charge around more. I hate sitting still. I'm the oldest by twenty minutes – the bossy baby who pushed out first.

(They laugh and fight. GRAN *enters. She walks with difficulty because of her arthritis.)*

GRAN: Girls, girls! Where is your dad? He should have been back ages ago. I've had the dinner turned down low for the last half-hour and my Yorkshire's gone all sad and soggy.

RUBY: Yorkshire pud – yummy yummy in my tummy.

GRAN: Yes, well, I just hope he hurries up. *(Exits.)*

GARNET: Dad *is* all right, isn't he?

RUBY: Of course he is. He's only been at a car boot sale, for heaven's sake. I expect he's bought piles of books and he's having trouble stuffing them all in the car. You know what he's like. Books, books, books, that's all he ever thinks about. We can hardly move in this house for books.

Play edition adapted for stage by Vicky Ireland (2004, Corgi Yearling), from "Double Act" by Jacqueline Wilson.

Snakes and Snails for Lunch

The Juniors pushed and shoved their way into the lunchroom, where the Infants were waiting in line.

'Food! Gimme food!' hissed Troll, licking his lips. He sneaked up on Sleeping Beauty. But just as he was about to pounce, the dinner lady looked up from her cauldron.

'What are you doing?' said the dinner lady.

'Nothing,' snarled Troll.

'Get back in line and wait your turn,' said the dinner lady.

Troll shoved his way back into the queue.

'Stop pushing,' said Jack.

Troll ignored him.

"Hit me! What did I say?" said Ugly Sister Two.

'Hit me,' said Troll.

Ugly Sister Two slugged him.

'Owwwww!' whined Troll. 'Why did you hit me?'

'You told me to,' said Ugly Sister Two.

'Grrrrrr,' said Troll.

'The choice today is turkey and peas or snakes and snails,' said the dinner lady.

'What? No roast children?' said Wicked Witch. 'I'll have to have the snakes, then.'

The dinner lady piled some on to her plate.

'Hmmmm, not bad,' said Wicked Witch, popping a fat juicy one into her mouth.

'Nothing for me. I'm on a diet,' said Jealous Queen.

'My mum won't let me eat vegetables,' said Troll.

'Don't you have porridge?' said Goldilocks.

'Not today,' said the dinner lady. 'What would you like, Cinderella?'

'Oh, whatever's left,' whispered Cinderella.

'Come on, dear, speak up for what you want, turkey or snakes?' said the dinner lady.

'Turkey please,' said Cinderella.

'If you don't blow your own trumpet no one else will,' said the dinner lady. 'Remember that.'

From "Don't Cook Cinderella" by Francesca Simon (2005, Orion Children's Books).

Adverbs and action cards

ADVERB CARDS	ACTION CARDS
sleepily	Walking his dog
happily	Reading a book
nervously	Playing basketball
excitedly	Making a cup of tea
slowly	Washing his car
impatiently	Playing on the computer

Introducing characters

Speech	Appearance	Actions	Likes/dislikes

Newspapers/ Magazines

This unit is based around newspaper articles and headlines. It is flexible enough to spread over three weeks. Some sessions cover a wide area and may be spread over two hours. There is opportunity for individual, paired and group work. Part or all of the third week could be used to produce a class newspaper that reflects aspects of real papers, with advertisements as well as articles and pictures. The unit will increase the children's experience of using commas within compound sentences, addressing *Grammar for Writing Unit 24*.

Hour	Shared text-level work	Shared word-/ sentence-level work	Guided work	Independent work	Plenary
1 Who? What? Where? When? Why?	Identifying style of text – structure, layout and purpose.	Demonstrating use of commas in sentences.	Looking at layout, level of formality and use of headlines in writing news reports.	Picking out key sentences that convey information.	Invite children to read their headlines. Discuss how effectively they grab attention.
2 Fun with facts	Looking at purpose of headlines, use of paragraphs.	Identifying and using past tense.	Creating headlines and inventing thematic news stories.	Writing a news report. Plan its newspaper-style layout and edit it using IT.	Share examples of effective use of commas. Consider degree of information in children's writing.
3 Pulling strings	Sorting fact from opinion.	Using dictionaries to help define and rephrase.	Finding examples of emotive language.	Writing an alphabetical glossary.	Listen to definitions of words and children's short, factual sentences.
4 Points of view	Developing awareness of different voices and features in newspapers including 'Letters to the Editor'. Scrolling online text to read.	Looking at journalistic style and voice; examining how points of view may be revealed or suppressed in a report.	Writing for a specific audience.	Using strong verbs and adjectives to write emotively and responding to previous text.	Reflect on *if* and *how* the children's writing reflects an emotional response.
5 Follow up	Writing and editing, using IT for a defined space.	Using commas to demarcate sentences effectively and grammatically.	Writing a factual report ensuring that the reader will find answers to questions.	Using direct speech as quotations within a report.	Review the use of commas in compound sentences.

UNIT 5

Hour	Shared text-level work	Shared sentence-/ word-level work	Guided work	Independent work	Plenary
6 Headlines	Identifying features of non-fiction texts; predict stories from headlines.	Recognising use of italics in text.	Identiifying features of effective headlines.	Anticipating text from headlines and checking for accuracy.	Sum up the purpose and effectiveness of headlines.
7 Doggie Dentures	Examining how headlines are used.	Looking at use of past and present tense in newspaper-style text.	Organising writing into newspaper-style paragraphs.	Spelling regular verb endings in present tense and present and past participles.	Look for headlines and text that complement each other; examine good use of paragraphs.
8 What can we sell you?	With special reference to advertising features, identifying writing that helps readers gain information effectively.	Studying newspapers' general layout and the use of advertising; eye-catching devices and selling voice.	Brainstorming catchy names of inventions to advertise and plan layout and content of advertising feature.	Think up snappy and memorable slogans, using linguistic devices such as alliteration or rhyme.	Assess product names, layout and content for ease of access to required information.
9 Fun run	Using IT to draft and lay out a report, comparing fact and opinion.	Spelling past tense verbs ending *ed* with annotated text.	Imagining headlines and captions based on textual content.	Punctuating an unpunctuated paragraph, with special attention to commas.	Discuss what editors look for in journalists' reports.
10 Fantasy news	Developing headlines into stories using IT, where the textual content satisfies the headline's suggestion.	Recognising verbs and be able to change them between present and past tense.	Working from draft to lay out, checking and editing own writing.	Checking subject and verb endings agree and that tense is consistent.	Compare stories with similar headlines. Discuss how well they match expectations.

Key assessment opportunities

- Can children use a comma correctly to demarcate sentences grammatically?
- Can they differentiate between fact and opinion and offer examples?
- Are they able to use IT to create and edit text, choosing and applying suitable font sizes and cases in a prescribed space and layout?

Who? What? Where? When? Why?

Objectives

NLS
T16: To identify different types of text, structure, style, layout and purpose.
T18: To pick out key sentences that convey information.
S5: To use commas in sentences for improved clarity.

S&L
39 Group discussion and interaction: to take roles within groups when discussing and planning.

What you need:
- Photocopiable page 59 (enlarged).

Shared text-level work

- Write the headline *Proud Penguin Promoted.* Ask how it grabs attention, for example: alliteration, anthropomorphism, use of capitals. Can the children predict the basic story?
- Display and read the report. Explain how this is *journalistic copy* – that is, text written by a reporter for, in this case, a national daily paper, *The Daily Telegraph.*
- Draw attention to the way numbers (from 11 upwards) are written in numerals, not as words. This is a universal convention of journalistic style.
- Ask what the number (67) means (*age*).
- Look at the division of text into paragraphs. All but one have only one sentence.
- Ask them if it is an important story? Examine the use of language. How does the reporter make it sound important? For example, formal, mock-heroic words like *bestowed* instead of *given*, elevating the tone; *flipper* in place of a human sleeve to emphasise anthropomorphism; *ignored* as if the bird chose not to respond.

Shared sentence- and word-level work

- Demonstrate the use and effect of commas, for example, could a band *play a penguin*? Write the sentence: *The penguin ignored a request.* Gradually expand this to recreate the original sentence, inserting commas.
- Write the question words: *Who? What? Where? When? Why?* Can the children find answers to any or all of these questions in the report?

Guided and independent work

- Ask the children to identify key points of information in the shared text. Under the five 'W' question word headings above, write brief notes to answer each question.
- Use the internet engines to investigate more stories about military mascots or other reports of the penguin, *Nils Olav.* Can the children find answers to these same question words in other news reports?
- Invite the children to use alliteration of animal names to generate news story headlines about a school mascot through brainstorming – for example, *Goat Goes Green; Chicken Chases Children.*
- Ask the children in groups to discuss possible stories. Allocate roles within the groups, including leader, reporter, scribe, mentor. Remind the children to try to answer the question words in their news story plan.

Plenary

- Allow group reporters to read out their headlines and ask other groups to choose which one sounds most interesting. Can children guess the story?
- Take suggestions on how to improve the less exciting headlines.

Differentiation

Less able
- Give children a starting headline and prompt them to brainstorm ideas.

More able
- Plan a 'photo-call' picture of their headline and write an attention-grabbing caption to go with the picture to support the storyline.

Fun with facts

Objectives

NLS

T16: To identify different types eg their content, structure, layout and purpose.

T24: To plan a newspaper style report with use of appropriate language, paragraphs and layout.

S5: To use commas in sentences for improved clarity.

What you need:

- Photocopiable pages 59 and 60.

Shared text-level work:

- Re-read the extract on photocopiable page 59.
- Invite comments about font, layout and captions. Why are headlines in a bigger font than the story itself?
- Ask what country Norwegians come from. Where is Edinburgh?
- Examine the use of paragraphs in this report. Would they normally have only one sentence?
- Has the brevity of this report influenced the unconventional use of single-sentence paragraphs?

Shared sentence-level work:

- What tense is used in the article? Remind children that tense refers to time. This is a story about a specific event that happened in the past.
- Ask the children why the Norwegian Guard were in Scotland at the time. Was it just to visit the zoo and make the award? Look at paragraph two for the answer and ask why the present tense is used here (*is taking part*).
- In the same paragraph, draw attention to the use of commas. Note how the change of tense occurs in parentheses - *as if to say, Incidentally...* .

Guided and independent work

- Following on from Hour 1, ask the children to choose an imaginary mascot animal for their school. Use this as a basis to plan a newspaper report about an award, given to the mascot, for example a title: *Chief Monitor; Sharpener in Charge of Pencils.*
- Distribute photocopiable page 60. Ask the children to develop the group ideas generated in Hour 1 individually, or to use new ideas. Ask them to think particularly about an eye-catching headline, opening paragraph, use of commas, and layout.
- Advise the children to plan a longer report than the shared text. They must put more than one sentence in their paragraphs.
- Use the layout design from the worksheet to transfer their text to computer.
- Ask the children to edit their story to fit onto a sheet of A4 paper, using a vertical newspaper-style half-A4 column width and incorporating a heading and a picture with a caption.
- Write captions for a supposed photograph of the school mascot to support and link with their reports.

Plenary

- Remind children of the question words: *Who? What? Where? When? Why?* Have they answered any or all of these questions in their opening paragraph or full report?
- Share some examples of the children's correct use of commas.

Differentiation:

Less able

- Allow children to work in pairs with an adult prompting discussion and/ or acting as scribe.

More able

- Insert suitable eye-catching sub-headings within the text of their report, editing as required for length and coherence.

Pulling strings

Objectives

NLS

T19: To understand and use the terms fact and opinion and begin to distinguish between the two, offering examples.

T21: To predict newspaper stories from the evidence of headlines and sub-headings.

W11 & W12: To use alternative phrases and wording to define meanings and use alphabetic sorting through dictionary use and glossaries.

What you need

- Photocopiable page 61
- internet access.

Shared text- and word-level work

- Write the headline from photocopiable page 61. Discuss how it achieves impact. Does it help the children to predict any elements of the news item? Remind them of the five question words beginning with 'W'. Which of these does the title and context begin to answer?
- Explain that it is an article from an imaginary paper, the *Antarctic Echo*, but based on stories that have been appearing in newspapers since the 1980s.
- Add the byline. What does *Air Correspondent* and the journalist's name suggest?
- Read the report together. Point out the use of direct quotations and speech marks.
- Remind the children of the convention of writing high numbers as numerals – compare *It is due to hatch in four days.*
- Re-read the first line. Ask the children to rephrase it in as few, simple words as possible. For example, *Petro is upset.* What is the effect of words such as *anguish, frantically, distraught, devastated*? Discuss how the use of emotive words might affect readers' feelings and responses.
- Identify which paragraph tells us the original myth that made pilots fly over on purpose. Where do we learn the nickname of this phenomenon?
- Encourage the children to identify opinions and value judgements among the facts, for example, the opening line *Anguish is evident in every feather ...*; *steel beasts* – an emotive metaphor; and *predatory helicopter* – a personifying adjective.
- Compare *bird baiters* and *crazy pilots* – one is within the report, the other within a quotation. How does the effect of emotive language differ in these contexts?

Guided and independent work

- Ask the children to use dictionaries to help write a glossary of some of the longer words in this article. Explain how to use second and subsequent letters to determine alphabetical order when looking up words, for example, *devastate(d)* before *distraught*.
- Encourage the children to select sentences from the text that include emotive language and rewrite in simple neutral terms.
- Ask the children to look up the term 'penguin topple' on internet search engines and compare published articles with the shared-text version. Demonstrate how to scroll online text.
- Note quotations and sources from these to demonstrate facts and opinions within the reporting and the use of emotive language.

Plenary

- Share glossaries and listen to definitions.
- Listen to the children's simplified sentences. Do they present the same facts but without emotive language?

Differentiation

Less able

- Ask the children to write captions to put on placards for demonstrating penguins.

More able

- Ask this group to arrange glossaries in alphabetical order.

Points of view

Objectives

NLS

T19: To recognise and distinguish between fact and opinion.
T23: To learn how to scroll when reading text on a screen.
T20: To be aware that newspapers have different features and voices.
W3: To break words into phonemes and look for spelling patterns.

What you need

- Newspaper pages of 'Letters to the Editor'
- photocopiable page 61.

Shared text-level work

- Note the use of the present tense when writing about the general situation and the change to past tense when relating specific events.
- Is this a serious or humorous article? Look how the author has used humour to echo journalistic style. What is in brackets instead of ages? Talk about adapting human-related phrases to anthropomorphise penguins, such as *waddled for my life, spokesbird, Court of Penguin Rights.*
- Invite the children to 'translate' [a] human terms, *ran for my life*, and so on, into, for example, fish terms (*spokesfish*).
- Explain that previous stories would supply the background. How and where has the writer achieved this here?
- Identify references to earlier articles about 'penguin topple'.
- Discuss whether this article is balanced. Does it give the pilots' views?
- Talk about 'Letters to the Editor' and read aloud some real-life examples. How does the tone and voice differ from the shared-text?

Shared word-level work

- List the following: *second, abandon, phenomenon, comforted, demonstrate, considering.* Demonstrate syllable division, after each consonant that follows a short vowel: *ab-an-don; phen-om-en-on*, and so on.
- Draw the children's attention to the *uh* sound of the letter *o* in all these words.
- Reinforce the long and short sounds of the digraph *ea*, finding examples from the text.

Guided and independent work

- Ask the children to work in pairs to draft a news story about when pilots first claimed causing 'Penguin Topple'. Write, this time, for a human audience.
- Explain that readers often respond to what they read, especially to emotive subjects. Look at real 'Letters to Editor' pages. Seek letters from readers with strong opinions. Look for differences in voice/style.
- Ask the children how those affected might feel. Write a letter to the editor of the *Antarctic Echo* from an annoyed penguin, an apologetic pilot or an unrepentant pilot.
- Ask children to preserve anthropomorphism in their writing, using strong verbs and adjectives.
- Ask the children to underline words containing *ea*. Sort and list them according to a long or a short *e* sound.
- Encourage the children to say and spell the multi-syllabled words.

Plenary

- Share examples of the children's writing. Have they retained a humorous tone? Used emotive language and appropriate tenses? Ask the children to support their comments with examples.
- Ask the children what they found most useful to get their message across – for example, strong verbs, adjectives, direct quotations.

Differentiation

Less able

- Ask children to tape 'Letters to the Editor' of the *Antarctic Echo* and guide them in transcribing and editing.

More able

- Edit articles and transfer to IT in newspaper format.

Follow up

Objectives

NLS

T24: To write a newspaper style report, editing stories to fit a particular space.

S5: To practise using commas to demarcate sentences grammatically.

What you need

- Photocopiable page 61 (enlarged) and photocopiable page 62.

Shared text-level work

- Re-read the article on photocopiable page 61. Invite the children to role-play the characters quoted in the article, each child reading their respective words of direct text.
- Examine the ratio of direct speech to plain reporting text. Note how the quotations break up the text and retain interest.
- Emphasise the importance of capital letters for personal names as well as names of organisations.

Sentence-level work

- Look at the use of commas in the shared text: before or after a name, when their role or status is included: *penguin, Petro*; *spokesbird, King Penguin*; *Petro's partner, Penny*. Also, after opening adverbs: *clearly, meanwhile, apparently, allegedly*.
- Write the following sample sentences:

> Clearly we need a comma in this sentence.
> Meanwhile we must work out where.
> Apparently it helps to get it in the right place.
> Children allegedly learn this at school.

Ask the children to explain where and why commas should be inserted.

- Do any sentences need more than one?

Guided and independent work

- Ask the children to invent a penguin colony's organisational names in keeping with the tone of the original article. These might relate to the young chick's life and his health and safety following his difficult start in life, for example, *SPOCE: The Society for the Prevention of Cold Eggs*.
- Use photocopiable page 62 for children to practise the use of commas in complex sentences and to begin to draft an article.
- Develop a longer article about the emotional reunion between penguin and egg – perhaps just as it's hatching. Remind the children to ask themselves all the 'W' question words. *What* happened to the missing egg? *Who* kept it safe and warm? *Where*? Till *when*? Encourage the children to use emotive language.
- Remind them of the strong verbs used and the direct quotations in the original shared text. Ask the children to try and use a similar emotive, yet humorous tone, in their writing.
- Transfer and further edit the text using IT.
- Re-read work to check for coherence and grammatical correctness.

Plenary

- Review the children's work. Slowly, read compound sentences from some written reports. Ask the children to raise a comma-shaped bent forefinger when they think a comma should appear. Address any errors.

Differentiation

Less able

- Make colour-coded cards of the sentence parts as they appear on photocopiable page 62, for the children to physically shuffle.

More able

- Encourage the children to experiment with a new title or add subtitles to their finished article.

Headlines

Objectives

NLS

T20: To identify features of non-fiction texts.

T21: To predict newspaper stories from the evidence of headlines, making notes and then checking against the original.

W4: To practise new spellings by Look>Say>Cover>Write>Check strategy.

What you need

- Photocopiable page 63
- selection of mounted newspaper and magazine headlines separated from articles, sorted into sets of six
- the headline FIDO AND THE DOGGIE DENTURES written large.

Shared text-level work

- Read the headline to the children. Clarify the meaning of dentures.
- Who is the news story about? Explain that *doggie* works in this headline as an adjective, describing the teeth.
- Ask the children to make brief notes based on the headline, guessing what the story might be about. Remind them to ask themselves questions, for example, *why would a dog have false teeth?*
- Read the whole poem. Who has guessed any correct elements of the text?
- Explain that although this is a poem, with strong rhythm and rhyme, it still tells a story.
- Ask which lines read like headlines. Which might need a word taken out, such as *Dentist makes (him) doggie dentures*? Note how headlines are catchy and brief.
- Consider why the poet chose to make the lines sound like headlines. What does it suggest to the reader?
- Discuss why some lines are printed in italics. These lines are also from a newspaper. Would they appear in a story column or an advertisement in, say, the 'Personal Column'?

Shared word-level work

- Identify words in the poem that contain silent, or lazy, letters. List them: *knocked, column, soften*. Read them aloud and establish which letters are silent. Think of similar words in each category, and invite the children to help you to spell them: *knee, solemn, listen.* Be prepared to explain variations in pronunciation as language changes (*often* with or without the *t* sounded).

Guided and independent work

- Ask the children to highlight lines or phrases, some spreading over the end of a line (enjambement), that read like headlines. Remind them to avoid highlighting words that would be better omitted. Point out that each headline must be able to stand alone meaningfully.
- Distribute prepared headlines and ask the children to make brief notes on what the story might entail. Ask them to find the missing article and note similarities or differences. Underline ideas that were correct and note other aspects of the story.
- Invent alternative headlines for stories they have read.
- Ask the children to practise the silent-letter words through *Look>Say>Cover>Write>Check* spelling strategy. Put the words in sentences to practise spelling in a context.

Plenary

- Write down a few lines from the poem that children have chosen. Discuss which words would require a capital letter in a heading or sub-heading.
- Encourage the children to suggest which phrases work best as headlines and explain why.

Differentiation

Less able

- Prepare simplified stories at a realistic reading level, with separate headlines.

More able

- Search stories on the internet. Note attention-grabbing headlines.

Doggie dentures

Objectives

NLS

T24: To organise writing into paragraphs, using headlines, in newspaper style.

W7: To spell regular verb endings s, ed, ing, recognising changes in tenses.

What you need

- Photocopiable pages 63 and 64
- enlarged copy of the first three verses from page 63.

Shared text-level work

- Display an enlarged copy of the first three verses of the poem, 'Fido and the Doggie Dentures'.
- Read each line aloud, consecutively numbering the start of each line that reads like a headline. Ask where number eight will begin? Halfway through the line, making *Dog learning how to beg* a separate headline.
- Look at lines 11 and 12, but do not number them. Alert the children to the way that the pronouns *they* and *them* require previous knowledge so would not work as stand-alone headlines.
- Choose ten children, each to read one of the first ten lines, reading the end of the third verse yourself.
- Reinforce that, as they read aloud, you want to hear each line sound like a newspaper headline.

Shared word-level work

- Discuss the use of capital letters in line seven – the judge's order, *Leave Dog's Teeth...* .
- Use different-coloured pens to highlight the following verb endings: *s*, *ed* and *ing*.
- Clarify how and why each ending is used and how they relate to tenses, present and past; passive and active.

Guided and independent work

- Provide copies of the poem and photocopiable page 64.
- Ask the children to retell the story of the dog and the postman as a newspaper report. Remind them to use paragraphs.
- Challenge the children to write a separate newspaper-style report about the speeding car that knocked Fido's teeth out. They could consider the following questions:

  Did the driver stop?
  Are the police appealing for witnesses?
  Was the driver charged with dangerous driving?
- Write the lines from the poem that include verbs ending in *ed*. Each is in the passive tense.
- Ask the children to rewrite them in the active present tense: for example, *A speeding car knocks out Fido's teeth*, and the active past tense, for example, *knocked out...* .

Plenary

- Assess the children's writing. Look for sub-headings that reflect the content of the ensuing paragraph. Do they match up? Are the main headlines broad enough for the whole story?
- Ask the children to read some of their speeding car stories. Are they written in a suitable style using paragraphs?

Differentiation

Less able

- Organise children to work in pairs.

More able

- Challenge children to write at greater length and read their articles to the class.

What can we sell you?

Objectives

NLS

T17: To identify features of non-fiction text that support the reader in gaining information efficiently.

T20: To examine the main features of newspapers, including advertisements.

S&L

39 Group discussion and interaction: To take roles within group discussion.

What you need

- Sample newspapers and magazines, including local 'freebie' papers
- photocopiable page 61 (enlarged).

Shared text-level work

- Look at the general layout of newspapers. Draw attention to the advertisements. What purpose do they serve? (Promotion for manufacturers, funds for publishers, information for readers.) Why are there more advertisements in a 'freebie' paper?
- Show examples of advertising features presented to appear like articles (advertorials). Look for small print that tells the reader it is an advertisement. Can an advertising feature be unbiased?
- Return to the 'Penguin Protest' article on page 61, used in earlier hours. Ask what might happen next? The pilots may not change their flight path or it could take time. How will the penguins cope?
- Brainstorm ideas for ways manufacturers could sell products to the penguin colony. Perhaps penguins might wear sound-proof bonnets or buy ready-constructed shelters. Consider attractive names for such items, such as *Instant Igloo*. Suggest egg nets - to stop the egg slipping when you waddle at speed.
- Write some of the claims of manufacturers of real items on the board. Consider the language of the adverts and how similar it is to that of a genuine magazine article . How does it differ in persuasive 'selling' tone?
- Talk about layout and use of captions, bullet points and other eye-catching devices to break up the text and draw in the reader. There might be endorsement from a famous penguin - *as used by King Penguin.*
- Imagine the reader is returning to the text to check on some major detail - is it easy to find? Why?

Guided and independent work

- Organise the children into groups, allocating roles to ensure that all members contribute to discussion and production.
- Ask each group to design an advertising feature for a product to help the penguins cope with the noisy helicopter flights. Encourage inventiveness and humour in keeping with the tone of the original article. Explain that their advert is for the same readership, the *Antarctic Echo.*
- Encourage the children to look closely at features of a variety of adverts to help plan their layout. Remind them to plan pictures and eye-catching captions.
- Draft a layout and make notes in preparation for paragraphs or lists to be included in the finished article.
- Think up a memorable slogan to associate with the proposed product. Support the children's efforts to use catchy language, such as using rhyme, rhythm or alliteration.

Plenary

- Share product names. Which ones immediately indicate the product's purpose? Ask a group spokesperson to explain how they plan to show who the feature is aimed at.
- Listen to some slogans. Ask which ones they think they will still remember tomorrow and why.

Differentiation

Less able

- Ask the children to tape-record an advert orally for their product for *Penguin FM Radio.*

More able

- Encourage the children to develop the design using word-processing and layout software.

Fun run

Objectives

NLS

T17: To imagine headlines and captions based on textual evidence.
T19: To compare the terms fact and opinion and distinguish between them.
T24: To use IT to draft and lay out reports.
S5: To practise using commas to mark grammatical boundaries.
W7: To spell regular past tense of verbs ending in ed.

What you need

- Photocopiable page 65 and 66.

Shared text-level work

- Read the *Fun run* news report but without giving any hint as to a headline. Ask what the article was about. Tell the children that they must think about a possible headline.
- Ask them to look at the picture in conjunction with the story and consider suitable captions.
- Re-read all but the final paragraph as children follow. Point to the punctuation, pausing exaggeratedly at commas with a lifted voice, at full stops with dropped voice, and adopting different voices or accents before and after direct quotations. Ask what is missing from the final paragraph.
- Talk about the facts and opinions contained in the report. Reveal how adjectives and adverbs can be used to qualify a verb and add opinion.
- Point out the use of justified text, easily achieved using IT. Look at the shape of the text from a distance and compare with real newsprint. Why are papers printed like that?

Shared word- and sentence-level work

- Draw attention to the regular past tense verbs ending *ed*. Cover the *ed* and read the stem verbs, *ask, admit* and so on. Point out the doubling of consonants.
- Ask the children to discern (or recognise) the journalistic rule about when to write a numeral and when to write a number-word.

Guided and independent work

- Distribute photocopiable page 66 explaining that the children are to concentrate on headlines, captions and punctuation, paying special attention to the use of commas.
- Challenge the children to imagine they were a fun runner in the *Flora London Marathon*. Who might sponsor them? Why? In aid of what? What costume would they wear and why? Make notes and produce some copy using IT.
- Write a journalist's style sheet, giving advice on writing articles. This could include how to notate numbers, present ages (bracketed), vary tag words, achieve snappy headlines, write captions, answer the five 'W' question words.

Differentiation

Less able

- Provide an enlarged copy of the final paragraph. Read aloud to the children, emphasising pauses.

More able

- Ask the children to imagine a funny incident during John Slogwell's run. Perhaps, took a wrong turning? Met a real astronaut? Lost his helmet? Ask them to add a paragraph to the article, retaining the style.

Plenary

- Ask the children to imagine they are the editor of a newspaper or magazine. What kind of stories would they expect their staff to report on? How would they judge their journalists' reports? Might they refer to the five 'W' words?
- Orally, name regular verbs: *play, jump, fill, skip, kick, wish, look*. Ask individuals to change them into the past tense (for example, *play: We played*) and spell the past participle.

Fantasy news

Objectives

NLS

T24: To develop headlines into paragraphs to a target story length, using IT to draft and lay out the text.
S2: To recognise verbs and understand how to change tense, past and present.

What you need

- 36 mix'n'match word cards: 12 in each of three colours allocated to subject nouns, verbs (past and present tense) and object nouns.

Shared text- and sentence-level work

- Before the lesson begins, write the following words on each set of cards:

Subject nouns	Verbs	Object nouns
man, baby, girl, police officer, clown, visitor, snowman, fairy, ghost, elephant, giant, bus driver	decorates, abandons, takes, chases, drops, paints, protected, soaked, baked, approached, bumped, wanted	car, goldfish, oak, bottle, television, pyjamas, forest, balloon, goat, skateboard

- Place the shuffled cards upside down and ask three children to pick one card from each respective set, holding them up in order. Ask the class to read the short sentence, for example, *Elephant Abandons Pyjamas*. Ask subsequent threesomes to make further selections. Note any that offer a possible funny story line. Return any uninspiring combinations to the shuffled pile.
- Experiment with the idea of the children changing places. Do the sentences still make sense? Can they be grammatically correct without making sense, for example, *Pyjamas abandons Elephant* – if the *pyjamas* were personified it could be grammatically correct if the verb ending was made to agree with the plural subject, *Pyjamas abandon Elephant*.
- Which sentences are present tense and which past tense? Clarify that it is the verb that determines the tense. Try changing the tense as one way of determining which word is the verb.

Guided and independent work

- Ask the children to draft a humorous news story based on their chosen 'mix'n'match' headline. They will either write a report in the present tense or a recount in the past tense.
- Give a word-count limit of 200-250 words, asking the children to edit to this length.
- Hear some opening lines read aloud. Invite comments on how interesting they sound. Do they whet the reader's appetite to read on?
- Encourage the children to read through and check their work. Ensure they have kept to their chosen tense, and that the verb endings agree with the subjects. Remind them that direct quotations can be in the present tense.
- When they have written their stories, ask them to swap headlines with a partner. See if their partner guesses what will happen in their report. They can then read each other's stories to find out.

Plenary

- Choose two or three children who have picked the same headline. Ask others to predict the story line. Ask the children to read their stories to see how similar they are. Do they all satisfy the headline's promise?
- Check for consistency of tense throughout each article.

Differentiation

Less able

- Discuss possible story lines and guide the children to write an opening line. Suggest sub-headings to help pace their story.

More able

- Remind children of the 'Proud Penguin' of Hour 1. Ask them to add an adjective to their headline in front of the subject noun.

Proud Penguin Promoted

by Tara Womersley

A KING penguin was promoted to the rank of honourable regimental sergeant major at Edinburgh Zoo yesterday.

The honour was bestowed by the Norwegian Guard, which is taking part in the city's military tattoo, and the insignia of office was attached to his right flipper.

But, as a band played, the penguin, named Nils Olav, ignored a request to inspect the 18 guardsmen standing to attention before him.

Nils Egelien, 67, a retired major who presided at the ceremony, said that only he and King Harald of Norway had known beforehand the rank that would be bestowed.

Mr Egelien visited the zoo in 1961 and fell in love with its large colony of penguins. The Norwegian army has been sponsoring a penguin there since 1972.

Penguin Nils, formerly a regimental sergeant major, was promoted because of "extraordinarily good" reports from the zoo.

From The Daily Telegraph ,18 August 2001

Non fiction unit 1 Phase 3

Fun with facts

- Sketch an animal school mascot in the box.

1. Write its name:

2. What has the mascot done to deserve an award?

3. What is the award?

4. Who is presenting it?

5. When?

6. Where?

7. Who else will be there?

8. Headline to grab readers' attention:

9. Opening paragraph – in the **past tense**.

10. Sketch a layout design for the text and any illustration opposite:

Key:

Area for large print headline

Areas of journalist's text or 'copy'

Space(s) for picture(s)

Non fiction Unit 1 phase 3

Penguin Protest

From the ***Antarctic Echo***:
PENGUIN PROTEST AT PILOT PRANKS by **Air Correspondent Bill Feather**

Penguin hunts for Egg

Anguish is evident in every feather of penguin, Petro. He is frantically searching for his precious egg.

"It was tucked on my feet, as usual," said the distraught bird (99.5cms), "when a deafening noise overhead scared me half to death. I was terrified and waddled for my life. That's when I … I …"

Petro was too distraught to go on. He is being comforted by friends and family as they continue their search.

"Petro would never abandon our egg. They've never been parted for a second before this helicopter arrived," said Petro's partner, Penny, who laid their egg over 60 days ago. "We are devastated."

Crazy Pilots

Emperor Penguins in Antarctica have to endure strong winds, plummeting temperatures to as low as –30° centigrade. Nothing warms eggs better than fathers' soft feathers as they huddle together. Experts are uncertain how long Petro's chick can survive without him. It is due to hatch in four days.

Meanwhile, penguins have had enough of pilot pranks. They were sparked by a rumour among pilots that, if they fly their helicopters low enough, penguins become mesmerised by the sight. Allegedly, they crane their necks looking up at the steel beasts, then topple over backwards.

"Apparently, the idea of a whole colony of penguins falling over backwards amuses these crazy pilots," said spokesbird, King Penguin, (35kg). "We would not be so stupid," he added. "We have fish to catch and eggs to hatch."

Adding Insult to Injury

Clearly, the pilots' antics are disturbing the peaceful colony. Every bird we spoke to denied the Penguin Topple phenomenon, so dubbed by the irresponsible pilots.

Following frequent disturbance, penguins have begun to demonstrate their anger at these bird baiters. Petro's lost egg is the latest incident to force action. A peaceful breed, the penguins do not wish to retaliate but they do say that enough is enough.

"We are considering taking our case to the Court of Penguin Rights," said one bird. "Until pilots change their flight patterns, we remain very stressed. The whole idea of Penguin Topple is a complete myth. It adds insult to injury to suggest that we would be so daft."

Even as he speaks, a distant whirring subdues the whole colony. As the racket increases, we look up to see another predatory helicopter looming just 1500ft above our heads. All the penguins go quiet and several turn to waddle away. It seems their troubles are not yet over.

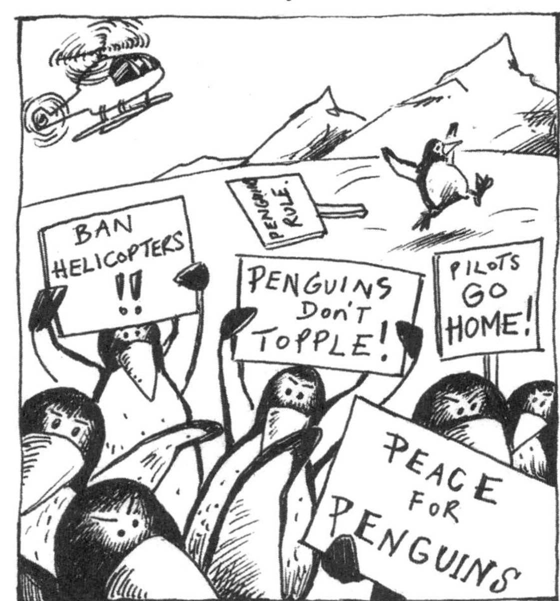

An abandoned placard gathers ice as penguin protester flees in panic.

Penguin Protest: follow up

- Mix and match these sentence openers, sub-clauses and sentence endings.
- Use some or all of them to continue the article in the space below.
- Remember where to use commas.

Subject starters	Sub-clauses	Sentence endings
Petro,	emotional and exhausted,	hugged the fluffy, grey chick.
Penny,	father of the lost egg,	was astonished and delighted.
A spokesbird,	found just in time,	declared himself thrilled to bits.
King Penguin,	who laid the egg,	checked all was well.
The chick,	friend of the family,	was already hatching.
Dr. Penguin,	popular in the colony,	said, "They were very lucky."

- Add new sentences, or alternative sub-clauses, to edit the story.

EMOTIONAL REUNION WITH EGG

This morning, just as hope was fading, Petro and Penny's lost egg was found.

Fido news report

- Read the story-poem 'FIDO AND THE DOGGIE DENTURES'.
- Highlight lines or phrases that would make a good newspaper headline.
- Choose one that reflects the WHOLE story as the main headline.

Reporter's Name:

Main headline ____________________

- Before writing the opening paragraph in the box below, think about the whole story.
- Choose other lines from the poem to use as sub-headings within the story.

- Add further paragraphs in each box, relating to the sub-heading and continuing the news report.

1st Sub-heading ____________________

2nd Sub-heading ____________________

- On another page add a further sub-heading and paragraph if you need it to conclude the news report.

Fido and the doggie dentures

Fido has some wild adventures
Teeth knocked out by speeding car
Dentist makes him doggie-dentures
Fido's bite now worse than bark

Another name for false teeth

Postman chased by grinning Fido
Dog takes bite of postie's leg
Judge now orders: Leave Dog's Teeth
At Home. Dog learning how to beg

Fido wins fresh court appeal
Teeth returned as doggie's right
Postman says they're worse than real ones
He should know: he's felt them bite!

Postie now wins compensation
Fido forced to take out loans:
Postman wants his reparation
Paid in cash and not in bones.

Payment to make up for what has happened to him
To make matters better for them

Fido longs to find an owner
Advertises in the end:
Dog who's tired of being a loner
Seeks a good two-legged friend

Now the postie sees the column:
Fido broke and all alone
Soon his heart begins to soften
Calls up Fido on the phone

Slang word for postman

Postie doesn't want a penny
Simply wants to share his home
With a dog who hasn't any
Teeth, but dentures – and a bone!

By Celia Warren

Fun run – headlines and captions (1)

- Read the story and think of a suitable headline to grab attention.
- Add a caption below the picture.
- Insert missing punctuation in the last paragraph.

- **Headline** ______________________________

You will need commas, full stops and speech marks.

,	.	“ ”
Comma	**Full stop**	**Speech marks**

John Slogwell (28) teacher at Tigworth Primary School, completed last Sunday's *Flora London Marathon* in just over six hours. Despite heavy rain showers, he says he enjoyed the challenge.

“The camaraderie was fantastic,” he said, “from fellow runners and spectators alike.” John's pupils have reason to be pleased, too, as he raised an amazing £350 for school funds.

“We are all very proud of Mr. Slogwell,” said headteacher, Miss Sally Floss, “especially his own Class Four who gave him lots of encouragement during his weeks of training before the event. They also sponsored him very generously.”

The course, which passes such famous landmarks as Tower Bridge and Canary Wharf, covers a distance of 26.2 miles.

“I have blisters on both feet,” John confessed, “but it was worth it. The atmosphere was indescribable. Everyone had such a wonderful time.”

“I was looking forward to seeing my picture in the paper,” he added, “but no-one will recognise me in my fancy dress.”

John one of thousands running alongside professional athletes celebrities from many walks of life and wheelchair athletes said he was certainly in the fun runner category Asked why he chose to dress as an astronaut John explained

If I hadn't been a teacher an astronaut is what I'd like to have been I was too hot in the costume he admitted but I thought I might go like a rocket if I wore that

Fun run – headlines and captions (2)

Speech marks for direct quotations from more than one speaker

Numbers up to ten written in words, unlike higher numbers

Opinion expressed through adjective

Text in columns justified to achieve evenly spaced format

John Slogwell (28) teacher at Tigworth Primary School, completed last Sunday's London Marathon in just over six hours. Despite heavy rain showers, he says he enjoyed the challenge.

"The camaraderie was fantastic," he said, "from fellow runners and spectators alike."

John's pupils have reason to be pleased, too, as he raised an amazing £350 for school funds.

"We are all very proud of Mr. Slogwell," said headteacher, Miss Sally Floss, "especially his own Class Four who gave him lots of encouragement during his weeks of training before the event. They also sponsored him very generously."

Fact

The course, which passes such famous landmarks as Tower Bridge and Canary Wharf, covers a distance of 26.2 miles.

"I have blisters on both feet," John confessed, "but it was worth it. The atmosphere was indescribable. Everyone had such a wonderful time."

"I was looking forward to seeing my picture in the paper," he added, "but no-one will recognise me in my fancy dress."

John, one of thousands running alongside professional athletes, celebrities from many walks of life and wheelchair athletes, said he was certainly in the 'fun runner' category. Asked why he chose to dress as an astronaut, John explained:

"If I hadn't been a teacher, an astronaut is what I'd like to have been. I was too hot in the costume," he admitted, "but I thought I might go like a rocket if I wore that."

Commas break up sentences grammatically

Opinion expressed through adverb

Past tense speech tag words varied – some sound over-dramatic for the context to make the report sound more impressive

SCHOLASTIC

Instructions

In this non-fiction unit children examine and create instructional texts. They will study the appropriateness of the present tense with special attention to imperatives and identify layout features and devices that enable easy retrieval of information. Hour 4 gives practice at using the internet for research and for text comparison purposes. This is a two-week unit and the lesson plans may be extended over this period. There is scope in the second week to allow children to develop instructional texts in topics of their choice or other curriculum areas. This unit also embraces *Grammar for Writing* Unit 20 objectives.

Hour	Shared text-level work	Shared sentence-/ word-level work	Guided work	Independent work	Plenary
1 Mask task	Identifying features of instructional text.	Using imperatives; sequencing text.	Designing a mask and writing instructions on how to make it.	Defining vocabulary in own words.	Checking recognition and use of imperatives.
2 Walk tall	Collecting imperative verbs for a specific purpose.	Spelling by analogy words ending *-alk.*	Planning layout of instructional text.	Writing clear instructions.	Testing spellings and effectiveness of instructions.
3 How to help	Recognising language, including imperatives, layout and purpose of instructions.	Observing the effect of changing verbs from present to past tense.	In groups: discussing and putting plan into practice.	Writing cohesive, clear instructions for a model.	Explaining decisions over use of language; revising imperatives.
4 The Countryside Code	Investigating how reading strategies are adapted for IT.	Comparing imperative and other verbs used in present tense; looking at use of logos.	Researching on the internet to develop content of own writing.	Writing a home behaviour code with outcome presented as key messages	.Comparing use of advisory and imperative verbs.
5 Ready, steady, go	Defining the purpose of instructions, listening to them and discussing effectiveness.	Determining tense of verbs for instructional purposes, especially imperatives.	Using link word *because* to create cohesive sentences.	Re-read own writing to assess effectiveness and identify and correct errors.	Looking at organisation of children's written instructions, noting imperatives.

Key assessment opportunities

- Can the children identify verbs written in the imperative?
- Can they justify which instructions match the desired outcome?
- Do they understand how logos can represent an instruction?
- Can they sequence instructions logically?

Mask task

Objectives

NLS
T22: To identify features of instructional text.
W11: To define vocabulary in own words finding alternative expressions.

What you need

- Photocopiable page 73 (enlarged)
- dictionaries
- an undecorated mask (or sketch) to support the written instructions, with one side trimmed; the other ragged; only eye holes cut to show later.

Shared text-level work

- Display photocopiable page 73. Clarify *three dimensional*. Which words in the title show that instructions will follow? What will be the outcome?
- How does layout affect how easy it is to follow instructions or find where you are up to?
- Examine how numbering clarifies that instructions are sequential.
- Are most sentences simple, that is, only one clause? Are they unambiguous?
- Are any instructions not explicit, for example, *how* to decorate the mask? Are there any clues in the list of materials?
- Reveal the prepared blank 3D mask (or sketch). Ask the children if it looks how they imagined. Support opinions from the text. Which instructions are demonstrated, for example, criss-crossing the paper for strength; cutting a crisp edge. Find evidence of instructions not followed.

Shared word-level work

- Highlight the first word in each numbered line. What kind of words are they? Introduce the term *imperative verb*. Offer more examples of verbs used as commands.
- Write the twelve verbs on cards. Give the children a card each and challenge them to stand with their cards in the correct sequence.

Guided and independent work

- Ask the children to plan a design for a blank mask. List the materials they would need to decorate it – think of colour, trimmings, hair-effects, ornaments, and so on. Is it to be a cartoon or real character, a generic character or simply a disguise? Make notes to develop into instructions.
- Challenge the children in groups to design a mask based on a paper plate for, for example: a phoenix; a fairy; a lion; a clown; a dragon. Ask one child to write the first instruction and pass it to the next to write the second, and so on.
- List the following words: *inflate, harm, expendable, abandon, puncture, embellish*. Ask the children to [a] define these words in their own words, then [b] find words or phrases within the shared text that mean the same thing. Write the quotations alongside to compare with their definitions.

Plenary

- Read out some group instructions and ask or invite questions where clarification is needed. Suggest amendments to tighten the text.
- Use some appropriate commands, commonly used in class, such as *Stop writing, Sit on the carpet*. Remind the children that these are verbs used in the imperative. Invite further examples, such as *Put your hands up, Sit still, Form a line, Find a partner, Remember your kit, Sharpen your pencil, Go home*!

Differentiation

Less able
- Scribe the children's instructions or ask them to draw sequential diagrams. Cut up the list and ask them to reorder the instructions and copy them below drawings.

More able
- Ask the children to write brief instructions on how to use the finished mask – sound affects, body movements, voice volume and annunciation.

Walk tall

Objectives

NLS
T25: To write clear instructions using conventions learned from reading.
T26: To use numbering and logos to help organise cohesive written directions.
W10: To spell *walk* from medium frequency list and similar words by analogy.

What you need

- Word cards: *sit, roll, crawl, shuffle, totter, rock, grab, hold, reach, stand, lift, move, step, raise, bend, lower, shift, balance, drop, lean, look, try, walk, run, hop, skip, jump, fly*. Plus some blank spares.

Shared text- and word-level work

- Ask the children what it would be like to have instructions for everything.
- Imagine a very clever baby who can read but cannot walk. What instructions could they write to guide the baby?
- Read the verb cards. Establish that they are imperatives. Begin sorting them into sequential stages, for example, what the baby does before it can walk. At what stage will the baby achieve the intended outcome? Can we discard any word cards?
- Invite the children to come out and hold up an opening imperative. Continue, inviting subsequent instructions, until you have a complete set.
- Write down each instruction as the children create it.
- Ask the children in turn to read out their own instruction until the complete set is read.
- Together decide on a suitable title for the instruction sheet.
- Look again at the mask-making instructions for Hour 1. Notice the tips. On blank cards, write some imperative verbs to use to insert tips. For example, *avoid* (*sharp corners*), *watch, mind, wear, keep, hold, check,* and so on.
- Practise spelling *walk* through the *Look>Say>Cover>Write>Check* strategy and similarly spelt words by analogy, with clues: *speak or utter, the stem of a flower, soft white mineral,* and so on.

Guided and independent work

- Plan a format for the baby's instructions on 'How to walk'. What decorations would attract the baby's attention or reflect its environment? What size font would a baby need? Could the font change colour with each step?
- Add humorous tips: *Don't grab dogs – they move! Never step on the cat! Limit your first walk to less than a kilometre.*
- Write a humorous set of instructions teaching a baby 'How to Annoy Older Brothers and Sisters', for example, *Take toys without asking; Tear book (Tip: make sure this is a favourite annual!); Scream louder than the TV set; Wet nappy for Dad to change, just as he's about to play football. (Tip: Make this a smelly one).*
- What might be a suitable safety tip? For example, *If things go badly, smile for the first time at your sibling and look your cuddliest!*

Plenary

- Read the children's sample instructions on 'How to Walk' and try them out. Amend any flaws or omissions.
- Ask the children some oral compound-word spellings using the *alk* trigraph.

Differentiation

Less able
- Provide word banks to help the children, and colour code imperative verbs.

More able
- Ask the children to find compound words, for example, sleepwalk, shoptalk, catwalk. Challenge them to think up clues and swap these with partners to guess and spell.

How to help

Objectives

NLS

T22: To identify features of instructional text.
T25: To write clear instructions based on conventions learned from reading.
T26: To improve the cohesion of written instructions and directions through the use of link phrases and organisational devices such as sub-headings and numbering.
S2: To develop awareness of how tense relates to purpose and structure of text.

S&L

39 Group discussion and interaction: To adopt group roles for discussion and implementation of plan.

What you need

- A selection of traditional stories and fairy tales
- photocopiable page 74 enlarged

Shared text-level work

- Look together at the instructional poster. How does the layout differ from previous instructions? Read each section.
- Ask the children who the target readership is.
- Look at the instructions again in context – do they seem harder now?
- Why do they think the safety warning appears in a star? What effect does background and layout have on the reader?
- What do the children recognise about the text – where is the idea from?
- Read and sequence key events to retell the original story. Identify links and references from the instructional poster.
- Identify the six components of the poster: *picture and caption; background information; highlighted advice or slogan; sequential instructions; safety warning; hints.*

Shared sentence-level work

- Discuss what tense the text is written in. Ask the children to change verbs to the past tense. Do they still sound like instructions?
- Ask which parts of the text are NOT instructions. Why are *things to remember* included? Can children explain why pronouns are omitted?
- Read the numbered instructions. In isolation, do they sound easy to follow? Consider quantity, sentence length, simplicity and opening imperatives. Which instruction sounds the easiest? Which the hardest?
- Discuss which words are identical to those in the traditional story.
- Why do they think the verb *grab* is repeated? Introduce the term *parody*.

Guided and independent work

- Ask the children to adopt the viewpoint of the gingerbread man and devise a simple set of instructions to help him escape.
- In groups, read stories to refresh memory of the characters, setting and sequence of events.
- Ask the children, in groups, to plan an instructional poster, giving advice to chosen character(s) in a traditional story. Allocate a story to each group. For example:

> *The Billy Goats Gruff* – How to cross the troll bridge
> *Goldilocks* – How to make the most of your visit to the bears' house
> *Red Riding Hood* – How to get to Grandma's house and home again
> *Cinderella* – How to prepare for a Prince's ball

- Decide whose viewpoint the group will address.
- Ask each group member to write one section of the poster but plan and produce the layout as a group.

Plenary

- Ask the children to explain how they chose what aspects of the original story to determine their sets of instructions, tips and slogans.
- Ask groups to read samples of their writing and ask others to identify the imperatives.

Differentiation

Less able

- Provide simplified versions of stories; arrange mixed-ability groups.

More able

- Encourage children to adopt a different viewpoint and prepare a set of sequential instructions for another character, such as *Sleeping Beauty: How to stay awake when under a spell.*

The Countryside Code

Objectives

NLS
T23: To investigate how reading strategies are adapted to suit IT properties.
T25: To write clear instructions using conventions learned from reading.
W11: To define familiar vocabulary in their own words.

What you need

- Photocopiable page 75 (enlarged and individual)
- access to the internet.

Shared text- and sentence-level work

- Look at the shared text on photocopiable page 75. Identify the broad readership.
- Explain that the information here is derived from direct quotations from the Countryside Access website. Find this website (www.countrysideaccess.gov.uk) and click on links to further information. Investigate how differently the text is presented; look at hyperlinks and scrolling text. Would all the website information fit on one sheet of A4 paper?
- Ask the children who else is addressed on the website? (land managers). Is this as broad an audience? How do these two readerships complement each other?
- Examine how logos can convey instructions in conjunction with or instead of words. To whom could this be useful?
- Write a dress code for walking in the countryside.

Shared sentence- and word-level work

- Ask the children to consider the word *code* - suggesting guidance rather than rules. Are imperatives used? Where? How else are verbs used: *it's best, you may, be prepared*? How does this affect the tone?
- Draw attention to the *Key Messages* - all imperatives. What about the verbs in the other box?
- Point out that on both the website and the poster certain words are in a larger font. Why? Which are verbs?
- Discuss meanings of words such as *restricted* and *local*.

Guided and independent work

- Ask the children to visit the *Countryside Access* website to find more details on the last five bullet points of the Countryside Code. What other advice is given, for example, on the danger of fires?
- Challenge the children to research areas of the *Countryside Code* on the internet. They should write an information sheet, expanding on one area. Suggest looking at safety matters, local weather forecasts, up-to-date information or maps.
- Invite the children to find information via the internet on the *VisitBritain* website. What kind of advice is given? Note sentences that contain imperative verbs.
- From the *Countryside Access* website, write the quotation: *Treat the countryside as you would treat your home*. Challenge the children to write a short *Home Behaviour Code* that satisfies the same *Key Messages* criteria: *Respect, Protect, Enjoy*. Consider environment care and preservation, home safety, consideration to others.
- Ask them to design and label appropriate *Home Behaviour Code* logos.

Differentiation

Less able
- Ask the children to colour the arrows as indicated on photocopiable page 75. Ask them to draw people on a country walk. In speech bubbles, add sensible rules to follow.

More able
- Challenge the children to design a website homepage to accompany their written work.

Plenary

- How has the class used verbs. Which are imperative? Which advisory?
- Listen to some of the children's rewordings of definitions and assess their accuracy.

Ready, steady, go

Objectives

NLS

T22: To use imperatives clearly with a pre-determined purpose.

T26: To improve cohesion of written instructions through use of link phrases.

S1: To reread own writing in order to correct errors.

S&L

Medium term plan: To listen to instructions and discuss their effectiveness.

What you need

- Paper and pencils
- red and black crayons and word cards (see *Differentiation*).

Shared text-level work

- Ask the children to imagine a school trip to the country. As you read instructions, they should make notes. Read the following:

> - So that we have a safe and successful day, listen carefully.
> - Do bring: a packed lunch, with no glass; a pair of binoculars, if you have them; waterproof clothing, wellies. The school will provide a picnic rubbish-sack.
> - Do not bring: money, toys, cameras or other valuables.
> - Before we go: Choose a partner to sit with on the coach; Take
> - travel sickness tablets if you need to.
> - On the day: Arrive at school by 8.30a.m. Remind your parents that we will be arriving back at normal school home time.
> - Remember NOT to bring umbrellas, only waterproofs.

- Ask the children what the purpose of these instructions is. How could it improve/spoil the day if children do/don't follow them?
- Ask, if it were a real trip, would the children have any questions?
- Invite the children to answer specific questions, referring to their notes: *What will we do with empty wrappers? Can I bring my teddy bear? When will we get back? Do we need pens? How much money do we need?*
- Do any instructions include justification? Are there circumstances where giving reasons could help? (For example, *Do not bring umbrellas because they could poke someone's eye.*)

Shared sentence- and word-level work

- Ask the children to determine the tense used in the instructions.
- Ask them which heading means the same as *Before we go*? Re-read the preparations under this heading and ask the children to tell you which words are the imperatives.

Guided and independent work

- Take each of the *Do not bring* instructions and ask the children to complete the sentence with *because* ... and an explanation. For example, *Do not bring toys because there will not be room or time for you to play with them.*
- Write four headings on the board: *Bring, Do not bring, Preparations, Transport.* Ask the children to write a school note aimed at parents about the school trip.
- Encourage the children to re-read their writing and check for coherence and accuracy.

Plenary

- Invite the children to read out a sentence from their school note. Can others guess which heading it comes under?
- Note the imperatives the children have used.

Differentiation

Less able

- Support the children to speak clearly in sentences by elaborating their words or phrases and by modelling complete sentences.

More able

- Encourage the children to use a greater range of vocabulary.

How to make a 3-D mask

YOU WILL NEED
a round balloon
petroleum jelly
a newspaper - torn into strips, approx. 15cm x 3cm
paste and a brush
scissors
elastic
acrylic paints (to decorate your finished mask)
bits of wool and string, etc.

Safety tip
If you use wallpaper paste make sure you wear protective polythene gloves. Such paste often contains an anti-fungal agent that can damage your skin.

1. Blow up a balloon. (Warning: You will be bursting this later so make sure it is not wanted!)
2. Spread petroleum jelly over the whole surface of the balloon.
   TIP: it's easiest to hold the balloon at the tied neck.
3. Wash your hands to remove grease. Lay strips of newspaper over the balloon. Make sure these criss-cross until the whole balloon is covered.
4. Apply a layer of paste.
   TIP: if you don't have a brush, use a piece of stiff card!
5. Continue to add strips of newspaper. Criss-cross and overlap in different directions from the layer below.
6. Allow to dry a little before adding further layers. Continue until your mask is about the thickness of thin cardboard.
7. Leave until the glue and paper is thoroughly dry. This may take a few days!
   TIP: it should sound hard and woody when you tap it!
8. Pinch the neck of the balloon and pierce with scissors to deflate. Remove and discard the balloon.
9. Trim the edge with scissors to neaten the shape, using one half.

10. Place it over your face and mark with a soft crayon the position of your eyes, nose and mouth
    TIP: ask a friend to help!
11. Ask an adult to help you to cut out eye, nose and mouth holes. Keep these small – you can always enlarge them later if you need to!
12. Fix elastic to each side of the mask so that it lies just above your ears.
    Your basic papier mâché mask is now complete. All you need to do now is decorate it as the character of your choice.

How to catch a gingerbread man

Things to remember about your gingerbread man:

- Tastes delicious, oven-fresh, so look there first.
- Smells mouth-wateringly tasty.
- Can run very, very fast.
- Is arrogant and over-confident.
- Will taunt you by singing a boringly repetitive song: DO NOT WEAR EAR-PLUGS! – Tempting as it may be, you NEED to hear the gingerbread man's song as it will lead you to him.

Run, run, as fast as you can
You can't catch me I'm the
gingerbread man

Follow that song!

1. **Put on oven gloves.**
2. **Open oven door slowly.**
3. **Grab, grab as fast as you can!**
4. **Eat and enjoy.**

SAFETY FIRST!
– the Gingerbread Man will be hot and keen to escape:
Hold him in oven glove to avoid burning bare fingers.
Take a bite only when you are sure you won't burn your tongue.

HINTS FOR SUCCESS IF YOUR GINGERBREAD MAN ESCAPES:

- Ask friends to chase your gingerbread man towards a river.
- Dress up as a fox and wait on the river bank – offer to ferry the gingerbread man across on your nose. BE READY TO BITE!

The Countryside Code

WELCOME!

Key Messages:

- Respect
- Protect
- Enjoy

The activities that can be enjoyed in the English countryside are as varied as the places you can visit. Most of them are free of charge and all of them are great for your health!

You can picnic, paint or take photos, walk the dog, or simply 'get away from it all'. From a gentle amble, to a long distance cycle ride; from paddling down a river, to climbing a mountain – there's something for everyone.

Even when going out locally, it's best to get the latest information about where and when you can go; for example, your rights to go onto some areas of open land may be restricted while work is carried out, for safety reasons or during breeding seasons. Follow advice and local signs, and be prepared for the unexpected.

You're responsible for your own safety and for others in your care, so be prepared for changes in weather and other events.

Part of the appeal of the countryside is that you can get away from it all. You may not see anyone for hours and there are many places without clear mobile-phone signals, so let someone else know where you're going and when you expect to return.

Footpath waymark yellow

Bridleway waymark blue

Byway waymark red

National Trails

Open Access

Refer to up-to-date maps or guidebooks.

Check weather forecasts before you leave, and don't be afraid to turn back.

Get to know the signs and symbols used in the countryside to show paths and open countryside.

The Countryside Code – advice for the public:

- **Be safe** – plan ahead and follow any signs
- **Leave** gates and property as you find them
- **Protect** plants and animals, and take your litter home
- Keep dogs under close **control**
- **Consider** other people

UNIT 7

Reports

This non-fiction unit looks at non-chronological reports and their purpose and target audience. There is special reference to the difference between specifics and generalities, and editing text to adjust the level of detail appropriately. The unit also looks at use of tenses, especially in Hour 2, with exercises that reinforce the use of the present tense. Then in Hour 3 the difference between fact and opinion is touched upon. The unit includes work on spellings to include the suffixes *al* and *ary* and addresses Grammar for Writing Unit 21 objectives.

Hour	Shared text-level work	Shared sentence-/ word-level work	Guided work	Independent work	Plenary
1 The wind	Identifying organisational devices and features that help the reader glean information.	Spellings derived from bases of compass directions; adjectives; adverbs.	Defining terms through rephrasing in their own words.	Retrieving information from a non-chronological report on *The wind*.	Reinforcing how layout aids efficient and speedy retrieval of information.
2 Then, now and forecast	Picking out key phrases that convey information.	Investigating and revising verb tenses.	Practice applying appropriate tenses contextually.	Writing in past and present tenses for different purposes respectively.	Review use of tenses and style, analysing why tense changes.
3 Busy fingers	Examining the impact of opening sentences; sorting fact from opinion.	Recognising and spelling the suffix ***ary***.	Writing a concise non-chronological report that is purely factual.	Re-reading and deleting unnecessary detail to keep report generalised.	Hear samples of precise writing and reinforce ***ary*** suffix.
4 In general terms	Developing recognition of key elements of non-chronological reports.	Recognising and spelling the suffix ***al***.	Writing a personal interest non-chronological report.	Finding adjectives ending in ***al*** in text and spelling by rhyme and analogy.	Checking for levels of detail and editing; practice spelling of the ***al*** suffix.
5 Look again	To re-read own work and identify errors and delete words and phrases to improve cohesion.	Developing awareness of how tense relates to purpose and structure of text.	Writing in groups, concisely, with use of lists and headings.	Writing a hints list with use of imperatives.	Role-play about a new pupil to test the effectives of writing aimed at a specific requirement.

Key assessment opportunities

- Can the children recognise the difference between a specific fact and a general fact and edit their writing to reflect this?
- Are they able to recognise and change the tense of regular verbs and the irregular verb *to be*?
- Can they create adjectives with the suffixes *ary* and *al*?

The wind

Objectives

NLS

T17: To identify features of non-fiction text.
T18: To pick out key sentences/phrases that convey information.
S4: To recognise and create adverbs.
W3: To build spelling from other words with similar patterns and meanings.
W11: To define familiar vocabulary in their own words.

What you need

- Photocopiable pages 82 and 83
- three coloured pens.

Shared text-level work

- Read photocopiable page 82 together. Draw attention to the words in bold. Look at the phrases that precede them: *sometimes known as...* ; *called a...* .What does this tell us about the highlighted words?
- Re-read the text, asking comprehension questions after each paragraph. *Is a region of low pressure an anti-cyclone or a depression*? Point out how the bold font helps to locate information.
- Why do they think, in paragraph three when *pressure gradient* is mentioned again, it is no longer in bold? Is it easy to check the meaning of the term? Why?
- Look at the layout of the Beaufort scale. Remind the children that this is 200 years old. Ask why it was, and still is useful.
- Draw attention to the table format; forces in numerical order; the range of speeds; the simple terminology and longer descriptions.
- Tell the children that a friend phoned and told you it was *very windy*. You wondered *how* windy was *very*! Then she said that bits of paper were blowing around. Who can tell you how windy it was on the Beaufort scale? Later, the friend rang to say the wind was Force 10. What do they think she was worried about?
- Based on the chart's information, would they feel safe playing out in a 20mph wind? Could they easily play tennis in a 35mph wind? Why not?

Shared word-and sentence-level work

- Write the words *west* and *westerly* on the board. Then write *east*. Can they guess the related adverb?
- Demonstrate how an adjective is created. Cover up *ly* and ask the children to read *west-er...* Explain that, *if you came from the west you would be wester...* Pause long enough for children to add the *n* to say *western*.
- Write the four main directions on the board. Create a table showing noun - adjective - adverb: *north northern northerly*. Invite the children to spell the missing words to complete the table, colour-coding each syllable.
- Explain the convention of using initial letters to represent directions.

Differentiation

Less able

- Draw a cross and the initial letters of directions for children to complete the words. Provide cloze procedure sentences, such as, *A wind from the N.... is a n........ wind.*

More able

- Challenge the children to discern and write directions such as *north-west(erly)*.

Guided and Independent work

- Ask the children to recreate the erased directions table. Start them off with headings: *noun - adjective - adverb* and initial letters.
- Invite the children to re-read the report, answering questions on photocopiable page 83.
- Encourage the children to write the meanings of phrases in bold, in their own words.

Plenary

- Ask the children to retrieve information at speed from the Beaufort scale.
- Reinforce how the layout and numbering helps to locate information.

Then, now and forecast

Objectives

NLS

T18: To pick out key phrases that convey information.

S2: To revise and investigate verb tenses.

What you need

- Photocopiable pages 82, 83 and 84
- writing materials.

Shared text-level work

- Re-read *The wind*. Establish that this is written in the present tense. Explain that tense means time. Wind blows all the time so the present tense is appropriate to describe its *general* behaviour.
- Can the children identify any verbs NOT in the present tense in the final paragraph? (*was* and *began*).
- Discuss the involvement of time and occasion in determining why these are past tense verbs.

Shared word-and sentence-level work

- Take a well-completed sample of photocopiable page 83.
- Refresh the children's memories of the picture, how the day began, what storm damage followed and why.
- Ask the children to picture themselves at the top of the hill. They can see the sea to the east and the valley and church to the west. Ask them about the wind. What *was* it like this morning? *On the coast, the wind blew ...* What *is* it like now (at noon)? What *will it be* like tonight? Scribe sentences underlining the verbs and reinforcing tenses.
- Ask the children to imagine that they are Josh. Ask: *What did you do this morning? What did you eat for breakfast?(I played ...; I ate ...) What are you doing/eating now? What will you do/eat later?* Emphasise the verb changes.
- Demonstrate how to create past, present and future tenses with regular verbs, such as *skip*, showing how to double the consonant before *ed* and *ing*.

Guided and Independent work

- Use photocopiable page 84 to help the children practise changing tenses and to write their own weather forecasts.
- Remind the children of the purpose of the original report. Ask them to imagine they visited Earth from another planet. On return to their own planet they write about Earth's winds.
- Point out that their report has a different purpose and audience. Ask them to revise the text (or a selected paragraph) of the original report from photocopiable page 82, using the past tense. *Wind occurred as air moved* ... and so on.
- Ask the children to write a contemporary nineteenth-century report, in the present tense, briefly describing what Francis Beaufort *is* working on and why. They might begin, *In these days of sailing ships ...*

Plenary

- Ask the children to read out some of their forecasts. Discuss how the style compares to the (present tense) non-chronological report. Invite them to explain why it can't all be in the present tense.
- Hear some of the *Alien* and *Beaufort* reports. Is the tense correct? Look closely at verbs. How do stem words compare?

Differentiation

Less able

- Provide a cloze procedure using word cards: blew, blows, blowing and blow with simple terms such as yesterday, today, tomorrow.

More able

- Research *Buys Ballot* and find out what law he discovered about the wind. Write a report in a chosen tense.

Busy fingers

Objectives

NLS

T18: To examine opening sentences that set scenes, capture interest.
T19: To understand and use the terms fact and opinion; and to begin to distinguish the two in reading and other media.
T27: To write a non-chronological report, deleting unimportant detail.
W9: To recognise and spell the suffix *ary*.

What you need

- Photocopiable page 85
- writing materials.

Shared text-level work

- Fill an A4 sheet with the opening sentence of the shared text. Is it difficult to imagine? Why not? Does it intrigue them, make them want to know more?
- Explain that it is the first line of the shared text. Write the title and ask if, with the sentence, this helps them to anticipate the subject.
- Ask the children to read the report. Examine which parts tell us about origami itself and which offer extra information. If they had to shorten the article, which parts might they leave out? For example, how long ago paper was invented or details of how to make a dart.
- Draw attention to the organisational devices of the text. Note how the brevity of hints makes the activity seem simple and achievable. What is the effect of numbering? The imperatives inform directly. Note how the key to symbols is easy to relocate. Look at paragraphs and opening lines.
- Compare statements such as, *Many (models) begin with the same set of folds* with *Origami is ... fun*. Which is fact and which opinion?

Shared word-level work

- Look at the opening word, *imagine* - a verb. Ask what other words in this paragraph come from the same root. (*imagination* - a noun; *imaginary* - an adjective). Write all three words, colour-coding the six stem-letters. Consider why *imaginary* is in brackets. (To remind readers of the earlier references to imagination?)
- Locate other words ending in *ary* (*primary, library, elementary*). Highlight the common letter string. Invite children to spell other words ending in the same suffix, for example: *ordinary, granary, summary, binary, secondary, burglary.*

Guided and Independent work

- Ask the children to underline facts rather than opinion. From these, ask them to write a brief, factual report, beginning *Origami is ...*, avoiding opinion.
- Encourage the children to compose a more interesting opening line, avoiding the word *Imagine*.
- Ask them to rewrite the hints to be succinct, avoiding explanation. Based on the content, can they add another hint, such as, *Never use scissors.*
- Encourage the children to swap reports and invite mutual suggestions of what text could be deleted.
- Ask them to practise spelling words with the *ary* suffix. Can they think of three proper nouns that also end in *ary*: two months of the year and a country beginning with *H*?

Plenary

- Listen to a selection of added hints. Are they practical?
- Invite oral and written spellings of words ending in *ary*.

Differentiation

Less able

- Pair with able readers. Ask them to write a simple definition of origami.

More able

- Challenge the children to research titles and authors of origami books and create a bibliography.

In general terms

Objectives

NLS

T27: To write a non-chronological report using organisational devices and generalising some details.
W9: To recognise and spell the suffix *al*.

What you need

- Photocopiable pages 85 and *86*
- writing materials.

Shared text-level work

- Continuing from the previous hour, look again at photocopiable page 85. Ask the children to describe its purpose, style and organisational devices.
- Remind the children of the meaning of origami and classify its nature, for example, interest, hobby, art, skill, pastime. Ask for examples of their interests and list them under headings: hobbies, clubs, pets, sports.
- Discuss how some fit under more than one heading, such as football club.
- Ask the children to think of opening sentences for factual reports about their interests. Share written examples and invite comments on their effectiveness.
- Consider sub-headings, numbered lists and other devices. Explain that specifics, such as match fixture dates, would be inappropriate in a general article on Under-11s football. General details, however, such as a typical training regime, would be appropriate.
- Draw on the original text for examples of generalised details. Pose questions, such as, Do you need any special tools? Is there more than one way to fold models? Compare specific questions. Who is the youngest person ever to design a new origami model? What is the symbol for 'Turn the Paper Over'? Are answers in the report? Reinforce the need to omit less important details and generalise others.
- Note how Or is used in paragraph two, but NOT as a connective. This is to generalise possibilities that could, otherwise, sound finite.

Shared word-level work

- Write add. Underneath, write addition. Add al, and read additional. Explain that it is now an adjective. Describe how the suffix adds additional letters.
- Distribute the shared text and ask the children to underline any word in the first paragraph that ends in al: central. Establish that this is derived from the noun (and verb) centre.

Guided and Independent work

- Ask the children to write a report about a personal interest, choosing a category discussed in the shared sessions. Remind them to generalise and be selective about the level of detail.
- Challenge the children in pairs to underline and list all the adjectives they can find ending in al in the shared text. Note: There are fourteen!
- Ask the children, in pairs, to take turns reading the list while the other writes the words. They should check and rewrite any with errors.
- Using photocopiable page 85, ask the children to spell short adjectives ending in al, by rhyme and analogy.

Plenary

- Listen to some reports. Discuss how details may be deleted if they become too specific or rephrased into more general terms.
- Check and correct spellings from the Normal Formal Clues worksheet.

Differentiation

Less able

- Provide small onset letters: *l, v, f, d, n, r* for use with photocopiable page 85.

More able

- Encourage the children to put their adjectives into sentences showing how they would modify the noun.

Look again

Objectives

NLS
T26: To improve the cohesion of written instructions and directions through the use of organisational devices.
T27: To write a non-chronological report including the use of organisational devices.
S1: To reread own writing to identify errors and consider alternatives.
S2: To develop awareness of how tense relates to the purpose and structure of text.

S&L
37 Speaking: To use ground rules for group dialogue, discuss, plan, draft and edit a report.

What you need

- The children's writing from the previous hour
- writing materials.

Shared text-level work

- Remind the children of the importance of generalising details and deleting less important specifics when writing a non-chronological report.
- From their writing in the previous hour, share good examples of sentences which demonstrate these criteria.
- Identify the use of powerful verbs.
- Consider examples of sentences that could be deleted without the report losing its flow. Invite suggestions.

Shared word- and sentence-level work

- Select a report that you feel is well written and follows the guidelines. Read it aloud to the class, or encourage its author to read it aloud.
- Invite comments on why it is successful. Look at the opening lines, use of interesting vocabulary, generalisation and also organisational devices. Explain that the children will be using these skills for a group report.
- List imperatives that could be used in an advisory capacity to a new child joining their class: *do, don't, arrive, go, leave, bring, remember, avoid, listen, look, put, try, sit.*
- Ask the children to improvise a helpful hint to follow each imperative. Write some as sentences, such as, *Do speak in a clear voice. Don't eat sweets in class.* Consider which tense suits the purpose and structure of the sentences.

Guided and independent work

- Organise the children into groups. Explain that they are to discuss and plan a concise report on *Life in Our Classroom.*
- Ask them to imagine that a new child joining their class is their target reader. Their report should give the newcomer basic information to help them to settle in quickly and confidently.
- Remind the children that sub-headings and lists may help in keeping the report concise and information easily retrieved.
- Ask the children to write a *Helpful Hints* or a *Dos and Don'ts* section to go with the report, using some or all of the imperatives from the shared list.

Differentiation

Less able
- Provide imperatives on word-cards for children to copy. Support them in writing sentences.

More able
- Ask the children to turn their initial report into a folded A4 pamphlet with a welcoming cover and title.

Plenary

- Invite the children to engage in role-play about a new pupil and for the new pupil to ask questions.
- Ask others to answer the questions from their written work, or to make notes of items that could be usefully added.

The wind

Wind occurs as air moves from a region of high pressure to a region of low pressure, sometimes known as **anti-cyclones** and **depressions**. The rate of change of pressure over distance is known as the **pressure gradient**. However, the actual direction of movement is not straight from high to low pressure. It is complicated by many factors but usually circles in to the centre, rather like water draining from a basin.

Air moves at different speeds and directions at different levels above the ground, or **altitudes**. We notice the low level winds most. A wind that usually blows steadily from one direction is called a **prevailing wind**. If you look how trees lean in exposed areas, you can often see the direction of the prevailing wind. The British Isles lie between the Atlantic Ocean to the west and the continents of Europe and Asia to the east. Here, the prevailing wind tends to be westerly.

The earth's spin, the pressure gradient, terrain, or **topography**, and altitude can all affect the wind direction. It is the differences in pressure that determine how hard the wind blows. The greater the difference between two areas, the faster the air will move, so the stronger the wind will blow.

Winds that build up great speed and strength are called gales, storms or hurricanes. In the days of sailing ships, being able to observe, predict and communicate the wind levels was very important. One way of describing the strength of the wind is to use a scale named after its British inventor and Royal Navy sailor, Francis Beaufort, RN who began its design in 1805. The wind levels are numbered from 0, **calm**, to 12, **hurricane**.

Jane A. Russell

THE BEAUFORT SCALE

No.	Speed in mph	Wind	Effect over land
0	1	Calm	Smoke rises vertically
1	1–3	Light air	Smoke drifts
2	4–7	Light breeze	Leaves rustle, wind felt on face
3	8–12	Gentle breeze	Leaves move, light flag is extended
4	13–18	Moderate breeze	Dust and loose paper blows about. Small branches move
5	19–24	Fresh breeze	Small trees sway a little
6	25–31	Strong breeze	Large branches sway, wires whistle
7	32–38	Moderate gale	Whole trees sway, hard to walk against the wind
8	39–46	Fresh gale	Twigs break off trees, very hard to walk into wind
9	47–54	Strong gale	Chimney pots and slates blown off. Large branches down
10	55–63	Whole gale	Trees uprooted, serious damage to buildings
11	64–72	Storm	Very rare inland, causes widespread damage
12	72+	Hurricane	Disastrous results

A change in weather

■ Look at this picture and then answer the questions. Explain your answers.

1. Which way is the wind blowing from near the coastline? (Ring one):

It is a northerly / southerly / westerly / easterly wind.

2. Is this the prevailing wind in this region? How do you know? ____________________

____

3. What number do you think the wind would measure on the Beaufort scale to the west of the hill? ____________________

4. Josh, playing on the beach, said, "I can feel the wind in my face". How would you describe the wind force using the Beaufort scale? ____________________

____

5. The following day it was a different picture. On the local news that night the reporter said, "The wind reached speeds of 50 miles per hour." How could you describe that wind?

____

Draw examples of damage that occurred that night.

6. Look at the pictures below. What force do you think the wind measured on the Beaufort scale?

____

Cloud shapes

blows

■ Improve these sentences.

1. Yesterday, the wind will blow so strongly that my hat blowed off.

Yesterday, the wind was ________ so strongly that my hat _______ off.

2. Today, there was no wind so no-one's hat is blew off.

Today, ____

3. Tomorrow, there was an easterly gale that may blowing trees down.

Tomorrow, ____

■ Write a weather forecast of your own. Begin by telling people what the weather *was doing*; then say what it *is doing now* and, finally, what tonight and tomorrow *will bring*.

At midnight last night ________________________________

____

At dawn this morning _________________________________

____

Now, this lunchtime, __________________________________

____

Tonight we can expect _________________________________

____

By tomorrow morning __________________________________

Busy fingers

Imagine a normal piece of paper, the same size and shape as this page. In your imagination, fold lengthways and re-open. Turn down the top corners to meet at the centre fold, and do the same again. If you now bend the straight outer edges back on themselves, to the central fold-line, what have you made? A paper dart. Throw it, and it should fly smoothly through the air. If you do this in the classroom, your (imaginary) dart will probably end up in the (imaginary) bin! Yet you will have been practising origami, the ancient Japanese art of paper-folding.

Origami has been around almost as long as paper itself – over a thousand years. Nearly everybody knows how to make a paper dart, but there are many more unusual models to make. The dart began life as a flat rectangle of paper, but most models start from a square. It may turn into a bird with flapping wings. Or a mouse.

Or a useful box. Enthusiasts create new designs for models all the time. Many begin with the same sets of folds – called the *bird base* and the *frog base.* Once you have learnt these primary folds (called after the bird and frog that they can turn into) the designs change direction. Using different folds after these bases leads to creating different models.

Origami is challenging and fun. It may begin as child's play, but there are adult addicts worldwide, remodelling old designs and creating new. Paper-folders can attend origami conventions where they share and compare their magical ideas. They help each other to refine their final designs. Animals are a favourite subject, but there is no one design of any one creature. For instance, over eighty different origami elephants were once collected and exhibited by one enthusiast.

The classical folds have names to identify them. Whether vertical, horizontal, or diagonal, *Mountain Folds* stick up – like the spine of an open book laid face down. *Valley Folds* sink – like the centre of an open book, face up. Simple diagrams in origami books (available from your local library) guide you through instructions to make models. They are like a code. A line of dots does NOT mean "cut along the dotted line". Scissors are NEVER used in traditional origami. Every tiny detail is achieved simply by folding. Give it a try and you will find there is more to paper-folding than the elementary paper darts – in or out of the bin!

Some basic origami symbols:

– – – – – – –	Valley fold
–·· –·· –··	Mountain fold

By Celia Warren

General hints:
Wash your hands to avoid sticky marks.
Rest your paper on a clean, flat surface.
Take your time. Accurate, crisp folds produce the best results.
If you can't afford special, thin origami paper, recycle old magazines.
Join a club, like *The British Origami Society*, formed in 1967, or start your own. Members help and encourage each other and share practical skills.

Normal formal clues

- Change the onset letter(s) of each word in column one to make a new word that rhymes.
- Read the clue and write the new rhyming words in column three. The first one is done for you ('f' changes to 'n')

Read the first word	Read the clue for the rhyming word	Write the new word
formal	Not odd or peculiar	**n**ormal
regal	About the law	
focal	Nearby; in your area	
herbal	Spoken aloud; voiced	
spinal	Last; ultimate	
mental	Relating to teeth	
fatal	At birth or nativity	
loyal	Of kings and queens	

SCHOLASTIC

UNIT 1

Narrative setting

Unit 1 is concerned with the way in which writers create an imaginary setting and place characters within it. This process is achieved through a focus on details that develop a setting which is similar to, but not actually, the real world we live in. Characters are people with whom the reader can relate, because they share common characteristics, attitudes and emotions. The unit will help children develop a writer's eye for detail and use of expressive language, and has five hours of planning, to be used over a two-week period, so that children can read across a range of genres and styles. The unit focuses on *Grammar for Writing* Unit 26.

Hour	Shared text-level work	Shared sentence-/ word-level work	Guided work	Independent work	Plenary
1 What is the setting?	Identifying where the setting is, who is there and what is happening.	Collecting adjectives and adjectival phrases. Identifying phonemes in text.	Collecting words with phoneme sound *eye*.	Drawing the setting, adding the objects, adding the characters.	Teacher says either *setting* or *character* and children offer their phrases or words for the correct one. Collect a word bank of words with phoneme sound *eye*.
2 Creating detail	Looking for words and phrases that create detail in the setting and develop character and events.	Collecting phrases that describe settings, characters and events. Looking for words with same root stem.	Building words using the same root stem.	Playing the 'connections game'.	Discuss words from the same root and collect them on the board.
3 Skeleton text	Using a 'skeleton text' to develop a setting and create atmosphere.	Using adjectives and adjectival phrases to create detailed descriptions.	Using the model piece of shared text, children collect unfamiliar words and test their own spelling.	Using skeleton text as a model for writing. Collecting similes that describe a colour.	Share skeleton text work with class and discuss choices of figurative language. Children offer their favourite phrases and justify their choices.
4 Using a photograph	Using a photograph as a stimulus for writing a setting.	Using comparatives and superlatives.	Using a photograph to stimulate writing. Develop skeleton text and then add descriptive language.	Looking at poems using comparatives and extended comparatives.	Discuss children's writing in response to photograph. Ask children to select their use of figurative language. Do the same with poems.
5 Draw the setting	Using a new extract and creating it through a drawing.	Collecting expressive phrases. Comparing texts.	Creating settings, characters and events orally and in written form. Comparing texts.	Writing their own version of the text in the first person.	Class discussions of group activities focusing on use of expressive language both orally and in written form.

Key assessment opportunities

- Are the children able to create a setting, characters and events that connect and influence the action?
- Can the children recognise and use defining adjectives and adjectival phrases appropriate to the setting, characters and events?
- Are the children able to model a writing style that they have encountered?
- Are the children able to develop an imaginary setting of their own using the writers' techniques developed in this unit?

What is the setting?

Objectives

NLS

T1: To understand how writers create imaginary worlds, particularly where this is original or unfamiliar, such as a science fiction setting and to show how the writer has evoked it through detail.
S1: To revise and extend work on adjectives from Year 3 Term 2 and link to work on expressive and figurative language in stories and poetry, constructing adjectival phrases.
W1: To identify phonemes in speech and writing; to segment words into phonemes for spelling.

What you need

- Photocopiable page 95
- plain paper and pencils
- whiteboards.

Shared text-level work

- Display an enlarged copy of the extract from *Kasper in the Glitter* by Philip Ridley (photocopiable page 95). Ask the class to listen carefully and write down the following information on their whiteboards or a piece of paper:
  a The setting – where does the action take place?
  b What is in the setting? Write down two or three objects that are in there.
  c Who is in the setting? Write down the names of the characters.
- Discuss what the class have found out about this extract and collect the information on the board under the three headings:-

Where	What	Who

- Re-read the extract and ask the class to draw the setting, the objects and the characters, as you read it.

Shared sentence-level work

- Ask the children to read through the enlarged extract with you and notice the words or phrases that describe *the setting, the objects* and *the characters*. Collect the words and phrases they suggest on the whiteboard and tell them that these are *adjectives* and *adjectival phrases*.

Guided and independent work

- In this guided session, ask the children to work in pairs. Give each pair a copy of the extract and a piece of plain paper. Each pair must read the text, look for information about Poodlecut and draw a picture of him. On the outside of the drawing they must write words or phrases from the text that describe what he looks like. On the inside of the drawing they must write words or phrases that describe what he does and what he says.
- Using the text for guidance, draw a picture of the objects in the palace and write down words or phrases that describe them.
- In this guided session, ask the children to work in pairs and look through the text for words which have the phoneme sound they would hear in the words *I* or *high*. Collect these and group them into sets with the same graphemes, for example, *aisle, light, why* and so on. They can test each other on spellings for different words with the same phonemes.

Differentiation

Less able

- Help the children find the words or phrases that describe either Poodlecut or the objects in the palace. Cut out and stick on the children's drawings.

More able

- Ask the children to use a thesaurus to collect alternative adjectives to those collected on the board.

Plenary

- Ask children to come out and underline or circle the words or phrases on the large extract, which describe Poodlecut as a character and his actions.
- Ask children to come out and underline the words or phrases that describe the palace and its the objects.

Creating detail

Objectives

NLS

T2: To understand how settings influence events and incidents in stories and how they affect characters' behaviour.

S1: To construct adjectival phrases.

W1: To segment words into phonemes for spelling.

S&L

(Term 3 44 Speaking: To tell stories using voice effectively.)

What you need

- Photocopiable page 96.

Shared text- and sentence-level work

- Explain that in this session you are going to look at how settings can influence the way characters behave.
- Read the extract from *Kasper in the Glitter* making sure that you speak the words of the characters in the way that the text informs you. Ask the class to tell you how you knew how to speak the words. Tell them that they are going to recreate the scene in terms of *speaking, listening* and *moving.*
- Choose a group to read the words spoken by Kasper and another group for Heartthrob.
- Choose two groups to be narrators, one for the setting and one for the characters.
- Choose a group to be Kasper and another to be Heartthrob. They are to listen carefully to the extract and move and react as described.
- Ask the children to tell you the adjectives and adjectival phrases that describe the setting and the characters' actions. Write these on the board and discuss how the phrases connect with what is happening in the extract.
- Play the 'Connections Game'. Draw three columns on the board with the headings *Settings, Characters, Events.* Write something in each column, for example under *Settings,* write *Garden shed,* under *Characters* write *Head teacher* and under *Events* write *Trapped by the tide.* Ask the children to contribute more ideas. Tell them that they need to create a scenario making connections between these three ideas. Ask them to make suggestions and write them down.

Guided and independent work

- Ask the children to play the 'Connections Game' using ideas from the shared session or creating their own. They should choose just one setting, two or three characters and one or two events, then write a brief outline of what happens when they make the connections.
- In this guided session, give children a copy of the extract. Ask them to underline the adjectival phrases that describe the setting and the characters under two headings, *Settings* and *Characters*.
- Ask the children to look for words in the extract that have the same root stem, but different functions, for example, *medicine, medical, medication.*

Differentiation

Less able

- Ask the children to draw Kasper in the position they think he is in at the beginning of the extract by using clues in the text. Write down the words or phrases that they used to find out this information.

More able

- Using the 'Connections Game', ask the children to create a short storyboard (3-4 pictures) connecting the *setting, characters* and *events.* They can write text underneath, using their adjectival phrases, and put the words spoken by characters in speech bubbles.

Plenary

- Read out adjectival phrases from the extract and ask the children to tell you whether the phrase describes the *setting* or the *character.*
- Say either *setting* or *character* and ask them to tell you an adjectival phrase that applies to the correct heading.
- Ask the children to share their phrases from the 'Connections Game' with the rest of the class.

Skeleton text

Objectives

NLS

T4: To understand how the use of expressive and descriptive language can, for example, create moods, arouse expectations, build tension, describe attitudes or emotions.

S1: To construct adjectival phrases.

W4: To practise new spellings regularly by Look>Say>Cover>Write>Check strategy.

What you need

- Photocopiable pages 93 and 97.

Shared text- and sentence-level work

- Use an enlarged copy of photocopiable page 93 to model the opening to a chapter or story, describing the *setting*, the *characters* and the *events*. Make sure that you remind the class to concentrate on creating the detail of their description through expressive language, using adjectives, adjectival phrases and similes. You may have to remind them quickly about similes.
- Use the skeleton text below and ask the children to think about which sentences or phrases create: *tension and expectation – mood and emotions – a character's attitude to events or situations.* There may be a combination of two or more in each phrase or sentence.

> Gemma is alone in her small bedroom. It is very dark. She had been crying in her sleep. She wakes. A shape appears on the wall. A voice calls to her. She hides under the bedclothes. The bed starts to lift off the floor.

- Ask the class to help you 'flesh out' this skeleton text, using adjectives and adjectival phrases, paying attention to sentence length and position of words, so that they create an atmospheric and interesting opening for a story.

Guided and independent work

- In this guided session, give the children a copy of photocopiable page 93 and ask them to put in a maximum of seven ideas for their setting. Underneath they should write down *adjectives, adjectival phrases* and *similes* that they might use to write the opening.
- Using the model piece of writing about Gemma, ask the children to write down words that they are unfamiliar with. They can then work in pairs to test each other's knowledge of spelling and meaning. They should use the *Look>Say>Cover>Write>Check* strategy.
- In this guided session, give the children a copy of the poem 'I asked the little boy who cannot see' (photocopiable page 97) and ask them to write down the *colours* and the *similes* which are connected to those colours. They should then write their own similes connected to colours.
- They can do this by choosing to use new colours or providing their own similes for colours that appear in the poem.

Differentiation

Less able

- Use the 'skeleton text' about Gemma as a starting point for discussing which ideas, phrases and adjectives they like from the model. Ask them to think of some of their own ideas to put into the model.

More able

- Help children to use the expressive language they have collected for the modelled skeleton text of Gemma to write one or two paragraphs for an opening to their story.

Plenary

- Ask the children to share their similes about the colours they have chosen with regard to the poem with the rest of the class.
- Ask the children to share the adjectives, adjectival phrases and similes they have collected for the Gemma skeleton text with the class.
- Discuss similes with the children and ask the group who have been using the poem 'I asked the little boy who cannot see' as a starting point, to share their similes with the class.
- Ask the children who have been 'fleshing out' the skeleton text of Gemma to share their writing with the class. Ask the children listening to see if they can remember some of the expressive language used.

Using a photograph

Objectives

NLS

T10: To develop use of settings in own writing, making use of work on adjectives and figurative language to describe settings effectively.

S1: To examine comparative and superlative adjectives; to compare adjectives on a scale of intensity.

What you need

- A photograph of your own choosing, preferably with one or two adults, and two or three children of school age, in the composition
- photocopiable page 94 (enlarged).

Shared text-level work

- Display an enlarged photocopy of the photograph you have selected. Ask what might be happening. Collect the children's interpretations under three headings, *setting, character* and *event.*
- Use children to model the children in the photograph. Model the adult yourself, or ask a child. Ask what the people in the photograph might have been thinking. Remind them to base their answers around *setting, characters* and *event.* Write these thoughts down.

Shared sentence-level work

- Enlarge page 94; the class is going to explore *figurative language* to make exaggerations. Ask the children to help write another four lines.
- Explain that you can take this further by adding another comparison to an idea, for example:

  My skin is softer than a pillow.
  My skin is softer than a pillow filled with a million feathers.
  My skin is softer than a pillow filled with a million feathers, floating on a bed of air.
- Ask for another example, then model comparisons and exaggerations.
- Explain that most superlatives end with *est.* Display the following:

  My mum is as strong as an elephant.
  My mum is stronger than an elephant who does weight training.
  My mum is the strongest – she can lift both elephants in one hand!
- Use other adjectives, for example, *clever, small.* Ask the children to suggest comparatives and superlatives. Write these on the board.
- Explain that some adjectives do not add *er* or *est,* for example, *fantastic, beautiful.* These add *more* or *most.*

Guided and independent work

- In this guided session, ask the children, in threes, to imagine they are waiting to have their photograph taken. Help them decide the *setting, people,* and *occasion.* They should discuss the task as a group and decide who will write about each aspect. They should write a paragraph each, using *figurative and expressive language* to create detail.
- Ask the children to use photocopiable page 94 as a starting point and add another four lines of rhyming couplets.
- Using the example modelled in the shared session, ask the children to work in threes and write their own comparisons, adding an exaggeration. They each begin with an initial idea, for example, *My Dad is hairier than a monkey...* and then contribute a comparison and an exaggeration to each other's starting points.

Differentiation

Less able

- Work with children to create comparisons they can use in a boastful poem about themselves: I am... Stronger than... Swifter than... Bigger than... Smarter than... .

More able

- Ask the children to use the photograph as a starting point and write their own individual paragraph about what was happening before the photographer arrived, including, the *setting,* the *characters* and the *occasion.*

Plenary

- Ask the groups to share their work on comparisons and superlatives.
- Ask them to tell you their favourite phrase.
- Ask the children who have written about the photograph to come and sit as if they are having their photograph taken. They each read their own piece to the class.

Drawing the setting

Objectives

NLS

T3: To compare and contrast settings across a range of stories; to evaluate, form and justify preferences.

T13: To write own examples of descriptive, expressive language, based on those read. Link to work on adjectives and similes.

S1: To examine comparative and superlative adjectives.

S&L

41 Speaking: To respond appropriately to the contributions of others in the light of alternative viewpoints.

(Term 3 44 Speaking: To tell stories using voice effectively.)

What you need

- Photocopiable pages 94 and 98
- plain paper, pencils.

Shared text- and sentence-level work

- Give each child a large sheet of paper and a pencil. Explain that you are going to read the opening to a story (photocopiable page 98). You are not going to tell them the title yet; instead they must draw the setting and the character, as you read. They must listen carefully for words and phrases that will provide the detail they need to draw.
- Ask a child to read the extract aloud and make your own drawing. Make sure that you talk out loud so that you can model the thinking behind your drawing. Emphasise the use of *adjectives, adjectival phrases* and *similes.*
- On your drawing, write the phrases that you and the children identified to help you create the setting and the picture of the character.
- Discuss the language clues in the text and their importance to the image.
- Ask them to guess the title of the story. (*The Iron Man*)
- Open up the discussion to all texts in this unit – what they have in common, and how they differ in style and in use of descriptive, expressive language.

Guided and independent work

- In this guided session, ask the children to work in threes. One child decides the setting, another introduces a character and the third decides on the event.
- Ask them to write expressive phrases to describe their element and then to tell the opening of their story in their own words.
- Give the children a copy of all the extracts in this unit. Ask them to discuss which one they preferred. Remind them to base their answers on:
  - *the writer's use of expressive language;*
  - *the way the writer has created tension, expectation, emotion and mood.*
- Ask the children to imagine they are 'the Iron Man'. They write the extract from his point of view, using 'I'.
- Remind them to look for clues to help them write about what the Iron Man is feeling as he comes to the top of the cliff, sees the sea for the first time and then crashes to the beach below.

Differentiation

Less able

- Using photocopiable page 94, help the children make more rhyming couplets using comparatives.

More able

- Ask this group to write the events in the extract from the point of view of a fisherman out in the bay, who sees the Iron Man appear at the top of the cliff and topple onto the beach below.

Plenary

- Ask the children to share their writing on *setting, character* and *event* by orally sequencing their phrases and descriptions in a way that creates a good opening. Then discuss the language used and which phrases or words the audience liked.
- Ask the children to report back their findings on the comparison of the three texts.
- Ask them to justify their choices by evaluating the *choice of language* and how the *tension, expectation, mood* and *emotions,* were generated by the writer.

Creating a skeleton text

■ Use the table to help you create your own skeleton text. Write down your scene-builders in the left hand column. Write down the *atmosphere*, *mood*, *attitude*, *tension* and *expectation* that goes with each scene-builder. Remember that there may be more than one for each scene-builder. Then collect your expressive language phrases in the box below.

Remember!
Setting – Character – Event!

Scene-builders	What you are creating: **tension**, **expectation**, **mood**, **attitude**, **emotion**.
1	
2	
3	
4	
5	
6	
7	

Expressive language Collect **adjectives** and **adjectival phrases** that will help you describe your scene-builders.
Setting
Characters
Events

Comparatives – using rhyming couplets

■ Below is the beginning of a poem. It is written in **rhyming couplets**. This means that each pair of lines rhyme at the end of the line. However, the rhyming words used to end lines changes with each couplet. The poem uses comparatives to make exaggerations.

■ Can you add more rhyming couplets to the poem below using the same structure?

I can jump higher than the roof of our house!
I can run faster than a rocket-propelled mouse!
I can laugh louder than my dad can snore!
I can keep my mouth shut tighter than a door!

I can ______________________ **than** ______________________

I can ______________________ **than** ______________________

I can ______________________ **than** ______________________

I can ______________________ **than** ______________________

Kasper in the Glitter (1)

Candles!

That was the first thing Kasper saw when he entered The Palace.

Hundreds of candles.

Candles illuminating everything with a gentle, flickering light.

And wooden pews.

Or, rather, piles of broken wood that used to be wooden pews. An aisle divided the piles of wood in two and at the end of the aisle was a huge chair made out of tin cans. It twinkled gold in the candlelight.

Jingo noticed Kasper staring at the chair.

'That's The Throne,' Jingo explained. 'Only King Streetwise is allowed to sit in it.'

Suddenly, a figure jumped out from behind The Throne and started running down the aisle towards them.

It was a boy with long, curly black hair and the largest ears Kasper had ever seen. They stuck out from the sides of his head like handles on a jug. His clothes were nothing but rags and, like Skinnybones, he was wearing a golden helmet!

'A moth!' he cried, coming to a halt in front of them. 'There's a moth in The Palace. I heard it flapping somewhere.' He cupped his hands round his ears to hear better. 'I've got to get rid of it'.

'This is Master Poodlecut,' whispered Jingo to Kasper.
'Another Argonaut.'

'Hello, Poodlecut,' Kasper said. 'Why have you got to get rid of a moth?'

'Because King Streetwise doesn't like them,' Poodlecut explained. 'He doesn't like the look of them, he doesn't like the sound of them and he doesn't like the feel of them. When he sees a moth he yells "YUK" at the top of his voice. It's my job to make sure The Palace is a moth-free zone. And there's one here now. I just know it, old bean.'

'My name's Kasper,' Kasper insisted. 'Not old bean.'

'Oh, I call everyone old bean,' said Poodlecut. He looked at Skinnybones and asked, 'Don't I, old bean?'

'You do, squire,' came the reply.

From "Kasper in the Glitter" by Philip Ridley (1994, Viking).

Kasper in the Glitter (2)

Kasper opened his eyes.

Darkness.

He took his fingers from his ears.

Silence.

He wasn't sure how long he'd been hiding in the toy cupboard. Fear had made him lose all sense of time. But the silence told him one thing: King Streetwise had gone.

Slowly, he pushed the toys aside, crawled out of the tin bath and opened the cupboard door.

And his fear was replaced by shock!

It was as if a whirlwind had hit the house.

All the lights had been smashed or broken, so the only illumination was the moonlight. And in this moonlight Kasper saw...

Wallpaper torn from walls.

Curtains yanked from windows.

Carpets pulled from floorboards.

Kasper walked into the kitchen, his feet crunching over shattered glass and crockery.

Cupboards had been smashed.

Food was splattered up the walls and across the floor.

The gas cooker was buckled, its door ripped off.

Kasper glanced through the broken window to look at the garden outside.

Or, rather what was left of it!

The once beautiful rosebushes had been totally ruined. There was nothing left but a trampled mass of twigs and branches. One or two bushes had even been dug up and thrown into the house.

Kasper went to the beauty salon.

The hairdryers had been ripped from the walls. All the magazines had been torn to shreds. The sunbeds had been broken beyond repair.

All except one.

Suddenly, it flickered on!

And, in the dazzling light, Kasper saw a face...

'Heartthrob!' gasped Kasper.

Heartthrob was curled in a corner, his face buried in his hands.

'The King got Hushabye, man,' Heartthrob said. 'And it's all my fault!

'No –' Kasper began.

'It is!' snapped Heartthrob, looking up. 'I ran away, Hushabye was right. I'm nothing but a scaredy-cat Heartthrob.'

From "Kasper in the Glitter" by Philip Ridley (1994, Viking).

I asked the little boy who cannot see

I asked the little boy who cannot see,
'And what is colour like?'
'Why, green,' said he,
'Is like the rustle when the wind blows through
The forest; running water, that is blue;
And red is like a trumpet sound; and pink
Is like the smell of roses; and I think
That purple must be like a thunderstorm;
And yellow is like something soft and warm;
And white is a pleasant stillness when you lie
And dream'.

the sound of leaves rustling is an onomatopoeia

Anon

The Coming of the Iron Man

The Iron Man came to the top of the cliff.

How far had he walked? Nobody knows. Where had he come from? Nobody knows. How was he made? Nobody knows.

Taller than a house, the Iron Man stood at the top of the cliff, on the very brink, in the darkness.

The wind sang through his iron fingers. His great iron head, shaped like a dustbin but as big as a bedroom, slowly turned to the right, slowly turned to the left. His iron ears turned, this way, that way. He was hearing the sea. His eyes, like headlamps glowed white, then red, then infra-red, searching the sea. Never before had the Iron Man seen the sea.

He swayed in the strong wind that pressed against his back. He swayed forward, on the brink of the high cliff.

And his right foot, his enormous iron right foot, lifted – up, out, into space, and the Iron Man stepped forward, off the cliff, into nothingness.

CRRRAAAASSSSSSH!

From "The Iron Giant" by Ted Hughes (1968, Faber and Faber Ltd).

UNIT 2

Audience

This unit is designed to stimulate children's curiosity in terms of the exciting range of stories available to them. This session gives them the opportunity to think about the target audience for books they review. They should, by the end of the unit be able to work collaboratively to plan and write stories in chapters, with a particular audience in mind. The sentence level work links to Unit 27 of *Grammar for Writing* and concentrates on the uses of the apostrophe.

Hour	Shared text-level work	Shared sentence-/ word-level work	Guided work	Independent work	Plenary
1 The same author?	To identify similar styles and themes in stories aimed at a target audience.	Using apostrophes to show singular possession.	Reviewing a story with reference to theme, setting, target audience.	Using apostrophes to denote singular possession. Categorising stories.	Discussion of story types and what appeals to the children as readers.
2 Target your audience!	Identifying themes/categories.	Using apostrophes to denote singular and plural possession.	Categorising stories, placing apostrophes in correct place to denote singular and plural possession.	Using apostrophes to show possession in singular and plural form. Categorising stories.	Discussion of type/ categories and target audience.
3 Books in a series	Looking at, and discussing books that belong in a series.	Using apostrophes for possession and contraction.	Using apostrophes to denote possession or contraction.	Writing advert for a series of books. Designing a survey on books for class use.	Report back on the design of a class survey. Discussion on adverts created by children to encourage reading.
4 A writer's brief	Looking at and contrasting books in a series aimed at different target audiences.	Using apostrophes for possession and contraction.	Using apostrophes to denote possession or contraction.	Vocabulary – using 'premier' as opposed to ordinary words. Using a 'writer's brief' to outline a new series of books.	Class discussion of main points to consider when creating a new series of books.
5 Write a book	Using a 'writer's brief' to model an opening setting.	Using descriptive, expressive language appropriate for the target audience.	Fleshing out ideas of a story line.	Groups working on chapters of a book, using the modelled 'writer's brief'.	Sharing favourite ideas, phrases and so on from own writing.

Key assessment opportunities

- Are the children aware of the audience that a writer targets in his or her work?
- Are the children able to identify the suitability of a books or series of books for a particular audience?
- Can the children identify particular genres of books?
- Are the children beginning to develop knowledge of the writing styles of particular authors?
- Are the children able to use the apostrophe correctly to show possession in either the singular or plural form?
- Are the children able to identify and use the apostrophe as a word contraction?

The same author?

Objectives

NLS

T9: To recognise how certain types of texts are targeted at particular readers; to identify intended audience, for example, junior horror stories.

S2: To use the apostrophe accurately to mark possession through: identifying possessive apostrophes in reading and to whom or what they refer.

S&L

41 Speaking: To respond appropriately to the contributions of others in the light of alternative viewpoints.

What you need

- Three contrasting opening extracts from school or class library fiction books (two by the same author)
- photocopiable pages 105 and 106.

Differentiation

Less able

- Using photocopiable page 106, ask the children to highlight the word in each sentence that includes an apostrophe. Can they complete the sheet by putting the apostrophe in the correct place in the next five sentences?

More able

- Give this group three extracts from books from the authors of two different series. Ask them to discuss the extracts and decide if more than one have been written by the same author.

Shared text-level work

- Tell the class that you are going to read short extracts from the openings of three books. Do not tell them the title or the author. Ask them to listen carefully and decide if any were written by the same author.
- Read the children the three extracts and ask them the following:

> - Were any extracts written by the same writer?
> - If yes, what made them decide which ones?
> - Talk about 'clues' in the writing, for example:
>   - the same or similar settings
>   - characters with the same name in each extract
>   - similar themes.

- Write the headings on the board: *Setting, Character, Theme.*
- Divide the class into three and give each group a task as you read the extracts again. Group 1 should listen for clues about the *setting* in each story, group 2, the *characters*, and group 3, the *themes*.
- Ask the children to tell you what category of story they would put the extracts in, for example, horror, folk tale, fantasy. Create a chart with *title, author, category, target audience*. Ask the children to suggest their favourite books and put these on the chart.

Shared sentence-level work

- Display an enlarged copy of one of your extracts (it needs to include apostrophes). Read the sentences to the children.
- Ask if they know what an apostrophe is.
- Ask a child to come out and circle an apostrophe. Repeat this until all the apostrophes are circled.
- Talk to them about the use of apostrophes to show possession, and how you have to re-phrase the sentence if you do not use an apostrophe.

Guided and independent work

- Give the children photocopiable page 105. Ask them to match the phrases to the sentences.
- In this guided activity, give the children a copy of the three extracts and ask them to use their knowledge about *setting, characters* and *theme* to write a short paragraph giving reasons why they would/would not be attracted to the books.

Plenary

- Use an enlarged photocopy of page 105 and ask the group who have been matching their phrases to the sentences to match their answers. Do the rest of the class agree with their choices?
- Ask the children to share their reasons for wanting or not wanting to read the books, based on the extracts they have read.

Target your audience!

Objectives

NLS

T9: To recognise how certain types of texts are targeted at particular readers; to identify intended audience, for example junior horror stories.

S2: To use the apostrophe accurately to mark possession through: identifying possessive apostrophes in reading and to whom or what they refer.

S&L

41 Speaking: To respond appropriately to the contributions of others in the light of alternative viewpoints.

What you need

- Three text extracts of your own choice. Two should be from the same genre (for example, *Goosebumps*).
- photocopiable pages 105, 106 and 107.

Shared text-level work

- Display an enlarged copy of your first chosen extract. Do not let the children know the title or the author. Read the extract to the class and discuss the *type, theme* and *target audience*.
- Tell the children that you are going to read them two more extracts. They are to listen and see if the extracts have anything in common.
- When you have read the extracts, invite the children to comment on the same three areas - *type, theme* and *target audience*.

Shared sentence-level work

- Display photocopiable page 106 and ask the children to look at the position of the apostrophe, that is, *before the s*. Emphasise the answer *- it is in this position to show that it belongs to one person or object.*
- Display photocopiable page 105. Can the children link the phrases without the apostrophe to the correct one using an apostrophe?
- Create sentences of your own that show the apostrophe's position when it denotes *plural possession*. Explain that this position for the apostrophe denotes a plural. Go through the examples and ask them to contribute some more.
- Show them examples of irregular plurals, for example, *children* or *mice*. Explain that these words, although they have a plural meaning, use an apostrophe *before the s* because they are not words that add an *s* for a plural.

Guided and independent work

- Ask the children, in pairs, to create sentences (up to ten) for their partners. They must leave the apostrophe out in each sentence, but know where to put it and if it is singular or plural possession. They should then swap sentences and complete each other's.
- In this guided session, give the children two extracts from books of the same genre. Ask them to answer the following questions by making notes:

> - Do these stories have a common theme? Category? Target audience?
> - Are the extracts by the same author?
> - What are the clues in the text that will help them decide? (for example, theme, characters, use of language and so on)

- Give the children copies of the three extracts and ask them:
  a To decide on a title for this genre/type of story
  b To discuss the reasons they like or do not like this type of story.

They should consider the *type of story, plot, characters* and the *style* and *language* during their discussion. They should make notes so that they can report back orally during the plenary.

Plenary

- Ask the children to report back on their reasons for either liking or disliking the extracts in the *Shared text-level* session.

Differentiation

Less able

- Give the children photocopiable page 107 and ask them to put the apostrophe in the correct place to show singular or plural possession.

More able

- Ask the children to write a paragraph about a favourite book. They must include information on the type of story and what audience the book is aimed at.

Books in a series

Objectives

NLS

T8: To review a range of stories, identifying, for example authors, themes or treatments.

T9: To recognise how certain types of texts are targeted at particular readers; to identify intended audience, for example junior horror stories.

S2: To use the apostrophe accurately to mark possession through: identifying possessive apostrophes in reading and to whom or what they refer; distinguish between uses of the apostrophe for contraction and possession.

W9: To use alternative words and expressions which are more accurate or interesting than the common choices, for example, got, nice, good, then.

What you need

- Sets of novels in the same series from the school or class library
- photocopiable page 108
- a large card with 'P' on one side and 'C' on the other and a class set of smaller 'P'/'C' cards.

Differentiation

Less able

- Ask the children to design a poster for their favourite book (or series) and to write an advertising 'blurb' on their poster that will make other people want to read that book too.

More able

- Ask the children to look at all the books on display in the classroom and create their own classification for them. For example, *horror, science fiction, school, comedy* and so on

Shared text-level work

- Show the class a collection of novels in the same series. Explain to the class that this is a series of books. Discuss what this means in terms of *characters, events* and *settings* with the class.
- Read a short extract from two or three of the books and ask the children to look for clues that tell them the age range of the target audience.

Shared sentence-level work

- Hold up the large card marked 'P' and 'C', showing each side. Ask the class if they can remember the other use of the apostrophe. Make sure that they all understand that 'P' is for *possession* and 'C' is for *contraction*.
- Create some examples of sentences that use an apostrophe to denote either contraction or possession. Give each child a card with 'P' on one side and 'C' on the other.
- Read out the sentences and after you have read each one, ask the children to hold their card up with either 'C' or 'P' facing you, depending on what they think the correct answer should be.

Guided and independent work

- Ask the children to design an advertisement for a series of books using pictures and words that will appeal to their target audience.
- In this guided session, give the children photocopiable page 108, which gives them a chance to show their understanding of the use of the apostrophe for possession and contraction. This worksheet requires the children to underline words with apostrophes, noting down whether it is *contraction* or *possession* and specifying *singular* or *plural*.
- Ask the children to design a survey sheet for the class to complete, in order to collect information about their most popular series of books. The survey sheet should include the following headings:
  - Title of the series
  - The author
  - One to five star rating for theme, setting, characters and plot.

Plenary

- Ask the children who have designed the survey sheet about collecting information about the popularity of books to talk to the class about what they have included on the survey sheet. The children in the class should be encouraged to suggest additional headings if they think they are needed; and the whole class should try and create a short written statement for each of the one to five star ratings so that when the survey is completed, everyone is using the same guidelines.
- Ask the children to talk to the class about the advertisements they have designed for their favourite series and the reasons for their choice.

A writer's brief

Objectives

NLS

T8: To review a range of stories, identifying, for example, authors, themes or treatments.

T9: To recognise how certain types of texts are targeted at particular readers; to identify intended audience, for example, junior horror stories.

S2: To use the apostrophe accurately to mark possession; to distinguish between uses of the apostrophe for contraction and possession.

W9: To use alternative words and expressions which are more accurate or interesting than the common choices, for example, *got, nice, good, then.*

What you need

- A series of books intended for very young children
- a teacher-prepared text with all the apostrophes removed
- photocopiable page 109.

Shared text-level work

- Using a series written for much younger children, talk to the class about the differences in *theme, character, setting, plot* and so on, between it and a series for their own age range. Make a list and write it on the board.
- Tell the children that you are going to create a 'writer's brief'. A writer has been asked to produce a new series of books and the publishers want to know the writer's ideas, for example, the *category* (*genre*) and the *target audience*. There are to be just two central characters, and the series must be based mainly in one setting.
- Model a pro forma with the following headings: *Category, Target audience, Series title*. Then create three columns headed with *Setting, Main characters, Storyline(s)*. Work with the children to fill in some initial ideas.

Shared sentence-level work

- Which apostrophe is which? Write some examples of your own on the board and ask the children, in pairs, to decide what the apostrophe has been used for in each sentence. Each pair must decide the correct use, that is, *possession* or *contraction*. They must copy the sentences and write either 'P' or 'C' at the end of each. Discuss the results.

Guided and independent work

- Give the children a piece of text with all the apostrophes missing! Ask them to read through and decide where to put apostrophes. They must mark their apostrophes with a 'C' or a 'P' and then, on the ones denoting possession, write *sing* or *plu* beside them to denote *singular* or *plural*.
- Using a thesaurus, ask the children to replace the underlined words on photocopiable page 109, with more exciting or interesting words.
- In this session, the children fill in a 'writer's brief' for a series of books for their own age group. They create a pro forma similar to the one in the *Shared text-level* session. Working in pairs, they use their knowledge of the target audience to complete the pro forma, giving brief details under each heading.

Plenary

- Ask the children to report back to the class on their review of their favourite series, emphasising their reasons for choosing this particular series.
- Ask the children to talk about their ideas for a new book/series for infants, using the pro forma scribed for them.
- Put up an enlarged copy of the text you gave the children, with all the apostrophes missing. Ask the class to help you fill them all in. The children who worked on the text in the independent work, can take the lead in the discussion.

Differentiation

Less able

- Using a book from a series for younger children, ask the children to discuss a new story using the same characters and settings. Scribe their ideas for them using the modelled 'Writer's brief' pro forma.

More able

- Ask these children to write a review of a favourite series for younger children. What is it about the characters that appeals to younger children? What do they think of the writing style and use of language?

Write a book

Objectives

NLS

T12: To collaborate with others to write stories in chapters, using plans with particular audiences in mind.
T9: To recognise how certain types of texts are targeted at particular readers; to identify intended audience, for example, junior horror stories.
S2: To use the apostrophe accurately to mark possession through: identifying possessive apostrophes in reading and to whom or what they refer; distinguish between uses of the apostrophe for contraction and possession.
W2: To identify mis-spelt words in their own writing: to keep individual lists (for example spelling logs) and learn to spell them.

What you need

- Completed 'writer's briefs' from Hour 4.

Shared text- and sentence-level work

- Take one of the 'writer's briefs' from the Hour 4 session and use this as a model for discussion with the class on writing a series of chapters for a new book in a series. Model the opening chapter on the board using the children's ideas to help you.
- Be sure to include the use of *descriptive, expressive language* when introducing the *setting, characters* and *complication/dilemma.*
- Decide on groups of children to write particular chapters when the *Guided and independent* session begins.

Guided and independent work

- Give each group in the class a chapter to write for the book. The model is on the board, as is the outline for each chapter. It would be unrealistic to expect the groups to produce a complete chapter in the time scale of 20 minutes; they should aim to flesh out the sequence of events and gather some expressive language, in phrases or sentences, to add detail to the characters, setting and events in their chapter. This could provide a basis for extended writing at a later date.
- Ask the children to identify words that are incorrectly spelt in their own writing. They should collect these with the correct spellings and add them to their individual lists.
- Work with the children to search through a book by their favourite author and see how she or he used the apostrophe in his or her own work. Can they identify the usage, for example, *possessive* (*singular* or *plural*) or *contraction*?

Plenary

- Ask the group who have been 'fleshing-out' their ideas for the storyline they developed in the previous session to share their work with the class. Ask the class to tell you what they liked best in terms of expressive language. Write these in the boxes.
- Ask the group who have been working on a 'writer's brief' from Hour 4 to share their work with the class. Again ask the rest of the class to listen carefully to the way in which the group has used expressive language. Ask them to try and remember ones they liked and write these on the board.
- Ask the group who have been writing chapters to feed back information on the events in their particular chapter. Ask them to share some of their favourite uses of figurative language – sentences or phrases – that they are particularly pleased with.

Differentiation

Less able

- Work with this group to 'flesh-out' their ideas for the storyline they developed in the previous session.

More able

- Using another 'writer's brief,' from the Hour 4 session, ask the group to flesh out a chapter each using the outline provided.

What belongs to who?

■ Draw a line from the sentence to the matching phrase. Each sentence uses **an apostrophe to show possession** and the phrases show possession without using apostrophes.

Sentences

The cat's food was all over the kitchen floor.

I saw the boy's football kit on the playground.

I pushed Julie's bike up the hill.

We found the dog's collar behind the sofa.

Who left the teacher's packed lunch behind?

Where are Darren's shoes?

Garry gave Andy's comic away.

Manminder wanted her sister's bracelets.

Leroy broke his brother's camera.

Jill left her Dad's birthday present on the school bus.

Phrases

the shoes of Darren

the camera of his brother

the comic of Andy

the food of the cat

the bracelets of her sister

the birthday present of Dad

the football kit of the boy

the bike of Julie

the packed lunch of the teacher

the collar of the dog

Highlight the apostrophe

■ Can you highlight the word containing an apostrophe in each of these sentences?

The cat's food was all over the kitchen floor.

I saw the boy's football kit on the playground.

I pushed Julie's bike up the hill.

We found the dog's collar behind the sofa.

Who left the teacher's packed lunch behind?

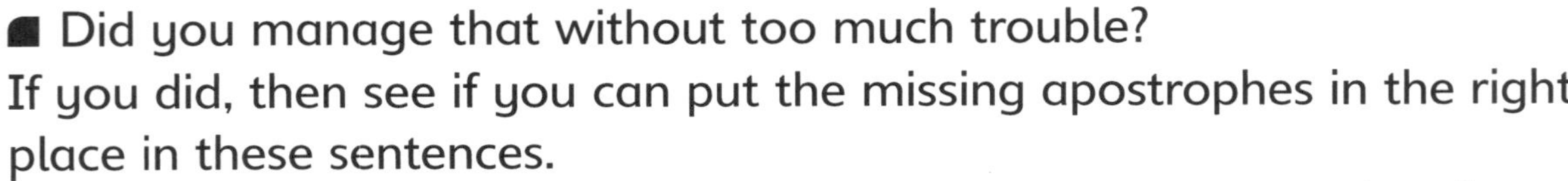

■ Did you manage that without too much trouble?
If you did, then see if you can put the missing apostrophes in the right place in these sentences.

Where are Darrens shoes?

Garry gave Andys comic away.

Manminder wanted her sisters bracelets.

Leroy broke his brothers camera.

Jill left her Dads birthday present on the school bus

Singular, plural or irregular?

- Here are some sentences. Put the apostrophes in the correct place.
- Then complete the box at the end of each sentence to show if the apostrophe has been used to denote:

Singular
Plural
Irregular plural.

Put either an **S**, a **P** or an **I** against each sentence.

Sentences	**S/P/I**
Eddys ball had gone over the fence.	
The girls football team lost the match.	
Everyones work was praised by the teacher.	
The school buss engine boiled over!	
All the school buses seat belts have to have a safety check.	
Kates mum was late fetching her from school.	
The schools head teachers held a meeting in the conference centre.	
The horses bridles had all been damaged.	
The cats whiskers twitched with excitement.	
The mens voices sounded fantastic when they sang together.	

Underling apostrophes

- Read the following passage of narrative.

Underline all the words that use an apostrophe.
Then, put these words into the correct columns below for either **contraction** or **possession** (singular or plural). Mark the latter **s** or **p**.

John's feet were freezing. He stamped them hard on the frosty pavement and wished he had not put on his brother's boots by mistake. They were far too big for his feet and his socks were crumpling round his heels. Suddenly, he heard a voice calling to him. "Hey! Jonno! What're you doing? There aren't any buses today." John looked round and saw Tom coming towards him. "I know," said John, "I'm waiting for Dad. Mum's car wouldn't start." Tom came and stood by John. "There's a bus strike," said Tom. " All the bus drivers have come out on strike. It's a bad end to a bad day. D'you think your Mum would give me a lift too? It's on the way." John smiled at Tom. He looked colder than a freezer full of ice. "Yes," he said and stamped his feet again, "I'm sure she will." Tom didn't look quite as cold anymore. He grinned at John and said, "did you hear about all the girls' bikes? Someone let all their tyres down!" Just as John was about to reply, he heard a car horn tooting. It was his Mum. The car's tyres swished through the slush, soaking them both with spray as it pulled up by the curb. They didn't mind! They could feel the warmth of the car's heater as they opened the rear door and hopped in.

Contraction	Possession (singular/plural)

SCHOLASTIC

Improve the text

■ Here is a piece of text for you to improve.

Some of the words have been underlined, because they are not very exciting uses of vocabulary and do not really describe either the person, the event, or what is happening, very accurately. You can use your own imagination or knowledge of vocabulary to find a better word. Alternatively, you can use a thesaurus, either in book form, or on the computer, to change these words and make the whole passage more interesting. Good luck!

Martin got to his feet and walked slowly towards the front door of his house. He rang the doorbell, but nobody answered it, so he bent down and looked through the letterbox. He called for his mother but nobody answered him. Martin did not know what to do. His foot was very painful and he could feel it getting bigger in his shoe. Carefully, he sat down on the step and tried to take off his shoe. He could feel it throbbing and the pain was getting worse. Then he thought back to what had happened.

It had been a nice day at school until a very big dog had run out of the park gates and pushed him over. The owner of the dog had come running out after it. She was very sorry and upset when she saw Martin lying on the ground. Martin could tell she was out of breath when she spoke to him.

"I'm really sorry," she said. "He's a very bad dog. Will you be all right?"

Martin felt his leg. "I think so," he said. "I only live across the road. I think I can walk to my front door."

"Well, if you are sure that you are all right," said the lady. As she spoke, the dog pulled the lead out of her hands and was running down the road. The lady said, "Come back Monty!" The dog went round the corner and the lady left Martin and went after the dog.

Martin sat on the step. "Oh well," he said to himself, "I suppose every dog must have his day! But why did it have to have its day when I was having such a nice day?" Then he heard his mum's voice. "Had a good day?" she said. Martin groaned!

UNIT 3

Poetry

This unit is based around two poems, one by Alfred Lord Tennyson and the other by Tony Mitton. It is designed to encourage children to respond to poetry - explore, interpet and reflect upon the imagery and structures used. The children will encounter some unfamiliar vocabulary and how poets use figurative language. The unit links to Unit 26 of *Grammar for Writing* which provides children with opportunities to explore comparatives and superlatives, which will help them when structuring their own poems.

Hour	Shared text-level work	Shared word-/ sentence-level work	Guided and independent work	Plenary
1 Flying carpet	Responding to poetry.	Rhyming words.	A visual interpretation of a poem.	Reflections on visualisation and imagery.
2 Performing poems	Exploring mood and feelings conveyed in poetry. Reading poetry expressively.	Spelling strategies for compound words.	Marking texts in preparation for presentation of a poem.	Share and evaluate. Picking up points from the introduction.
3 The Splendour Falls	Identifying rhyming patterns.	How can we tell that this is an older poem? Words that have changed over time.	Generating rhymes. Rhyme races.	Feeding back on rhyming activity. Identifying aural and visual rhymes.
4 Repeating structures	Shared writing. Using repeating structures to make poems.	Adjectives, comparatives and superlatives	Writing poems using comparatives and superlatives.	Sharing poems. Identifying examples of effective rhyming. Discussing the difficulties with rhyming.
5 Multimedia poems	Multimedia presentation of own poems.		Multimedia presentation of a poem. Allocating tasks in groups, such as finding sound files, finding images.	Evaluating multimedia poems using criteria of appropriateness and sensitive interpretation of the poem.

Key assessment opportunities

- Can the children demonstrate the ability to rhyme orally and to find appropriate rhymes for poems?
- Are they able to orally present a poem? How successfully have pitch, power, pause, pace, emphasis, action and instrument been used?
- Can the children present a poem using multimedia? Have they selected appropriate images, WordArt, sound files, sensitive use of presentational software tools for transitions and so on?

Flying carpet

Objectives

NLS

T5: To understand the use of figurative language in poetry and prose; compare poetic phrasing with narrative/descriptive examples.

T7: To identify patterns of rhyme and verse in poetry, eg choruses, rhyming couplets, alternate line rhymes and to read these aloud effectively.

W6: To spell words with common endings *-ight*, and so on.

What you need

- A selection of the teacher's favourite poems
- photographs of cloud shapes and pictures of carpets, rugs or quilts (try looking on the internet)
- photocopiable page 116
- dictionaries.

Shared text-level work

- Ask the children what they already know about poetry and then list their ideas.
- Check the children's understanding of the terminology that is used when discussing poetry; *collection, anthology, anthologist, performance poet,* and so on.
- Read the children two or three poems that you particularly like. Talk to them about your reasons for liking these particular poems - for example, *content, use of expressive language, use of rhyme, imagery,* and so on.
- Ask the children if they have any favourite poems and why they like them so much.
- Use an enlarged copy of the poem 'Flying carpet' and introduce it. For example: *This is a poem about giving an ordinary object (the carpet) extraordinary qualities.*
- Read the poem expressively. Use statements and tentative thinking as well as questions to encourage children's responses. You might use prompts such as:
  - This poem makes me think about... What does it make you think about?
  - Which were your favourite lines?
  - I wonder why Tony Mitton wrote whispers of sky?
  - Does this poem rhyme?

Shared word-level work

- Identify pairs of rhyming words in the poem and use a highlighter pen to mark them on the enlarged copy.
- Draw attention to any words that are unfamiliar, for example, *tassels, woven, hover.* Ask for definitions and check the meanings in a dictionary, revising dictionary skills as appropriate.

Guided and independent work

- In pairs, the children practise reading the poem aloud to each other.
- Select favourite images from 'Flying carpet' and use a range of materials to make a poster. Incorporate lines from the poem in the image. Some poetry posters displayed in the classroom will help to stimulate ideas.

Plenary

- Invite the children to read the poem aloud.
- Ask the children to share their pictures based on the poem and explain how the images are suggested by the words of the poem.
- Comment on favourite images. Encourage the children to reflect on how drawing contributed to their understanding of the poem.

Differentiation

Less able

- Work with these children to find images in the poem, for example, *whispers of sky, twitters of birds.* Ask them to draw images of the flying carpet based on the poem's images.

More able

- Give these children an everyday object, for example, a piece of jewellery, a picture of a patterned quilt or rug, a cloud image. Ask them to collectively write some descriptions that give these objects a magical or mysterious quality.

Performing poems

Objectives

NLS
T4: To understand how expressive and descriptive language can, eg, create moods, arouse expectations, build tension, and describe attitudes or emotions.

S & L
41 Speaking: To respond appropriately to the contributions of others in the light of alternative viewpoints.

What you need

- Photocopiable pages 116 and 117
- a pre-selected range of poems suited to the task and learner-ability.

Shared text-level work

- Re-read the poem 'Flying carpet'. Discuss the range of moods from the matter-of-fact statement *Colourful carpet*, to the magic and mystery of *whispers of sky*.
- Consider ways to read expressively. Encourage children to think about the meaning of lines before making suggestions. Put up an enlarged copy of *Spoken poetry: prompt sheet (*photocopiable page 117) and discuss the key factors for reading aloud, referring to the original poem.
- Demonstrate how to mark the poem to aid expressive reading, for example, highlighting the words to be emphasised.

Shared sentence- and word-level work

- Examine the structure of the word *whenever*. Ask the children if they notice anything about it. Explain that it is a compound word made from two root words, *when + ever*.
- Ask if they can find any words in the poem that can become a compound word by adding another word. For example:
  - *hover + craft = hovercraft*
  - *silk + worm = silkworm*
  - *bird + song = birdsong*.
- Start a class compound word collection to which the children can add new words as they find them.

Guided and independent work

- Give each pair or group a pre-selected poem and photocopiable page 117. Ask them to prepare to read the poem for a performance to the class.
- They should complete the prompt sheet as modelled in the *Shared text-level work*.
- Then, give each pair or group a pre-selected poem and ask them to look for compound words within the text, and words that can be used to make compound words by adding another word.

Plenary

- Invite the children to comment on how easy or difficult it was to complete the prompt sheet for reading aloud.
- Ask the children to read their poem aloud to the class using their own interpretation of the text based on their prompt sheets.
- Discuss with the class the expressive methods used by the readers. How did it help make the meaning clearer?

Differentiation

Less able
- Work with this group using appropriate pre-selected poems and page 117. Help them complete the prompt sheet and interpret the poem as a performance.

Less able
- Give this group more challenging pre-selected poems and page 117. Ask them to complete the prompt sheet in pairs and agree an interpretation to prepare for reading aloud.

The Splendour Falls

Objectives

NLS

T6: To identify clues which suggest poems are older, eg language use, vocabulary, archaic words.
T7: To identify patterns of rhyme and verse in poetry, eg choruses, rhyming couplets, alternate line rhymes and to read these aloud effectively.
W11: To understand that vocabulary changes over time, eg through collecting words that have become little-used and discussing why, eg wireless and frock.

What you need

- Photocopiable page 120 (enlarged) and page 118
- a set of rhyming dictionaries.

Shared text-level work

- Tell the children that you are going to read them a poem called 'The Splendour Falls'.
- Read the poem aloud without expression. Invite suggestions for improving the reading. Mark the poem and read it aloud together.
- How does this poem make the children feel? Do they notice any patterns in the way the poem is written?
- Highlight the pairs of rhyming words. Explain that this pattern of rhyme is called *rhyming couplets.*
- Compare the rhyme scheme with the poem 'Flying carpet'.
- Model writing a new rhyming couplet for the last two lines of verse one. Explain that you are going to use words that rhyme with *flying* and *dying.*
- Ask the children to suggest their words that rhyme with *flying* and *dying.* Can they use the same structure as Tennyson to supply new line endings for each verse?

Shared word-level work

- Ask the children if they think the poem was written recently or a long time ago. Why?
- Check their understanding of words and ideas that may be unfamiliar (for example, *summits; cataract; glens; yon*).
- Explain that new words are added to language every day and some words drop out of use (such as *yon*).

Guided and independent work

- In pairs, ask the children to play rhyming races, using photocopiable page 120. How quickly can they find two rhymes for each word? Use the rhyming dictionary to extend the activity.
- Investigate how word usage changes over time. What words do the children use that adults do not use in the same way? Ask them to make a list of words common in youth culture, and ask adults what these words mean to them.

Plenary

- Take feedback from the rhyming races. Ask for rhymes found for *blue*, such as *glue.* Some words rhyme by sound and sight, others have a different spelling pattern.
- Ask if they found rhymes for all the words? Are there any that don't have rhymes?
- Ask how the poem would sound if it didn't rhyme? Encourage intuitive responses.

Differentiation

Less able

- Start with an 'I spy' rhyming game: *In this room there is something that sounds like door (floor).* Develop the game by providing clues rather than a rhyming word: *In this room there is something that sounds like a hairy animal (chair).* If they can't guess the word, supply more clues.

More able

- Provide more challenging sets of words for the rhyming activities.

Repeating structures

Objectives

NLS

T11: To write poetry based on the structure and/or style of poems read, for example, taking account of vocabulary, archaic expressions, patterns of rhyme, choruses, similes.

T13: To write own examples of descriptive, expressive language based on those read. Link to work on adjectives and similes.

S1: To revise and extend work on adjectives from Year 3 Term 2 and link to work on expressive and figurative language in stories and poetry: relating them to suffixes which indicate degrees of intensity.

What you need

- A poem written with rhyming couplets
- a collection of dictionaries and word banks
- photocopiable pages 116, 118, 119 and 120.

Shared text-level work

- Read a poem with rhyming couplets. Invite the children to supply the second rhyme in each couplet.
- Explain that a poet, Adrian Mitchell, wrote a poetry book called 'The Thirteen Secrets of Poetry' containing ideas to help children write poetry. One was that all writers can learn from other writers. As he put it, *Like a poppy-field poppy be happy to copy.*
- Explain that many poems have a repeating structure – show them 'Flying carpet' and 'The Splendour Falls'. Ask them to find the repeating structures. For example, the opening line in 'Flying carpet' is the same in each verse. Tennyson uses a repeating structure for the rhyming couplets at the end of each verse in 'The Splendour Falls'.
- Tell the children that you are going to create a poem using words at the beginning of each line that rhyme. For example: *Flying like a wind trapped kite / Sighing like a last regret.* Ask them to create similes for each new initial rhyming word that you give them. (At this stage the simile lines do not have to rhyme with each other.)
- Ask the children in pairs to use this repeating structure to write rhyming couplets. (Rhyming dictionaries can be used.) Ask the class to choose the best ideas, then complete the frame and demonstrate how to cut words that do not add to the meaning. Ask them to consider vocabulary choice, making improvements on verbs and adjectives.
- Once completed, re-read the poem and make any changes needed.
- In pairs, ask them to brainstorm new words for the poem that all rhyme with *flying, sighing, dying,* and so forth. Make a list and display it.

Shared sentence-level work

- Explain that you are going to show them another structure that they can use to create rhymes and play with words. You are going to use *comparatives* and *superlatives* – put up some examples of these. Now display the following structure (from page 119): *Quick as a flash / Quicker than a dash / Quickest of all is the way I spend my cash.*
- Ask the children to suggest some words such as *slow* and *fast,* to see if they can use the same structure to create three-line rhymes.

Guided and independent work

- Ask one group to use the structure from the *Shared text-level work* to create rhyming couplets which have a word at the beginning of each line that rhymes. (They can use the top-half of photocopiable page 119.)
- Other groups can use photocopiable page 119 to make poems using the three-line structure. They could work in threes and contribute a line each.

Plenary

- The children share poems in small groups and feedback to the class. Which did they like? Ask them to justify their preferences. Were effective rhymes used? Guide them to consider appropriateness using context.
- Were there any words that were difficult to find rhymes for? Ask if they have learned anything new about the way poets use rhyme.

Differentiation

Less able

- Work with these children to help them complete *Rhyming races* on page 120.

More able

- Explore more complex rhyme schemes, noticing how some make visual and aural rhymes but others do not have the same spelling pattern. The very able may be guided to identify half- as well as full rhymes.

Multimedia poems

Objectives

NLS

T11: To write poetry based on the structure and/or style of poems read, eg taking account of vocabulary, archaic expressions, patterns of rhyme, choruses, and similes.

S & L

43 Group discussion and interaction: To use time, resources and group members efficiently by distributing tasks, checking progress, making backup plans.

What you need

- An ICT suite with networked computers or a data projector/interactive whiteboard in the classroom
- a prepared presentation of a poem using presentation software, with a completed version of the planning sheet on page 121
- photocopiable page 121.

Differentiation

Less able

- Multimedia work may present an opportunity for children who experience difficulties with verbal expression. Grouped sensitively and with some adult intervention, most children should be able to participate in this activity.

More able

Multimedia work can provide the problem-solving challenge that suits the more able. Ensure that a stimulating range of poems is available to allow for a guided choice of material.

Shared text-level work

- Review poems written in the previous hour. Briefly talk about ways in which poems could be presented to an audience, for example, *oral performance*, *a collection* or *anthology*. Explain that in this instance you will be using presentation software to give a slideshow for an audience.
- Using Tony Mitton's poem 'Flying carpet', demonstrate how a poem can be presented as a slideshow using images, sound files, WordArt titles and the lines from the poem and transitions between slides. Show a presentation that you have prepared and invite children's comments.
- Use an enlarged copy of the planning sheet (photocopiable page 121) that you have prepared to model your thinking, explaining the choices you have made for:

- the title slide
- images
- sounds
- transitions.

- Model your thought processes by outlining ideas that you considered but rejected and your reasons for this.
- Show the children how to search for and capture copyright-free images and sound files.

Guided work and independent work

- Work with a group to show how the ideas about expressive reading (Hour 2) can be applied to creating a voice-over narration for the slide show. Create such a voice-over narration for the slideshow that you have already prepared.
- Individually, or in pairs if preferred, the children use a blank planning frame (page 121) to prepare presentations of their poems, making notes about the images and sound files that they would like to use. After planning they will need time to search for images and sound files to enhance their presentation.

Plenary

- In pairs, share and evaluate work in progress. Ask for one or two comments about how effectively the ideas would enhance the poems. (Note: Extra ICT time will be needed for finishing the presentations.)
- Review the list of ideas produced at the beginning of the week. Ask what they have learned about poetry and what they can now add to the list. Suggestions might include the following type of responses:

- Some poems rhyme and some do not
- Rhyming poems have different rhyme schemes
- Some rhymes have the same spelling patterns but others do not
- You can use the structure of an existing poem to help you write your own
- Poems can be presented in a variety of ways. How many can you suggest?

Flying carpet

Colourful carpet,
your curious patterns
are woven with whispers of sky.
No wonder you float
like a beautiful boat
whenever you hover and fly.

Colourful carpet,
the silk of your tassels
is twisted from twitters of bird.
No wonder you fly
to the end of the sky
whenever I give you the word.

Tony Mitton

Illustration © Peter Bailey

Spoken poetry: prompt sheet

- When we read poetry aloud we can make it sound more interesting by using our voices well.

- Below are some things for you to think about when preparing your poem.

- Complete the marking grid with your own symbols.

Pace	Reading faster or slower.	
Pause	Leaving a space or pause.	Mark ^ to show a pause.
Pitch	Using a higher or lower pitch than the normal pitch of your voice.	Mark ▲ to show higher pitch. Mark ▼ to show lower pitch.
Power	Varying the power of your voice: loud, soft, shouting, whispering, firm, gentle.	
Emphasis	Making one or more words in a line more important than others.	Underline the words you want to emphasise.
Movement	Adding simple movements for emphasis.	
Sound effects	Using voice, body parts or percussion.	

- Try different effects and then choose the version you like best.

The Splendour Falls

The splendour falls on castle walls
And snowy summits old in story;
The long light shakes across the lakes,
And the wind cataract leaps in glory.
Blow, bugle, blow, set the wild echoes flying,
Blow, bugle; answer, echoes, dying, dying, dying.

cataract – meaning a cascade

O, hark, O, hear! how thin and clear,
And thinner, clearer, farther going!
O, sweet and far from cliff and scar
The horns of Elfland faintly blowing!
Blow, let us hear the purple glens replying,
Blow, bugle; answer, echoes, dying, dying, dying.

scar – craggy part of a mountainside

O love, they die in yon rich sky,
They faint on hill or field or river;
Our echoes roll from soul to soul,
And grow for ever and for ever.
Blow, bugle, blow, set the wild echoes flying,
And answer, echoes, answer, dying, dying, dying.

yon – old-fashioned word for 'over there'

Alfred Lord Tennyson

Poetry frame – repeating structures

- Write a poem using rhyming words for the first word in each new line. For example, using **crying, sighing, lying**:

> Crying like a new born baby
> Sighing like a leaf in the wind
> Lying like a fallen tree

- Here is an incomplete example. Complete the lines with phrases of your own. Can you turn any of the lines into rhyming couplets?

Flying like a ______________________

Trying like a ______________________

Drying like a ______________________

Frying like a ______________________

Comparatives and Superlatives

- Most comparatives add 'er' and most superlatives add 'est'. For example, 'wise', 'wiser', 'wisest'; 'short', 'shorter', 'shortest'. Use comparatives and superlatives to make three-line poems based on this structure:

> Quick as a flash
> Quicker than a dash
> Quickest is the way I spend my cash!

- Add the comparatives and superlatives to these adjectives:
short tall bright dark empty red old.

- Use the structure below and make three-line poems. If you can make the last word in each of the lines rhyme, it makes it more fun – but you don't have to!

Short as a ______________________

Shorter than a ______________________

Shortest of all is the ______________________

- Now try making poems with the other comparatives and superlatives.

Rhyming races

- Are you a super-fast rhymer? Race your partner and see how quickly you can write two rhymes for each of these words. Are you ready? Get set, Go!

- When you have finished, use a rhyming dictionary and find some more rhymes for the words.

	Rhyme 1	Rhyme 2	Dictionary words
night			
day			
bear			
bull			
sock			
shoe			
far			
near			
king			
queen			
sky			
water			
soon			
later			
nine			
ten			
owl			
hawk			
blue			
orange			

Planning Sheet

Title Page Words Image	Slide 1 Words Image
Slide 2 Words Image	Slide 3 Words Image
Slide 4 Words Image	Slide 5 Words Image
Slide 6 Words Image	Slide 7 Words Image

UNIT 4

Notes and information texts

This unit has ten hours allotted to it to give the children enough opportunities to develop their skills in this area of literacy. It will help them gain knowledge and understanding in two areas, both of which are very demanding. The first area is developing children's understanding that the order of words in a sentence conveys its meaning. They will have practice in reducing sentences to key words, creating simple and compound sentences and playing with word order. The second skill is sifting information from texts and diagrams. Both these activities are allied closely with Unit 28 of *Grammar for Writing*.

Hour	Shared text-level work	Shared word-/ sentence-level work	Guided work	Independent work	Plenary
1 How many words?	Looking for words that convey the key meaning in a sentence.	Looking at how words can be ordered and re-ordered to retain or alter meanings.	Extracting key words for meaning.	Making freeze-frames of key meanings and making a variety of sentences from word jumbles.	Sharing the sentences created. Showing freeze-frames of key meanings.
2 Freeze-frames	Conveying meaning in as few words as possible. Freeze-frames of key meanings.	Looking at how word order conveys meaning.	Searching for key words to convey meaning in a group of sentences.	Finding key words in a sentence. Re-ordering jumbled headlines to convey meaning.	Sharing work on finding key words and the re-ordered headlines.
3 Scanning books	Scanning non-fiction books for information using a research frame.	Making simple sentences from key words. Creating compound sentences.	Playing with word order to create sentences without destroying the meaning.	Using a research frame to sift books for information. Reducing an extract to essential words to convey meaning.	Sharing of work on the skills needed to research for information. Sharing of reduced and elaborated sentences.
4 Key words in fiction	Making notes on key words from a fiction extract.	Using connectives and conjunctions to create more elaborate sentences.	Using a thesaurus and dictionary to make differing definitions of a single word.	Looking for key words, headings and phrases to develop note-making skills.	Sharing the work undertaken on word definitions.
5 Key words in non-fiction	Looking at non-fiction texts for key words, phrases and headings.	Looking at how word order can affect meaning.	Using a combination of two nouns and a verb to create simple and more elaborate sentences.	Note-making from non-fiction texts.	Sharing the sentences created from the three key word starters.

Hour	Shared text-level work	Shared word-/ sentence-level work	Guided work	Independent work	Plenary
6 Research	Using a research frame to collect information.	Emphasising word order.	Collecting research information from a designated website.	Using a research frame for information gathering.	Discussing the methods used for information gathering.
7 Notes on the planets	Using research from non-fiction to generate a diagram with information boxes.	Again emphasising that word order in text conveys meaning.	Creating sub-headings, key words or phrases in an information box.	Again, collecting information, using information boxes, sub-headings, and so on, to create diagrams.	Sharing the diagrams the children have created and discussing the reasons for selection of information.
8 Notes on eclipses	Creating diagrams in a physical form with the children using selected information.	Reinforcing the use of word order to convey meaning.	Collecting and sifting information from an extract to collect key words, and so on.	Creating a diagram to display information.	Using the children to physically represent their diagrams.
9 Notes into prose	Using a diagram or chart to create a piece of connected prose.	Emphasising the use of word order, connectives, and so on, to convey correct meanings.	Working with information from a website diagram to create connected prose.	Using a chart or diagram to create connected prose giving the same information.	Comparing their connected prose versions with the diagrams and discussing what they have selected and how they have used word order.
10 Information on Mars	Note-making from a non-fiction extract that has been read to the class.	Emphasising use of word order and connectives.	Creating a wall chart or diagram to display information.	Again, creating a wall chart or diagram to display information.	Sharing and comparing the wall charts and labelled diagrams that the children have made.

Key assessment opportunities

- Can the children reduce sentences to their key words and create simple sentences from a reduced sentence, without altering the meaning?
- Can they make compound sentences using commas, full stops and connectives to re-order the words without changing the meaning?
- Can the children take key words, phrases and headings from non-fiction texts in order to generate diagrams and charts to display information? Can they scan through information books knowing how to find out, quickly and efficiently, if the book (or website) contains the information they need?
- Can they use a diagram or wall chart containing notes and headings, to help them write connective prose on the same topic?

How many words?

Objectives

NLS

T14: Notemaking: to edit down a sentence or passage by deleting the less important elements, for example, repetitions, asides, secondary considerations and discuss the reasons for editorial choices.

S3: To understand the significance of word order.

What you need

- Some example sentences of your own, which are modelled on the examples in the shared text and sentence level work.

Differentiation

Less able

- Give these children some simple sentences, such as, 'Emma fell over and cut her knee.' Ask these children to choose the main words that convey the meaning of the sentence. Can they make one freeze-frame to tell the story of each sentence?

More able

- Give these children an extract from a class reading book. Ask them to edit down the sentences to the most important words that convey meaning. They should then write their abbreviated version. Remind them that they must retain the same word order and convey the same meaning. Ask them why they selected some words and edited out others.

Shared text-level work

- In this session you are going to show the children how to 'cut the clutter' from text. This is an essential note-making and editing skill, used to identify the essential facts within a text. Display this example:

  Tom was running down the road when he saw the man fall over.
- Ask them to help you find the least number of words in the sentence that can still convey the meaning to the reader. Write down the key elements, for example, *Tom saw the man fall.*
- Explain to them that the meaning could be altered if you change the word order. *The man saw Tom fall* changes the meaning completely.
- Use this example to emphasise the process: *Karen was in such a hurry that she put the wrong shoe on the wrong foot.* This could become *Karen put the wrong foot on the wrong shoe.* Play with the word order and see how it not only changes the meaning but can also create nonsense sentences!

Shared sentence-level work

- Explain to the class that you are going to look at how words can be re-ordered to retain meaning or change meaning. Sometimes, re-ordering words can destroy the meaning but sometimes the word order can be changed to alter meaning, but still make sense. For example:

  The dog bit the man / The man bit the dog.
- Display the following in random order on the board:

  The cat / the fence / and / on / over / jumped / the dog / landed.
- Write each word/pairs of words down on a single piece of paper and give one piece of paper to various children. Ask these children to come out to the front and stand in line so that the class can see every word.
- Ask the class if they can move the children around to make a sentence that has meaning. Can they re-order the words into different sentences that make different meanings?
- Write their various sentences on the board. Talk about whether or not each sentence makes sense and/or conveys a different meaning.

Guided and independent work

- Work with the children. Give them a selection of sentences like the ones modelled in the *Shared text-level* session. Ask them to highlight the key words and then reduce the sentences to their key meanings, using the same word order. The sentences must make sense. They can compare their editorial and note-making skills with each other.
- Give the children the same sentences as in the above activity. Ask them to isolate the key words that convey meaning. Now ask them to make one freeze-frame per sentence to show the key meaning.

Plenary

- Ask the children to report back with their edited sentences.
- Then ask them to perform their freeze-frames, and discuss the meanings, and how words and pictures have been edited or composed to show meaning.

Freeze-frames

Objectives

NLS

T14: Notemaking: to edit down a sentence or passage by deleting the less important elements, for example, repetitions, asides, secondary considerations and discuss the reasons for editorial choices.

S3: To understand the significance of word order, for example, some re-orderings destroy meaning; sentences can be re-ordered to retain meaning (sometimes adding words); subsequent words are governed by preceding ones.

What you need

- Photocopiable page 134
- a collection of newspaper headlines
- a range of fiction books.

Shared text-level work

- Explain that you are going to look at conveying essential meaning from sentences or groups of sentences, in as few words as possible, but retaining meaning. Display the example sentence below:

  The survivors from the plane crash were spotted, floating in their dinghy off the west coast of Scotland.

Ask for volunteers to make a freeze-frame of the most important moment in the sentence. Ask if they can reduce the sentence to a newspaper headline (show them examples). Display their suggestions and talk about which words have been chosen and why.

- Give one of the headlines below to each group and ask them to make a freeze-frame showing the meaning of the headline. They must not show their headline to the rest of the class, because you want to see if the others can guess the headline.

FIREMAN SAVES KITTEN
BLIZZARD CREATES ROAD CHAOS
MAN EATS GIANT APPLE PIE
PLANE FLIES UNDER BRIDGE

Shared sentence-level work

- Explain that word order conveys the meaning of a sentence. It brings ideas together in the way the writer intends. Tell them that they are going to play with newspaper headlines, reversing the order of words.
- Ask the children to reverse the headline in a freeze-frame, for example, KITTEN SAVES FIREMAN. Ask for volunteers to create a freeze-frame as you ask the rest of the class to help reverse the other meanings and write them on the board.

Guided and independent work

- Using the top half of photocopiable page 134 (Silly headlines), ask the children to re-order the words so that the headlines make sense.
- Using fiction books, select, or ask the children to select, a paragraph each (six or seven sentences). Work with them to read each sentence and select the key words to convey meaning (three or four). They must then reduce each sentence by editing out the clutter. Remind them that when re-writing they must retain the word order and it must make sense.

Plenary

- Ask the children to share the key words from their re-written paragraphs. Can the rest of the class fill out the rest of the sentence with phrases that enhance the meaning and give more information?
- Ask children to share their silly headlines with the class.

Differentiation

Less able

- Give these children a card each with three words on each one - noun-verb-noun such as, *man - ran-road.* Ask them to fill out each key word card using the same word order, to make a simple sentence, for example, *man- ran - road* could become *The young man ran quickly down the main road.*

More able

- Ask the children to use conjunctions, connectives, commas and full stops to create a more interesting narrative using photocopiable page 134.

Scanning books

Objectives

NLS

T15: To appraise a non-fiction book for its contents and usefulness by scanning for example headings, content list.

S4: To recognise how commas, connectives and full stops are used to separate clauses; to identify in their writing where each is more effective.

W15: To build up speed, for example, particularly for notes, drafts, lists.

What you need

- A display of non-fiction books related to other curriculum areas
- a model research frame with the following headings: *TITLE - AUTHOR - CONTENTS - INDEX PAGE NO.*

Shared text-level work

- Use a non-fiction book related to another curriculum area. Explain that you are going to model a quick method of scanning books to see if they will be useful for research. Display an enlarged copy of your research frame and then complete the following exercise with the class:

> - Book title - is it on the correct subject? If so, add title/author to the frame.
> - Contents page - are there chapter headings that look useful? Make a note.
> - Index - are there words that are linked to the topic? If so, write them down with the relevant page numbers.

Shared sentence-level work

- Explain that you are going to look at a simple sentence, reduce it to its key words, and then make it into a compound sentence by adding more information. The meaning of the sentence will not be altered.

> - Example sentence: *The boy watched the burglar enter the house.*
> - Reduced to three key words it would be: *Burglar - entering - house.*
> - To make a more interesting sentence, words and phrases can be added:
> *The boy watched the masked burglar stealthily enter the old, deserted house.*

- Emphasise that the essential meaning is the same. Now show them how to re-order this sentence and add words that change the emphasis from the burglar to the boy. Point out that the meaning remains the same.

  Although the masked burglar entered the house stealthily, the brave boy stayed and watched him.

Guided and independent work

- Give the children information books on a topic from another curriculum area. Using the research frame you modelled in the *Shared text-level* session ask them to complete the frame using two or three books from the ones given to them, in the way you demonstrated.
- Work with these children and using the same process from the *Shared sentence-level* session, give them some simple sentences to play with:
  - Can they reduce each sentence to three key words? (They may have to alter the ending of the verb to do this.) For example, *Burglar - enter**ing**- house.*
  - Ask them to fill out the sentences adding more descriptive detail, but keeping the same word order.
  - Now see if they can change the word order around to shift the emphasis, but still retain the essential meaning, as in, *Although the masked burglar...* .

Differentiation

Less able

- Work with the children on a selected information book and help them scan for information in the correct way and enter it onto the frame.

More able

- Ask these children to select non-fiction books and scan them for information on a required topic. They can create their own research frame, based on the one you modelled. Are there any other headings they think should be included? Ask them to use their frame to compile research from books.

Plenary

- Ask the children to talk to the class about their method of collecting research information.

Key words in fiction

Objectives

NLS

T17: To scan texts in print or on screen to locate key words or phrases, useful headings and key sentences and to use these as a tool for summarising text.

S3: To understand the significance of word order, for example, some re-orderings destroy meaning; sentences can be re-ordered to retain meaning (sometimes adding words); subsequent words are governed by preceding ones.

W15: To build up speed, for example, particularly for notes, drafts, lists.

What you need

- Two suitable extracts, fiction or non-fiction (about a paragraph). The second extract should be written in short sentences. You could create this example yourself.

Differentiation

Less able

- Create a research frame for these children, similar to the one used in Hour 3. Work with them to select books and scan them. They can fill in their book titles, authors and comments on the pro forma.

More able

- Using the research frame created in Hour 3, children should add two new columns headed: *WHAT I KNOW* and *WHAT I NEED TO KNOW*. Ask them to write down information they already know, then a series of questions to ask.

Shared text-level work

- Tell the children that you are going to read an extract to them. They are to listen carefully and jot down key words that jump out at them as you read.
- Ask the children to suggest the key words in each sentence.
- Using their key word prompts – can any of them tell you what the sentence meant, using their own words, but keeping the word order they have noted down.

Shared sentence-level work

- Using the second extract ask them to help you use *connectives, conjunctions, commas* and *full stops* to connect the passage together in fewer sentences, but still retain the meaning.

Guided and independent work

- Using either a short passage from a class or child's reading book (fiction or non-fiction) or a piece of text from a suitable website, ask the children to model the work from the *Shared text-level work* and look for *key headings, key words* or *phrases* in the passage. They should use these to help them write a brief summary of the text.
- Work with the children and give them a list of familiar words that you may be using in a class word bank and ask them to do the following:

> Using either a thesaurus and/or a dictionary (class-based or on a computer), define each word using:
> - four words
> - three words
> - two words
> - one word.

This will give them an opportunity to research alternative words or single words that could be used to transmit meanings more effectively.

Plenary

- Ask the children to share their findings about defining words, using one to four words with the rest of the class. The class can then offer suggestions as to how some of these various combinations of words can be used within a sentence to create more effective meanings.
- Ask the children who have been looking for key headings, key words or phrases in a given passage to share their work with the class. Firstly, ask them to tell you their key headings, key words and phrases and write these down on the board. Secondly, ask them to read out their own summary of the text. Now read the original text and ask the class to compare the two. Has the group left anything important out?

Key words in non-fiction

Objectives

NLS

T18: To mark extracts by annotating and by selecting key headings, words or sentences, or alternatively, noting these.

S4: To recognise how commas, connectives and full stops are used to join separate clauses; to identify in their writing where each is more effective.

What you need

- Teacher's choice of text from another curriculum area which the children are studying. You will need a text that can be reduced into headings and brief notes to make statements.

Shared text-level work

- Using your own extract, model for the children how you would sort out and select the main statements.
- Give the children photocopies of the extract and ask them to work in pairs to highlight key words or phrases that they think are important. Note the selections on the board and discuss why they have selected these particular ones.

Shared sentence-level work

- You are going to look at how words can or cannot be moved in a sentence. Using the example below, build a simple sentence:

Cat - chased - dog

- Emphasise the *subject, verb* and *object* sequence.
- Write a simple sentence such as *The cat chased the dog.*
- Now add words/phrases to make the sentence more complex without altering its sense, such as *The old, tabby cat chased the young dog around the tree.*
- Experiment with the word order so that you shift the sentence around to change the focus, for example, *The young dog, who was barking excitedly, was chased around the tree by the old, tabby cat.*

- Display the three words *cat - stalking - mice* and with the children's help ask them to make a simple sentence, then make a more elaborate sentence by adding additional phrases/words. Finally, ask then to alter the sentence around to make the mice the focus, but without destroying the meaning of the sentence.

Guided and independent work

- In the guided session ask the children to make a pile of noun cards and verb cards. Put the cards face down. Each child chooses two noun and one verb and puts them in noun-verb-noun order.
- Now ask the children to use the techniques modelled in the *Shared sentence-level work* to build simple sentences, complex sentences and experiment with word order.

Plenary

- Children who have made sub-headings/notes can talk about the key phrases and words they have chosen.
- Those who have made new sentences from 'three word starters' can share their writing with the class.

Differentiation

Less able

- Ask the children to suggest nouns and verbs. Write these down. Help them to put their words in noun-verb-noun order. Point out that the noun before the verb is the subject and the one after is the object. Help them to compose simple sentences from these three words. Then help them to elaborate their sentences.

More able

- Give these children three words each - two nouns and a verb. Ask them to make as many elaborate sentences as they can with just those words. Then see if they can re-order the words to swap the subject and object round but still retain the meaning.

Research

Shared text- and sentence-level work

- Using an enlarged version of your research frame, tell the children that you are going to model a method of collecting information, based on what is known and what you need to find out. Some children will have experience of this from Hour 4 so ask them to take the lead.
- Using the frame and a selected topic, invite the children to contribute statements about what they already know and write these on the form.
- Now ask them to think of questions on the topic that they might want to research. Write these on the frame.
- You can either model the process of looking for information from books on the topic, or, if you have sufficient texts, give the books to the children and ask them to help you find appropriate material and note down the references on the frame.
- Re-emphasise the process:
  book title -author - contents -index - page numbers.

Guided and independent work

- Work with the children to help them find appropriate websites from which to gain research information.
- They must first write down what they already know and then list some research questions of their own. They should use their note-taking skills to help them cut and paste their selections, then print these out and enter their facts onto their research frame.
- Using a photocopy of the modelled research frame, ask the children to write down facts they already know about the given topic, write down some research questions, and then start to select books. They should write down suitable titles, authors and information on the frame.
- Ask the children to select one chapter heading from a book appropriate for their topic. Then ask them to create sub-headings in information boxes and write short notes, key words or phrases in the boxes.
- Can the children draw arrows between the boxes to show the correct sequence of information? Emphasise that correct word order is necessary to maintain meaning.

Plenary

- Ask the children to share their findings with the rest of the class. but emphasise that they must be able to back up their findings with editorial judgements about what they have selected and what they left out.
- The groups who have been creating research frames and research questions for collecting information from websites should talk about the advantages and disadvantages of collecting information on screen.
- Ask the children involved in selecting information for research frames to discuss the reasons for making new editorial judgements in terms of what they selected and why some information was not included.

Objectives

NLS

T16: to prepare for factual research by reviewing what is known, what is needed, what is available and where one might search.

W15: to build up speed, for example, particularly for notes, drafts, lists.

What you need

- Photocopiable enlargement of the research frame created by the more able pupils in Hour 4
- a selection of non-fiction books from the school or class library, and/or designated websites chosen by the teacher.

Differentiation

Less able

- Work with this group on a selected chapter from a non-fiction book. Help them to determine key headings and make information boxes for them. Then help them select key words or phrases to go in the boxes.

More able

- Ask these children to use a photocopy of the research frame they helped to devise and divide their tasks as follows. (1) Contribute a statement each to the column 'WHAT I KNOW. (2) Agree one or two questions for further research. (3) Scan books for relevant information. (4) Create information boxes and note key words/ phrases. They then all discuss and agree the sequence of information and draw arrows between boxes to show sequence.

Notes on the planets

Objectives

NLS

T21: To make short notes by abbreviating ideas, selecting key words, listing, or in diagrammatic form.

What you need

- Photocopiable page 135
- a website or a book from either the school or class library that gives information about Uranus, Pluto and Neptune.

Shared text-level work

- Using an enlarged version of photocopiable page 135, read through the text: *Opening paragraph - Our location - Orbiting around a star - A range of planets.*
- Tell the children that you are going to show them how to make short notes, how to abbreviate ideas, select key words and then to draw a diagram to show the essential facts.
- Work with the class to collect *headings, sub-headings* and *key words and phrases* but not in any sequence. List these on the board.
- Tell the children that you want them to draw information boxes with headings in. Demonstrate this process but leave the boxes empty.
- Tell them that in the *Guided and independent* session, they are going to complete the task and that they can use the information on the board to help them.

Shared sentence-level work

- Remind them that word order in the text is very important and even if they abbreviate complex sentences, they must ensure that the meaning is retained.

Guided and independent work

- Give one group of children the passage from photocopiable page 135, with the heading *Our location.* Ask them to work in pairs to read the extract.
- Work with them to help them create sub-headings in information boxes and decide on key words or phrases to enter into the boxes. They should draw arrows between the boxes to show the correct sequence of information.
- Give a second group the passage from photocopiable page 135, with the heading *Orbiting around a star.* Ask them to work in pairs to read the text, write down sub-headings, create information boxes and put in key words or phrases. They should draw arrows between the boxes to show the correct sequence of information.
- Give a third group the passage from photocopiable page 135, with the heading *A range of planets.* Ask them to work in pairs to read the text, write down sub-headings, create information boxes and put in key words or phrases. They should draw arrows between the boxes to show the correct sequence of information.

Differentiation

Less able

- Work with this group using the introduction on photocopiable page 135, *The nearest star to Earth...* Help them select key words and phrases, create information boxes with headings and then link the boxes in the correct order.

More able

- Give this group a page from a book about Mars (such as pp18-19 from *Astronomy* by Rachel Firth, Usborne Publishing). Ask them to work together to decide key phrases and words, create information boxes, and link their diagram together in the correct sequence.

Plenary

- *Our location* – ask the children involved in this activity to bring out their charts and justify the sequence of information they have created through the use of arrows and boxes.
- Ask the groups who have been looking at *Orbiting around a star* to discuss their selection of key words and phrases from the text.
- Ask the children who have been collecting information on *A range of planets* to discuss their reasons for choosing sub-headings and key words and phrases.

Objectives

NLS

T21: To make short notes by abbreviating ideas, selecting key words, listing, or in diagrammatic form.

What you need

- A website or a book from either the school or class library that gives information about solar and lunar eclipses, Uranus, Pluto and Neptune.

Notes on eclipses

Shared text-level work

- Using an enlarged version of a text you have chosen about eclipses, read the passage to the class. Ask children to volunteer to be the sun, the moon and the Earth.
- See if the class can help these children move into the correct positions for each of the three types of eclipse, as you read the passage to them again. Ask them if they remember any key phrases that helped them to make their decisions.
- Now ask the children to draw a diagram of each of the eclipses as you read the passage again.
- Then ask them to help you draw a labelled diagram based on their own diagrams, so that you can label it correctly.
- Explain to the children that sometimes a diagram with labels can be a very quick way of collecting important information.

Shared sentence-level work

- Reinforce to the children the previous work you have done on word order and meaning. Tell them that they must be just as aware of using the correct order of words when they are extracting information to put onto a diagram, as when they are producing a text.

Guided and independent work

- Give one group of children a page from a book that includes information about eclipses (for example, pages 18–19 from *Astronomy* by Rachel Firth, Usborne Publishing). Ask them to collect sub-headings, key words and phrases. They could work in pairs, taking a section each.
- Ask a second group to draw a diagram of the solar system with labels to define each planet.

Plenary

- Ask the children who have been creating the diagrams of the eclipses, to bring their work out in front of the class and talk through the eclipse using the headings, key words and so on, as prompts.
- Ask the children who have made a diagram of the solar system to come out and for one child to pretend to be each of the planets. They should put themselves in the correct places.
- Then ask this group to write down the key points from their work on the solar system on the board. They can write bullet points under each planet or use these as prompts to talk to the class about what they have discovered.

Differentiation

Less able

- Work with this group to help them create a diagram of the eclipses used in the *Shared text-level work* and put the relevant key words and phrases in information boxes.

More able

- Give this group a book or books containing information about Uranus, Pluto and Neptune. Ask them to select information, draw a diagram of the planets within the solar system, label them and put information boxes next to each one.

Notes into prose

Objectives

NLS
T22: To fill out brief notes into connected prose.
S4: To recognise how commas, connectives and full stops are used to join separate clauses; to identify in their writing where each is more effective.

What you need

- Photocopiable page 135.

Shared text-level work

- Using one of the children's diagrams and notes on the Solar System (from Hour 8), model how you would take the basic information from this and turn it into connected prose.
- Emphasise that they already carry additional information in their heads from their own research, note-taking and diagrams. These can act as good prompts from which to elaborate their notes and diagrams.

Shared sentence-level work

- Remind the children about the use of commas and connectives when they are writing prose.
- Also reiterate that they need to make sure that they always use words in the correct order so that what they write makes sense.

Guided and independent work

- Ask the children who created diagrams based on eclipses (in Hour 8) to use these and their brief notes to write a description of one of the three types of eclipse. They can share their information with each other, and then select the most appropriate notes, phrases and so on to use in their prose on their chosen eclipse.
- Ask the children who have been working on the Solar System (in Hour 8) to use their diagrams and notes to write connected prose on the subject of the Solar System.
- Again, they can share information and make appropriate selections from the pooled information.
- Using a diagram from a designated website selected by the teacher on a topic covered in another curriculum area, work with the children to use the diagram and notes to relay the information in connected prose.

Plenary

- In this session the children should have an opportunity to compare the different versions of the information they have used from diagrams and note-making.
- The guided discussion should be aimed at identifying the editorial choices they have made in selecting connectives and phrases to endorse and elaborate their text.
- Ask the children who have been writing prose on the solar system to discuss their editorial choices and their chosen sequence of presenting information in text.
- Ask the children writing about Uranus, Pluto and Neptune to read their work to the class. Ask the children listening to see if they can remember any good connectives and phrases used by the writers in order to make their writing more entertaining.
- Discuss the difficulties of changing brief notes and information boxes into connected prose.

Differentiation

Less able
- Work with this group and help them to use their own diagrams and notes from Hour 8, to write a brief piece of connected prose about one or two of the information boxes they completed.

More able
- This group can use the diagrams and notes they made on Uranus, Pluto and Neptune to write a connected piece of prose about these three planets. Ask them to do this individually.

Information on Mars

Objectives

NLS

T23: To collect information from a variety of sources and present it in a simple format, for example, wall chart, labelled diagram.

What you need

- Photocopiable extract from an information book on Mars
- a collection of information and reference books
- research frames from previous hours in this unit and/or websites designated by the teacher.

Shared text- and sentence-level work

- Using an enlarged copy of a photocopied extract about Mars, read the information to the class, asking them to write down any words that they think may be key ones.
- Read the information again and model how you would read and re-read sentences, looking for words and phrases that seem to be the key ones.
- Decide on your selection and create information boxes with headings.
- Explain that key words and phrases may be 'hidden away' in complex sentences. They will have to be very observant!
- Now draw a picture of Mars, and with the children's help, add the relevant information in the correct locations.

Guided and independent work

- The tasks in this section will apply to all groups. Explain that this is their last session in this unit and that they have developed a great many skills during each of the other hours. Now is an opportunity for them to share those skills with each other.
- Every child will use the information that they have collected in previous sessions including diagrams, research frames from earlier sessions and their own notes and information boxes. They can work in pairs or groups and pool their information.
- They must decide on a suitable method of presenting this information, as either a wall chart or a diagram. Explain that time is of the essence! They can cut-out and stick-on information to display it to its best advantage. In addition they may need to add one or two other bits of text or diagrams to make their finished presentation complete.

Plenary

- Ask the children to bring out their wall charts and diagrams so that they can be seen and shared. This is an opportunity to discuss working methods within the group and how they selected the relevant pieces of information.
- Discuss with the children the following points:
  1. How did they set about making notes on their texts?
     a. Did they read it all first?
     b. Did they scan it quickly to look for key words?
     c. Did they underline or highlight key words and phrases?
  2. Did they all agree on the information to select?
  3. Did they agree on a format for their presentation, for example a wall chart or diagram?
  4. Did some children find one method of displaying the information easier to do? Were they more comfortable working in a wall chart or a diagram?
  5. Why did one method appeal to them more than another?

Differentiation

Less able

- Help them decide their format – wall chart or diagram. Then help them to sift information and select key points for display.

More able

- Select suitable websites on the same topic then work together to collect information. They could try to create a display unit, a wall chart and a diagram. Which one is best?

Silly headlines

FRUITCAKE RUNS OFF WITH BOY AND STEALS SPOON

KITE LOSES MAN IN NEW WORLD RECORD HEIGHT BID

Station deserted in mystery at ghost train disappearance

NIGHT CONFUSION OF VILLAGE IN SMALL HOTEL

MAN MOUNTAIN TAKES BIKE AND PEDALS OFF

School football team play girls in right to win

SAUSAGE CREATES CRISIS IN SUPERMARKET SHORTAGE

SCHOOL FOOTBALL TEAM PLAY GIRLS IN RIGHT TO WIN

The bald facts

■ **Use connectives, conjunctions, additional phrases, commas and full stops to 'fill out' these sentences. You must keep the meaning, but you can re-order words.**

Adam and Katy left their friend's house. They walked home. They walked along the road. It was late. They phoned Mum. She told them to wait outside the post office. She would collect them. They waited outside the post office for Mum. It was six o'clock. Adam dropped his football. It bounced into the road. He ran after it. Katy tried to stop him. There was the sound of brakes. A car skidded. Adam's football was flattened. The man got out of his car. He said that Adam was lucky. It could have been worse. Mum arrived in her car. Adam told her what had happened. Mum was not pleased. She told Adam to say that he was sorry. Adam apologised to the man. The man smiled and reached into his car. He took out a football. He told Adam that he was the Manager of the local football team. He gave Adam the football. He told Adam that football should be played on grass, not pavements. Adam was very pleased. He thanked the man. The man got in his car. He drove away. Adam, Katy and Mum went home.

Astronomy

The nearest star to Earth is the **Sun**, a bright yellow **star** that produces plenty of light and heat. Our star is fairly unusual, only about five percent of stars produce as much heat and light as the **Sun**. There are nine planets orbiting the Sun. Our star and its **planets** make up what is known as the **Solar System**.

OUR LOCATION

The Sun is located in one of the spiral arms of the **Milky Way Galaxy**. A galaxy consists of billions of stars held together by the force of **gravity**, and most galaxies also contain vast clouds of dust and gas. The Milky Way Galaxy is shaped like a huge lens – fatter in the middle than at the edges. The whole galaxy is rotating, and this rotation has produced several spiral arms that extend from the centre. The Milky Way Galaxy measures about 100,000 light years in diameter. The nearest similar galaxy is the Andromeda Galaxy about two million **light years** away.

ORBITING AROUND A STAR

Held by gravity, the planets orbit around the Sun as if they were attached to it by pieces of invisible string of varying length. Earth is the third planet from the Sun. Mercury and Venus are closer, and the other planets are further away. Earth orbits the Sun at a distance of about 150 million km, and takes one year to complete one **orbit**. Jupiter orbits at a distance of about 780 million km, and one orbit lasts nearly 12 Earth years.

A RANGE OF PLANETS

The planets in the Solar System can be divided into two basic types, small rock planets and large gas planets. Mercury, Venus, Earth, and Mars are rock planets. Jupiter, Saturn, Uranus and Neptune are gas planets. Pluto is too distant for scientists to be certain exactly what it is. Most of the planets have one or more moons (natural satellites) orbiting around them. Jupiter is by far the largest of the planets. With a diameter of about 143,000 km, it is one-tenth the size of the Sun. Jupiter contains more than twice as much mass as the other nine planets put together.

From "The Science of Searching for Life in Space" (2004, ticktock Media Ltd).

UNIT 5

Explanation texts

In this unit the children will develop their skills in writing explanation texts. They will look at how texts are ordered in a sequence of paragraphs to clarify meaning. They will learn about the conventions of writing explanatory text using the present tense and the passive voice. They will look at the skills of identifying key features from a text and use a writing frame to sequence information. They will practise adapting texts to create diagrams and using diagrams to generate explanation texts, and within their writing they will have to be aware of using connectives. This unit is closely linked with Unit 29 of *Grammar for Writing.*

Hour	Shared text-level work	Shared sentence-/ word-level work	Guided work	Independent work	Plenary
1 Using paragraphs	Looking at explanation texts. Identifying key meanings in paragraphs.	Identifying and using connectives.	Re-ordering texts into paragraphs in the correct order.	Writing paragraph headings with brief explanatory notes.	Verbal résumé of text headings using children's own notes.
2 Complex sentences	Identifying key features in explanatory text.	Use of connectives.	Putting text into the correct order.	Turning text into a labelled diagram.	Discussing the labelled diagrams and the correct sequence of paragraphs.
3 The parts of a guitar	Identifying use of passive voice and present tense.	Use of connectives of time and cause and effect.	Sequencing texts into main paragraph headings.	Creating labelled diagrams with brief notes.	Using the children to physically create the diagram and labels.
4 The water cycle	Using a frame for writing an explanatory text.	Awareness of connectives within the frame.	Using a writing frame for explanatory text.	Using a writing frame for explanatory text.	Sharing the work produced from the writing frame and listing connectives.
5 Turning diagrams into text	Re-ordering a text into the correct sequence: introduction, sequential paragraphs and conclusion.	Awareness of connectives and how they are used.	Working with a website diagram to turn it into a connected piece of explanatory text based on the frame.	Using non-fiction books with diagrams to create connected prose for an explanatory text based on the frame.	Discussing the explanatory texts and the use of connectives, passive voice and present tense.

Key assessment opportunities

- Are the children able to recognise key meanings in paragraphs, and to sequence an explanation text from introduction to conclusion using paragraphs appropriately?
- Do they have confidence in converting text to a diagram and vice versa?

Using paragraphs

Objectives

NLS

T19: To identify how and why paragraphs are used to organise and sequence information.

T24: To improve the cohesion of written explanations through paragraphing and the use of link phrases and organisational devices such as sub-headings and numbering.

S4: To recognise how commas, connectives and full stops are used to join and separate clauses; to identify in their writing where each is more effective.

S&L

43 Group discussion and interaction: To use time, resources and group members efficiently by distributing tasks, checking progress, making backup plans.

What you need

- Photocopiable page 142.

Shared text-level work

- Using photocopiable page 142, 'The classical guitar', talk to the children about how an explanation text is written:

  - Use of paragraphs
  - Use of present tense
  - Passive voice
  - The purpose - to explain a process or to answer a question
  - Structure - introduction followed by sequential explanation
  - Use of connectives.

- In the extract, the writer has forgotten to use paragraphs. Ask the children to help you identify where new paragraphs might begin.

Shared sentence-level work

- Explain to the children that a clause is a group of words that expresses an event. It usually contains a subject and a verb, for example, *He was hungry.*
- Explain that a simple sentence contains one clause.
- Now tell them that a compound sentence has two or more clauses of equal weight and that both are main clauses. Look at these two simple sentences: *He was hungry. He ate some food.* These sentences can be changed into a compound sentence by adding one of the following joining words: *and, or, but, so*. Which one do they think should join these sentences?
- Ask the children to suggest two more short sentences that could be made into a compound sentence by removing the full stop and adding a joining word.

Guided and independent work

- Give the children a copy of the extract and ask them to make a list of all the connectives used. Ask them to write a new opening paragraph for 'The classical guitar' using some of these connectives.
- Ask the children to work in pairs. Each partner must write ten two-statement sentences, separated by a full stop. When they have finished, they exchange sentences and see if they can remove the full stop and use *and, or, but* or *so* to make the simple sentences into compound sentences.
- Ask the children to work in pairs on the extract. One child completes the task on computer, the other on paper. Ask them to break the text up into an *introduction, sequential paragraphs* and a *conclusion*, adding key headings and making notes. Tell them to work closely as a pair and check progress. If the computer-generated version does not work, then they have the backup plan on paper.

Differentiation

Less able

- Cut-up a copy of the text into jumbled-up paragraphs. Give the children numbered sub-headings and ask them if they can match the jumbled paragraphs to the correct heading.

More able

- Give these children the jumbled-up paragraphs of the text. Ask them to put these into the correct order and to create a sub-heading for each paragraph.

Plenary

- Ask the children to report back to the class on their breaking the text into paragraphs and adding key headings and notes, and to give a brief résumé of the piece in their own words (taking a paragraph each).

Complex sentences

Objectives

NLS

T20: To identify from the examples the key features of explanatory texts: purpose - to explain or to answer a question; structure - introduction followed by sequential explanation, organised into paragraphs.

S4: To recognise how commas, connectives and full stops are used to join and separate clauses; to identify in their writing where each is more effective.

What you need

- Photocopiable pages 142 and 143.

Shared text-level work

- Using the text 'The classical guitar' (page 142), model the process, with help from the class, of identifying the following from the extract:

- The structure
- The sequence of explanation
- The organisation into paragraphs
- The language features
- The presentation.

Shared sentence-level work

- Remind the children about the differences between a simple sentence and a compound sentence as discussed in Hour 1.
- Tell them that in this session, they are going to look at complex sentences.
- Tell them that a complex sentence consists of a main clause and a subordinate clause. For example, *Although it was sunny, I wasn't hot.*
- Ask them to tell you what the punctuation mark is that links the two clauses in this sentence.
- Explain to them that economy in writing is achieved by using a compound sentence, but that explicitness is better achieved by using subordinate clauses. Display some of your own examples of compound sentences, and then of complex sentences.
- Ask the children if they can identify each type, and then ask them to make suggestions of their own and state which type of sentence each one is. Are they correct?

Guided and independent work

- Give the children a jumbled-up version of photocopiable page 143 by re-ordering the paragraphs (by cutting, pasting and photocopying). Ask them to put it into the correct order, following the pattern: *introduction - sequence of paragraphs - conclusion*.
- Give the children the jumbled-up extract and ask them to draw a labelled diagram of 'The water cycle'.
- Working with the children, choose some suitable extracts from the class or school library; then give them a photocopy of one of these extracts. Ask them to identify and underline all the simple sentences in blue, compound sentences in red and the complex sentences in green.

Differentiation

Less able

- Work with this group to put the sequence of the extract together from introduction to conclusion, making their own headings for each section.

More able

- Ask this group to work together so that some make a diagram while others put the paragraphs in the correct order. They can check their conclusion with the work from the other groups in the *Plenary*.

Plenary

- Ask the children to show their labelled diagrams of 'The water cycle' to the rest of the class and explain how they were produced using the text.
- Ask the children who have been sequencing the paragraphs to contribute their findings. Have all the groups got the extract in the right order?
- Ask children who have worked with the extracts from the library to explain how they have underlined the different types of sentences.

Objectives

NLS

T20: To identify from the examples the key features of explanatory texts: language features - usually present tense, use of connectives of time and cause and effect, use of passive voice; presentation - use of diagrams, other illustrations.

S4: To recognise how commas, connectives and full stops are used to join and separate clauses; to identify in their writing where each is more effective.

S&L

41 Speaking: To respond appropriately to the contributions of others in the light of alternative viewpoints.

What you need

- Photocopiable page 142 (enlarged).

Differentiation

Less able

- Work with this group to make labels for each part of the guitar. They should investigate the text to find the information.

More able

- Ask these children to work together to put the text into the correct order and write a brief paragraph under each heading using passive voice, present tense and connectives.

The parts of a guitar

Shared text -level work

- Read an enlarged photocopy of page 142, displaying 'The parts of the guitar'. Ask the children what is wrong with it (*no sequence of paragraphs, no use of passive voice, not enough use of present tense*). Write these reminders on the board and write a class version of the introduction, using all the key features of explanatory text.

Shared sentence-level work

- Revise the work on compound and complex sentences from the previous hour using the children's examples.
- Write these on the board and ask the children if they can identify which type of sentence you have written down.
- Tell the children that a compound sentence can contain more than two clauses. For example:

  He was late for school.
  He ran all the way.
  He got there just in time.

Using connective words this can become a compound sentence:

  He was late for school so he ran all the way and got there just in time.

- Ask the children to offer three simple sentences that could be joined in this way.

Guided and independent work

- Ask the children to work in pairs. Each partner should create ten examples containing three simple sentences. They then exchange sentences with their partner and ask them to turn each one into a compound sentence using the correct joining words. How many of them can use *or*?
- Give the children a copy of the text on 'The parts of the Guitar'. Ask them to see if they can identify the main sequence: *introduction - sequential paragraphs - conclusion.*
- Ask them, in pairs, to discuss the headings for each paragraph and the key features to include. Remind them that in a discussion they should be aware of the appropriate language to use*: I think that is a good idea. I'm not sure you are right but let's look at it again. Had you thought about this?* and so on.
- Ask the children to use the text to draw a diagram of the guitar and label the main parts with a brief note about what their function is.

Plenary

- Ask children who have been making labels to come and stand with their labels in the shape of the guitar, including the machine head, the nut, the neck, the body, the strings and the bridge.
- Ask all the children to contribute information to the parts of the guitar from their own investigation of the text.

The water cycle

Objectives

NLS

T25: To write explanations of a process, using conventions identified through reading.

S4: To recognise how commas, connectives and full stops are used to join and separate clauses; to identify in their writing where each is more effective.

W4: To practise new spellings regularly by Look >Say>Cover>Write>Check strategy.

What you need

- Photocopiable page 143.

Shared text -level work.

- Using photocopiable page 143, model a process for the class using the following frame:

> - The first thing that happens...
> - This means that...
> - After that...
> - As a result...

- Put brief headings and summaries for each section into a 'paragraph box' and write down a list of useful connectives.

Shared sentence-level work

- Remind the children of the work covered in the previous session.
- Explain that writers keep their readers' interest by varying the style and length of each sentence. Use examples from books in the classroom to demonstrate. In particular, look for examples that contain *prepositional* and *adverbial phrases*. Point these out to the children.
- Tell them that prepositional phrases modify the verb and can be re-ordered without destroying the meaning of the sentence. *He worked all through the night* can be modified to *All through the night, he worked.* Point out the comma. Ask which sentence is more interesting.
- Explain that the same process can be used with adverbs. *She was smartly dressed* can be modified to *She was dressed smartly.*
- Ask if they can think of any more sentences using prepositional or adverbial phrases. Discuss what they think, as readers, if you re-order these sentences.

Differentiation

Less able

- Using photocopiable page 143, help these children put each section under the writing frame model. They can cut and paste paragraphs in order to do this. Ask them to highlight or underline the connectives that are used.

More able

- Using a diagram from a non-fiction book of their own choice or website (designated) ask these children to create their own writing frame for an explanation text, using the one in the unit but making it more sophisticated. They can add a list of connectives and paragraph boxes with headings and notes.

Guided and independent work

- Work with the group to select a non-fiction book. In pairs, they should model the process from shared work. Each child should have a specific responsibility; one might collect good connectives, the others make paragraph boxes with headings and brief notes. They should arrange their paragraph boxes and selected connectives into the writing frame used above, using either numbers or sub-headings to order their work.
- In pairs, each child writes down ten sentences using prepositional or adverbial phrases. They exchange sentences with their partner, asking them to re-order the sentences without destroying the meaning. Which version do they prefer?
- Give the children a copy of photocopiable page 143 and ask them to underline words unfamiliar to them. They should write these down and use the *Look>Say>Cover>Write>Check* strategy to check spellings.

Plenary

- Ask the children to share their work using the writing frame with each other and see how the model works. A list of connectives from each group could be written on the board for future reference. Can they think of other phrases they might need to add into the frame?

Turning diagrams into text

Objectives

NLS

T25: To write explanations of a process, using conventions identified through reading.

S4: To recognise how commas, connectives and full stops are used to join and separate clauses; to identify in their writing where each is more effective.

What you need

- Photocopiable page 142.
- non-fiction books from the classroom and/or teacher-designated websites showing diagrams of information that the class are working on in this curriculum area.

Shared text-level work

- Using the extract 'The parts of the guitar', ask the children to help you write a sequence of paragraph headings. Using the extract as a model, ask the children to offer their knowledge of writing explanation texts to re-order this piece into sequential paragraphs and a conclusion.
- Remind them that the introduction was written in Hour 3. Use it as a reminder about the use of *connectives, passive voice* and present tense.

Shared sentence-level work

- Display some examples of sentences using an *adverbial* or *prepositional phrase*.
- Ask the children to help you re-order them. You can use some examples from their work from Hour 4.
- Display the following beginning to a story.

> It was dark. Peter was afraid. He stood silently watching the deserted, old house. Did he see someone at the window? Was it just the shadow of a tree?

Ask the children to help you write the opening paragraph to this story. They can re-order it if they wish.

- Remind them to think about compound and complex sentences, and about the use of prepositional and adverbial phrases.
- Also tell them that sometimes a short simple sentence can add to the pace and flow of the writing.
- Play with word orders as you write the piece and ask the children which orders they like best.

Guided and independent work

- Work with the class to take information from a designated website that uses a diagram to explain a process, so that they can generate an explanation text using the model (*paragraph boxes* and *connectives*).
- Ask the children to use a non-fiction book to take a diagrammatic explanation of a process and turn it into an explanation text – using *paragraph boxes, phrases* and *organisational devices* such as *sub-headings*.
- Ask the children to write the opening paragraph to a story using a combination of simple, compound and complex sentences. Remind them that using prepositional and adverbial phrases can enhance their writing. Tell them not to be afraid to play with the word order.

Plenary

- Ask some children to read out their explanation texts and involve the class in discussing how they have been written. Do they use the *correct sequence? Passive voice? Present tense? Connectives?*
- Ask the children to share their story openings, then discuss the use of different types of sentences, prepositional and adverbial phrases, as well as the word order writers have selected. How well does it work?

Differentiation

Less able

- Work with this group using 'The water cycle' diagram or their labelled version of 'The parts of a guitar' to write a brief introduction, sequential paragraph and conclusion as an explanation text. You can help them by using the original extract and pointing out various sections to them.

More able

- Ask this group to choose a diagram each from a non-fiction textbook and working alone, create an explanation text, observing the correct conventions.

The classical guitar

The writer of this text has used some of the correct features for an explanatory text, but has left one very important one out: *paragraphs*!

The classical guitar is a fretted instrument with six nylon strings tuned in EADGBE and is played with the fingers and thumb. The guitar has a great range of notes and a variety of tones, which makes it ideal for the solo performer. This versatility is, possibly, one of the reasons the guitar is such a popular instrument.
The exact origins of the classical, and indeed, all modern guitars, are not really known. However, as long ago as 1400 BC the Hittites were playing an instrument with a long neck and a body with a waist. It was not until the eighteenth century that the guitar came to resemble the modern instrument that we know today. Then the guitar had six strings, but was much smaller and quieter. In about 1840, a Spanish carpenter named Antonio de Torres began making guitars. He gave the instrument a much bigger body than had previously been used and he was very sensitive to the acoustic quality of wood. Although much of the wood he used came from furniture, which he dismantled, few makers since have been able to equal the sound and character of his instruments. It was not until the second half of the twentieth century that the classical guitar became very popular. This was due to the explosion of a popular music culture and also the arrival of steel strings, which gave the modern acoustic guitar a much 'bigger' full-bodied sound.

The parts of the guitar

If I was going to describe the main features of a classical, or any other guitar for that matter, I would say the following. The guitar has a wooden body with a waist. It was always made from wood. The main body of the guitar is what we call the sound chamber and the hole in the middle is called the 'rose'. I've got six strings on my guitar and these are connected at each end to what is called the 'bridge' and to the 'machine heads', which are at the end of the neck. Oh, and by the way, the things on the neck, the metal bits running across, are called 'frets'. You use them to put your fingers in between to make the notes you want to play. You push the strings through the bridge and wind them round the pegs. These are on the machine head and have a hole in the cylinder to put the string through. You tighten the strings by turning each peg. The strings pass across a bit at the end of the neck, at the bottom of the machine head, called the 'nut'. Don't know why! Then they go all the way down the neck and are attached to the bridge, which is stuck on the soundboard. You pluck or strum the strings with your fingers to make the sound. Easy as that!

By Campbell Perry

SCHOLASTIC

Water cycle

About two-thirds of the Earth's surface is covered in water. Some 97% of this occurs as salt water in the seas and oceans. More than half of the remaining fresh water exists as glaciers and ice caps, so a very small amount of fresh water occurs as lakes, rivers and groundwater. Groundwater accounts for 0.6% of the distribution of water on Earth.

Water is a continuous cycle, powered by the sun. Water evaporates from surface water and is transpired by plant foliage. The water vapour condenses, forming clouds, and then precipitates as rain or snow. Some of this collects as run-offs in the streams, rivers and, eventually, the oceans.

Much of the rain filters into the ground to form groundwater. Some of the water in the ground is absorbed by plant roots, then carried up to the leaves and returned to the atmosphere by transpiration. Most of the water stays in the ground, slowly moving through the aquifers and eventually in streambeds, springs and oceans.

An aquifer is a layer of rock, which can absorb a large quantity of water. It can do so because it is porous or because the rock is broken up with crevices that hold the water.

From the website www.highlandspring.co.uk (Highland Spring Limited).

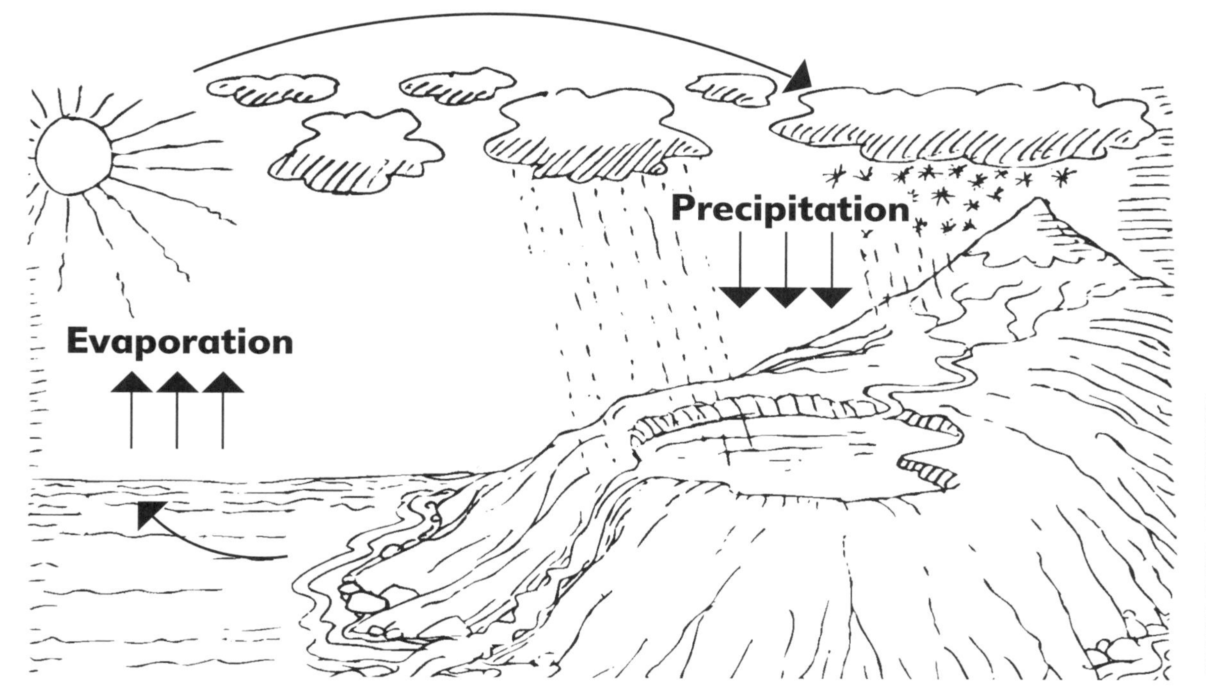

UNIT 1

Poetry

In this unit children will have the opportunity to explore a range of poetic styles from limericks and clapping games to poems with a verse/chorus structure and poems written in stanzas. They will work with different rhyming patterns and rhythms as well as exploring the use of imagery. The sentence-level work is based around Unit 30 of *Grammar for Writing* and the children are given opportunities to explore how word endings can significantly change the classification and use of a word.

Hour	Shared text-level work	Shared sentence-/ word-level work	Guided work	Independent work	Plenary
1 Limericks	Looking at different types of poems, rhyme, chorus, rhythm.	Understanding that words can be put into a different category by using different endings.	Working with words. Creating different categories by adding different endings.	Writing limericks and adding to a poem, using the original as a model.	Sharing and discussing limericks and the additional verses for an existing poem.
2 Clapping and skipping rhymes	Knowledge of stanzas rhyming sequences, rhyming couplets.	Using the same root word to make different categories of word by adding different endings and applying them in sentences.	Using the same root word and adding different endings to make different categories.	Working with clapping and skipping rhymes. Using an original poem as a model to create a new stanza.	Performance of clapping rhymes, discussion of rhyme and rhythm used.
3 What type of words?	Comparing three poems in terms of structure, imagery, and rhyming sequence.	Working with words collected by children. Placing words in a sentence so that the correct category of ending is used.	Review of poems based on knowledge of structure, rhyming pattern, imagery used.	Looking at rhyming patterns in poems. Making nonsense words by mismatching words and endings.	Sharing the nonsense words collected by the children and classifying them into categories.
4 Favourite poets	Teacher choosing some favourite poems to share and discuss with class, looking at structure, rhyme, rhythm and use of language.	Making up nonsense sentences with words with the correct endings, but which do not fit in the category.	Comparison of two poems by the same writer.	Children writing about their own reading habits. Using words out of category to make sentences.	Discussion of favourite poems, concentrating on style and structure. Sharing nonsense sentences.
5 Pull a face	Discussion of structure, rhyming pattern and use of figurative and descriptive language in poems – looking for polished expressions.	Revising, deleting and adding words and phrases to create a polished piece of writing.	Interpreting the poem through physical and facial expression.	Using an original poem as a model for writing. Reviewing a favourite poem.	Sharing original poems within the class and discussing the structure and use of language.

Key assessment opportunities

- Are the children able to recognise different poetic forms?
- Are they aware of the way poems can be structured in terms of verses, stanzas, rhyming patterns and the numbers of syllables in a line?
- Are they able to interpret poems?
- Are they able to write their own poems using a model structure provided for them?

Limericks

Objectives

NLS

T4: To understand the following terms and identify them in poems: verse, chorus, couplet stanza, rhyme, rhythm, alliteration.
T5: To clap out and count the syllables in each line of regular poetry.
T14: To write poems, experimenting with different styles and structures, discuss if and why different forms are more suitable than others.
S1: To understand that some words can be changed in particular ways and others cannot, for example changing verb endings, pluralisation and that these are important clues for identifying word classes. (*Grammar for Writing* Unit 30)
W3: To spell by analogy with other known words.

What you need

- Photocopiable pages 150–152.

Differentiation

Less able

- Work with this group to complete the limerick at the bottom of 'Limerick maker' (page 152).

More able

- Ask these children to write their own limericks. They can work alone, or in pairs: One pair takes the opening two lines, the second pair take lines three and four and they all work together to write the last line.

Shared text-level work

- Read the poem 'Ready Neddy?' from photocopiable page 150 to the class. Discuss with them: the type of poem (limerick), the number of lines and rhyming sequence. Clap the syllables in each line. What do they notice? Ask them if they know any other limericks.
- Create a class limerick on the board.
- Read the poem 'It's a dog's life' also on page 150. Put an enlarged copy on the board. Talk about the structure – verse and chorus and the rhyming sequence.

Shared sentence-level work

- Display an enlarged copy of 'Endings' from photocopiable page 151.
- Explain that the class is going to explore word endings because these often tell us what sort of as word it is – for example *ing* and *ed* are usually verb endings, *er* and *est* make adjectival comparisons, adverbs end in *ly*.
- Using the enlarged sheet go through the text and find some more examples.

Guided and independent work

- Using the 'Limerick maker' on photocopiable page 152, ask the children to write their own limericks. Display a set of rules for writing limericks such as:

> - You have a set number of lines and a set rhyming sequence.
> - The first two lines rhyme with each other and also with line five.
> - Lines three and four rhyme, but not with lines one, two or five
> - In lines one, two and five there are usually about ten syllables
> - In lines three and four there are about five each.

- In this guided session give the children 'Endings 1' on photocopiable page 151 and ask them to collect some words that can be put into different categories by using a different ending.
- Give the children a copy of 'It's a dog's life' and ask them to write another verse using the same rhyming sequence and number of syllables per line as the original.
- In the poem 'It's a dog's life' point out the words *coat* and *goat*, and see how many words you can collect that use the same spelling patterns.

Plenary

- Ask the children to share their limericks with the class and explain the structure of this poetic form.
- Ask the children to read out their extra verses for 'It's a dog's life' and explain the structure of the poem to the class.

Skipping and clapping rhymes

Objectives

NLS

T4: Understand the following terms and identify them in poems: verse, chorus, couplet, stanza, rhyme, rhythm, alliteration

T7: To recognise simple forms of poetry and their uses, for example the regularity of skipping songs, the chorus in songs.

S1: To understand that some words can be changed in particular ways and others cannot, for example changing verb endings, pluralisation and that these are important clues for identifying word classes. (*Grammar for Writing* Unit 30)

What you need

- Photocopiable pages 151, 153 and 154.

Shared text-level work

- Display an enlarged copy of the poem 'If Stan was a man'. Discuss the structure of the poem, the rhyming sequence, that it has five stanzas, and that each verse has a rhyming couplet.
- Display an enlarged copy of *Skipping and clapping rhymes* (photocopiable page 154). Ask the children to clap the rhythm of the rhymes as you say them.

Shared sentence-level work

- Using 'Endings 2' on photocopiable page 151 discuss the example word on it (*love*) and discuss the uses the word can have by creating sentences with the class for each category.
- Now collect some more words that have the same root but can be used in each category. If you are not sure or it doesn't work – mark them 'not sure' [?] or 'doesn't work' [x].

Guided and independent work

- Ask the children to work out their own clapping sequence to either or both of the clapping games used in the *Shared text-level work.*
- Ask the children to look closely at the poem 'If Stan was a man'. Work with them to identify the structure of each stanza. Ask: *How does each stanza always begin? How is each stanza structured in terms of rhyming sequence?*
- Help them to identify that after the repeated lines *If Stan / Was a man* the following line rhymes with the last line, and the middle lines rhyme with each other. (AABCCB)
- Now ask the class to use what they have learned about the verse structure to add another stanza to the poem.
- Ask the children to use 'Endings 2,' and collect more words that have the same root, but can be put into different categories.

Differentiation

Less able

- Ask this group to work out their own clapping sequence to either or both of the clapping games used in the *Shared text-level work* and learn the words so that they can perform it to the class.

More able

- Using either the clapping games or the skipping rhyme from the *Shared text-level work* as models, ask the children to write their own skipping or clapping rhyme.

Plenary

- Ask the children to share their skipping or clapping rhymes with the class.
- Discuss these as a class looking at the use of words, rhyme and rhythm.
- Ask the children to read out their additional stanzas for 'If Stan was a man'. Discuss whether they have got the correct structure.
- Ask the children to give their personal views on which of these new verses they particularly like and why.

What type of words?

Objectives

NLS

T4: To understand the following terms and identify them in poems: verse, chorus, couplet, stanza, rhyme, rhythm, alliteration.
T14: To write poems, experimenting with different styles and structures, discuss if and why different forms are more suitable than others.
T6: To describe how a poet does or does not use rhyme, for example every alternate line, rhyming couplets, no rhyme, other patterns of rhyme.
S1: To understand that some words can be changed in particular ways and others cannot, for example changing verb endings, pluralisation and that these are important clues for identifying word classes. (*Grammar for Writing* Unit 30)
W4: To practise new spellings regularly by *Look > Say > Cover > Write > Check* strategy.

What you need

- Photocopiable pages 151, 155, 156.

Differentiation

Less able

- Using 'Endings 2', help the children find words that have the same root but can be used in different categories. Can they use these words correctly in sentences?

More able

- Give these children copies of the poem 'Love at First Sight!'. Ask them to create a poem of their own using the exact same number of words and the same line structure and rhyming pattern.

Shared text-level work

- Look at the three different poems together – 'I am Cat', 'Bobdog' and 'Love at First Sight!'. Discuss each poem, looking at structure, use of rhyming patterns, use of figurative language – alliteration and so on.

Shared sentence-level work

- Using photocopiable page 151 'Endings 2', ask the children who worked on this task in Hour 2 to suggest some of the words they found.
- Emphasise that you can put words into more than one category. Ask the children to suggest sentences for the words that work and to write them on the board.

Guided and independent work

- In this guided session, give the children copies of the three poems. Ask them to write a short review about these poems saying what they like or do not like about them. They must base their answers on the structure and the use of language.
- Ask the children to look at the three poems and to comment on the rhyming patterns used in each poem.
- Using photocopiable page 151 'Endings 2', ask the children to find words that do not fit into other categories. For example 'happy', cannot be a verb or a noun. Can they make nonsense sentences using the word incorrectly?
- Give the children a copy of the three poems and ask them to write down any words that they are unfamiliar with. In pairs, they can test each other's spelling, by using the *Look > Say > Cover > Write > Check* strategy.
- Using one of the three poems, can the children write a similar poem about a cat or dog that is based on the same structure and rhyming patterns as their chosen poem?
- Ask the children to work in pairs and write a brief summary of one of the poems about cats and dogs used in this unit. They must concentrate on what they liked or did not like about the structure, rhyming patterns and use of language in the chosen poem. They both then listen to their partner read their summary and identify the main points raised.

Plenary

- Ask children to come and write on the board words that didn't fit into categories on 'Endings 2' (page 151). Discuss the categories that the children have used these words in.
- Ask some children to read aloud their reviews of the three poems. Concentrate on discussing the use of language and how the poems are structured.
- Ask children who have been writing similar poems to share their work with the class.

Favourite poets

Objectives

NLS

T9: To read further stories or poems by a favourite writer, making comparisons and identifying familiar features of the writer's work.
T10: To describe and review own reading habits and to widen reading experience.
S1: To understand that some words can be changed in particular ways and others cannot, for example changing verb endings, pluralisation and that these are important clues for identifying word classes. (*Grammar for Writing* Unit 30)

S&L

46 Group discussion and interaction: to identify the main points of each speaker, compare their arguments and how they are presented.

What you need

- Photocopiable pages 151 and 157.

Differentiation

Less able

- Using words that can be used variously to mean different things in a sentence, ask the children to make up more sentences like the ones modelled in the *Shared sentence-level work*.

More able

- Using words with the same root, for example *cook*, can the children create sentences using this word alliteratively in different categories? For example:
The cook cooked cold, crumbling cucumber con carne on the cooker.

Shared text-level work

- Choose three of your favourite poems and share them with the class.
- Try to choose poems that have very different structures, for example:
  One that rhymes
  One that has no rhyming sequence
  One that has a verse and chorus structure (maybe a song lyric).
- Discuss what you like about them, concentrating on style, structure, and the use of language.

Shared sentence-level work

- Display an enlarged copy of 'Endings 2' (photocopiable page 151).
- Ask the children who worked on it in Hour 3 to tell you words they found that did not fit into categories.
- Then, with the class, make up some nonsense sentences using these words and ask the children to identify their use, For example, verb, adjective, noun and so on.
- Use a word that does fit most of the categories, to make a sentence with as many uses of that word in it as possible. For example: *The end word we chose for the ending, ended the end of the book with the words 'The End'.*

Guided and independent work

- Ask the children to write about their own reading habits, using photocopiable page 157 ' My reading habits'.
- Invite the children to choose two poems by a favourite poet. How would you know they were by the same writer? Challenge them to spot the similarities or differences in both pieces of work.
- Ask the children to research the life of their chosen poet using the library and the internet. Can they draw a simple timeline of the poet's life including some of the dates of his or her work?
- Using words out of category, make-up some nonsense sentences, for example, *Tomorrow I will be poeting all day*. Write by each word, which category it is being used in.

Plenary

- Invite the children who have been choosing two poems by a favourite poet to share their findings with the class. Make sure that you include the following in your class discussion: *The similarities, if any, in each poem; the differences between the poems.*
- Then ask the children to talk about their favourite poet and tell the class which clues they found in the writing that helped them recognise this person's work. These may include *subject matter, style, use of language* and *structure.*
- Compare some of the timelines. Are any of the poets about the same age? Are any of the poets no longer alive?
- Ask the children to share some of their nonsense sentences and see if the rest of the class can tell which categories they have put the words into.

Pull a face

Objectives

NLS

T15: To produce polished poetry through revision, for example deleting words, adding words, changing words, reorganising words and lines, experimenting with figurative language.

What you need

- Photocopiable page 158 (enlarged copy).

Shared text-level work

- Display the poem 'Face' (photocopiable page 158) and read it aloud to the class.
- Discuss the poem's structure and the use of figurative and descriptive language.
- Go round the class and ask the children to make a face to the person next to them. Can the person next to them tell what kind of a face is being pulled? Draw the faces on the board, for example, *happy, angry, bewildered, thoughtful* and so on.
- Refer back to the poem and ask the children if they can create phrases beginning with *like a* and *as a* to describe the words for facial expression that they have collected. They can use the opening two lines in the poem as a model.
- Can they create rhyming couplets with their phrases?

Shared sentence-level work

- Collect some examples of nonsense sentences from Hour 4 that the children created by knowingly putting inappropriate word endings on words that do not fit into that category.
- Now talk about how you could use this technique to create a nonsense poem. Decide on the structure (for example, a four-line stanza, limerick) and the rhyming sequence employed (if any) and with the children's help, create a short nonsense poem.

Guided and independent work

- Using the 'Face' poem as a model, can the children replace some phrases, to make their own poem?
- In this guided session, ask the children to see if they can interpret the poem using actions/movement, while another child reads it out.
- Ask the children to write a paragraph about the poem they have liked best in this unit. They should base their writing on the style, rhyming pattern and use of figurative language of the poem they choose.

Plenary

- Ask the children who have been interpreting the poem 'Face' to come out and show the actions they have devised to accompany the poet's words.
- Talk about any similarities and differences between the movement sequences.
- Ask the children who have been writing poems that are based on 'Face' or 'Hands' (see *Differentiation*) to share their work with the class.
- Discuss the use of language within the new poems.

Differentiation

Less able

- Help the children to take digital pictures (or draw) each other showing two contrasting expressions. (For example, happy, sad.) Ask them to write two phrases to describe each face, for example:

  Face, sometimes........ like a....... .

  Face, sometimes.........as a....... .

More able

- Using the 'Face' poem structure and rhyming sequences, ask these children to write a similar poem entitled 'Hands'.

It's a dog's life

They call me Spot
But I've not got
A single one upon my coat.
As you can see
The joke's on me!
It really gets my goat!

Chorus
It's a dog's life being me.
It's a dog's life you must agree.
It's such a bore fetching sticks,
Shake a paw! Do some tricks!
It makes me sick!
Yes, it's a dog's life.

I bark and growl,
I snarl and howl,
I always try to do my best.
To earn my keep
I never sleep!
A watchdog never rests.

Chorus
It's a dog's life being me.
It's a dog's life you must agree.
It's such a bore fetching sticks,
Shake a paw! Do some tricks!
It makes me sick!
Yes, it's a dog's life.

But this old pooch — *slang word for dog*
Would rather mooch — *wander aimlessly*
Around the streets by day and night.
Before you guess
I must confess
My bark's worse than my bite

Chorus
It's a dog's life being me.
It's a dog's life you must agree.
It's such a bore fetching sticks,
Shake a paw! Do some tricks!
It makes me sick!
Yes, it's a dog's life.

Campbell Perry

Ready Neddy?

There once was a racehorse named Neddy
But for racing he wasn't quite ready.
I'm sorry to say
He ran the wrong way
'Cos he didn't know his tail from his 'heady!'

Campbell Perry

SCHOLASTIC

Endings

Use this page to model the way in which a word can change its classification or category by adding a different ending.

Endings 1

Certain endings are typical of certain word categories:

- verbs often end in 'ed' or 'ing'
- adjectives usually add 'er' and 'est' to make comparatives
- 's' is usually added to make plurals.

Let's see if we can choose some words and put them into one of the categories below, then see what happens if we change or add an ending.

Endings 2

Make words in each of the categories by adding an ending. If it does not work by using the rule for adverbs, put a cross at the end [x]. If you are not sure, then put a question mark (?).

NOUN	VERB 'ed'/'ing'	ADJECTIVE	ADVERB 'ly'
Example:			
love	loved / loving	lovely	lovingly

Limerick maker

- Write a limerick!

Think about words to end lines **one**, **two** and **five** first. Make yourself a list! It's no good choosing a word to end line one if you can't think of words to rhyme with it for the ends of lines two and five.

Now make a list of different words that rhyme well together for lines **three** and **four**. Limericks are laid out as below and often begin with:-

There was a/an ______________ from ______________.
(young man/old lady/old man/young girl) (place name)

Who ______________ (rhyme with line one)

S/he/it ______________ (five syllables)

____
(five syllables and rhyme with line three)

____
(ten syllables and rhyme with lines one and two)

- Work in pairs to write a limerick. One person writes lines one, two and five and the other person writes lines three and four. You can also write a limerick in a group of five. This is what you do:

1. Agree the words that rhyme with each other to end lines one, two and five.
2. Agree the two words that rhyme with each other to end lines three and four.
3. Agree how it will start, for example, 'There was a...'
4. Cut a piece of paper into five strips and put the number of your line and your end word on the paper.
5. Now you all write your line without letting anyone else know what you have written.
6. When everyone has finished put the limerick together! It should give you a good laugh!

- Complete a limerick!

I couldn't think of some of the endings so I have left them blank. Can you help?

Sammy sweet-tooth

Sammy Sweet-Tooth had a ______________ that was ______________

Chocolate was all he would ever eat!

But I'm sorry to ______________

One ______________, summer's ______________.

Sammy ______________ away in the ______________ .

SCHOLASTIC

If Stan was a man

If Stan
Was a man
And not a family pet,
Do you think he'd prefer that?
Being a man, not a cat.
But! Could he ever forget?

If Stan
Was a man
He'd drive a Mercedes-Benz.
Purr smoothly into town
Eye the birds up and down,
Toot the horn at all his friends.

double meaning – birds is a slang word for girls, but also a cat's favourite prey

If Stan
Was a man
He'd live in a mansion house.
Drink milk by the bucketful,
Keep fish in his swimming pool!
And for a pet? Why! He'd have a mouse!

If Stan
Was a man
He'd play an electric guitar.
Be a cool cat who swings,
Caterwaul when he sings,
And become a rock and roll star!

a slang word for someone who enjoys a good time

a loud miaowing noise made by cats

If Stan
Was a man
He'd drive a Mercedes-Benz.
But he's not! He's a cat!
So that really is that!
And that's how this poem ends!

Campbell Perry

Skipping and clapping rhymes

Clapping Rhymes

Lotte was a lot of fun
A lot of fun was Lotte!
She caught a soldier by the leg
And smacked him on the botty!
B.O.T.T.Y
Cross my heart and hope to die
If I should ever tell a lie!

Tommy was a mate to me
A mate to me was Tommy.
Kissed his sweetheart on the lips
And never told his mummy!
M.U.M.M.Y
Cross my heart and hope to die
If I should ever tell a lie!

word play 'Lotte' and 'lot of' (lotta)

alliteration

common abbreviation of the word bottom

abcbbdd rhyme

Campbell Perry

Skipping Rhyme

Usher, gusher, beetle crusher.
Skip to Poland or to Russia.
Catch a king or catch a crook,
Be a duchess or a cook.
Spring, summer, autumn, winter,
Blushing bride or lonely spinster.
Summer, autumn, winter, spring
What will the future bring?

internal rhyme

alliteration

rhyming couplets

Campbell Perry

SCHOLASTIC

Bobdog

Most dogs love to eat *rhyming couplets*
Munchy biscuits, tins of meat,
Juicy bones to crack and crunch,
Your dad's socks, the Sunday lunch!
But not Bobdog. *repeated refrain*
Oh no!
He's an odd dog
Is our Bobdog.
He likes:
Eating plaster off the wall,
Chewing the paper in the hall.
Curry, teabags, frozen rolls,
Wire wool, flowerpots, plastic bowls!
He's an odd dog
Is our Bobdog.
Is he a bit like your dog?

Most dogs like to chase *rhyming couplets*
Next door's cat all over the place.
Sniff other dogs' bottoms, bark and growl. *repeated refrain*
Chase their tails, whine and howl.
But not Bobdog.
Oh no!
He's an odd dog
Is our Bobdog.
He likes:
Chinese food and watching the telly,
Dozing, dreaming, scratching his belly. *alliteration*
Eating chocolates sent though the post,
A cup of tea, a slice of toast!
He's an odd dog
Is our Bobdog.
Is he a bit like your dog?

Campbell Perry

Love at First Sight!

Tabby cat

Sat

Licking fur;

Saw

Cat

Next door,

Began to purr.

Hearing that

Cat

Siren –song!

Poor

Cat

Next door

Said, " I'm off! So long!"

Campbell Perry

I am Cat

I am cat. — *self assurance*
Wild or tame,
Domestic or Divine;
Am I the same?
Hunter, pet, talisman, sign. — *a lucky charm*
I am poise. I am grace.
The unfathomable face. — *too deep to measure*
Favourite of Pharaoh;
Honoured in life, death and myth.
The beckoning cat, Maneki Neko — *Maneki Neko is a lucky cat from Japanese folk tales*
Of Japanese legend, a story to bequeath.
Good fortune on those who believe.

I am cat.
I beguile — *charm and fascinate*
In silky movements,
But without a smile.
Devotion? Or mere pretence?
I am omen. I am lucky charm; — *a warning sign*
Bringing good fortune, foretelling harm.
I am what you see.
The cat who sits on your lap at night
And purrs affectionately.
The stealthy stalker, who with spit and bite
Hunts the darkness, eternally.
I am cat.

Campbell Perry

My reading habits

■ Here is a chart to help you put down some thoughts about you, the books you like, and your reading habits.

My favourite time and place to read	
What makes a book/story/poem good to read?	
What do I like best? Fiction/Non-fiction	
My favourite book/story/poem	

Face

Face!

Sometimes bright like a bouncy beach ball. *alliteration*

Face!

Sometimes blank as a concrete wall.

Actively reflecting

What is truly real?

Or passively deflecting *opposite of line 5*

The way I really feel

Face to face?

Two faced? Or interface? *two faced – metaphor for someone who says or pretend one thing but means something else*

interface – computer term for making a connection

North face, *used to describe sides of a mountain*

South face,

About face, *instruction to face the opposite way*

In your face! *metaphor for someone who won't leave you alone*

Campbell Perry

Issues and dilemmas 1

This unit is all about choices. The children will have opportunities to encounter characters in stories with choices to make and identify the key issues they encounter. This unit has close links with *Grammar for Writing* Unit 31. Children will explore the identification of word classifications and how the addition of different endings can give the word a new classification, or how it may make a classification that does not work.

Hour	Shared text-level work	Shared sentence-/ word-level work	Guided work	Independent work	Plenary
1 Dilemmas	Identifying issues and dilemmas in a story.	Identifying classification of words depending on their endings.	Identifying issues and dilemmas within paragraphs of a story.	Highlighting words in a text so that they can identify their classification.	Discussing the identified dilemmas in a story and why the characters make them.
2 Drummingly!	Creating freeze-frames to show dilemmas and putting a short script to them.	Discussing word classes and the endings which identify them.	Summarising dilemmas in a paragraph into two or three short sentences.	Looking for word classifications that do not work when the correct ending is applied.	Creating freeze-frames to accompany headings and paragraph summaries.
3 The point of paragraphs	Creating a summary of key issues within each paragraph of a text. Discussing the reason for paragraphs and chapters.	Looking at dilemmas of applied word endings to the same root word. Why don't they work?	Creating paragraph headings for a text extract and summaries with notes.	Changing word endings in a poem to make them 'nonsense'.	Discussing 'nonsense' words created in poems by adding word endings.
4 Punctuation cards	Model the way you would respond to issues and dilemmas within a text.	Identifying and responding to punctuation uses in a story extract.	Identifying and collecting punctuation marks from the text and knowing what they do.	Working out alternative choices that confront characters in stories and developing consequences.	Discussion of the choices and consequences the children have created for a character.
5 What are the consequences?	Investigating choices and consequences for a character by building alternative sequences of consequences for them.	Modelling an opening paragraph to demonstrate the use of punctuation and how the reader should respond to it.	Working with three given consequences. Writing a paragraph for each and using punctuation to enhance clarity.	As before, working with three given consequences. Writing a paragraph for each and using punctuation to enhance clarity.	Sharing and discussion of paragraphs written. The choices and consequences the writers have created.

Key assessment opportunities

- Can the children identify key issues and dilemmas confronting characters in stories?
- Are they able to create issues and dilemmas for characters, giving them alternative choices and writing paragraphs that develop the consequences of their actions?
- Can the children identify the classification of words by their endings and change that word classification by adding another ending?

Dilemmas

Objectives

NLS
T1: To identify social, moral or cultural issues in stories, for example the dilemmas faced by characters, or the moral.
S1: To understand that some words can be changed in particular ways and others cannot, for example changing verb endings, adding comparative endings.
W4: To practise new spellings regularly by *Look>Say>Cover>Write>Check* strategy.

S&L
44 Speaking: to tell stories using voice effectively, for example, identifying the ways presentational features contribute to message and impact.

What you need

- Photocopiable pages 165 and 166 (enlarged).

Differentiation

Less able
- See if they can identify the main dilemma in paragraphs one, two and three of the story. Using freeze-frames and captions, can they create two freeze-frames per paragraph to show dilemma and solution?

More able
- Ask this group to create a script for paragraphs one, two and three, dealing with: Amul and his mother's discussion about drumming and going to market; Amul's mother at the market; Amul's drumsticks and his meeting with the old woman.

Shared text-level work

- Tell the children that you are going to read them the story *Amul and the drum*. It has dilemmas for characters, who have to make decisions about what to do.
- Ask them to listen to the story and identify dilemmas as you read. Make sure that you use your voice effectively for the narrative and to distinguish each character.
- Ask the children if they can remember any of the dilemmas. Write these on the board. Then display an enlarged copy of the story and read it again, highlighting the dilemmas.

Shared sentence-level work

- Display an enlarged photocopy of the grid 'Endings' (photocopiable page 166).
- Tell the children that certain endings are typical of certain word classes: *ed* and *ing* and many verbs *er* and *est*. Demonstrate how to make adjectives into comparatives. Explain that singular names often add *s* to make a plural.
- Use the example of drum. Ask what class of word it is. Can they put other endings on it to make different word classes, for example, *drum* (*noun*), to *drum* (*verb*), *drummer, drumming*?
- Now try this with other words from the story, for example, light, sorrow and hungry.

Guided and independent work

- Cut the story into paragraphs. Give each pair one of these and ask them to read and identify: *the dilemma; the choices facing the characters; the solution.*
- Ask the children to take a paragraph each. They should note down the sequence of events in it and then rehearse telling their part in their own words. They must use a narrative voice and create other voices for characters.
- Give the children a copy of the grid 'Endings' from photocopiable page 166 and ask them to collect words from the story and see if they can: *identify the class of the word; put this word into a different class by adding an appropriate ending.*
- Using the story, ask the children to highlight words that are new or unfamiliar to them. They should write these words down (up to ten) and practise their spellings using *Look>Say>Cover>Write>Check.*

Plenary

- Ask the children to report their findings on the cut-up paragraphs and to discuss the choices facing the characters and the decisions they make.
- Ask the children who have been working as storytellers to tell the story in their own words. Have they used different voices to create maximum impact?

Drummingly!

Objectives

NLS

T24: To summarise in writing the key ideas from for example a paragraph or chapter.

T20: To summarise a section or paragraph by identifying the most important elements and rewording them in a limited number of words.

S1: To understand that some words can be changed in particular ways and others cannot.

What you need

- Enlarged photocopiable pages 165 and 166
- class copies of page 165.

Shared text-level work

- Display the enlarged copy of *Amul and the drum* (photocopiable page 165). Ask children who created freeze-frames and a script for the first three paragraphs in Hour 1 to come out and make their freeze-frames as you read the paragraphs. Then repeat the freeze-frames and ask the children who wrote the scripts for the paragraphs to read them as the first group create the frames.
- Ask the class if they can identify the most important elements from each paragraph. Write these on the board. Discuss with the class the phrases and words that give the key meanings of each paragraph. Now see if they can help you write these sentences, summing up the opening paragraphs.

Shared sentence-level work

- Display the enlarged photocopy of 'Endings' from Hour 1 (photocopiable page 166). Ask the children to give you some examples of classifying words. Draw these with the class.
- Now look at words the children have found which do not work, for example, drummingly (adverb). Put this into a nonsense sentence, with ideas from the class. Now ask for suggestions for sentences with words that work and words that do not.

Guided and independent work

- Give the children a copy of the story *Amul and the drum* and work with them to summarise each dilemma of the remaining paragraphs into two or three key sentences.
- Ask the children to work in pairs to create two or three freeze-frames to summarise in pictures the key points in the remaining paragraphs.
- Give the children the 'Endings' grid (page 166) and ask them to find words from the story or think of examples of their own which do not work when re-classified. For example, *corner* (*noun* and *verb*) *cornerly* (*adverb*); *She came round the bend cornerly!* Ask them to make a nonsense sentence with some of these words they suggest.

Plenary

- Ask some children who have worked on the first two tasks in the last section to come out to the front of the class. Some children should hold up the chapter headings and the children who have worked on making freeze-frames do their actions to the appropriate heading; the children who summarised each paragraph dilemma should read out their work by each freeze-frame and heading.
- Discuss the selection of phrases and words that they have used and what they have had to leave out.

Differentiation

Less able

- Ask children to create paragraph headings for the remaining paragraphs, writing these as chapter headings for the next episodes of the story.

More able

- Give children this example of how to make fun sentences, with as many different endings as possible for one word. The sentence must make sense and be grammatical. *Imagine having an imaginary imagination, which imagined, in its imaginary imagination, having an imaginary imagination.*

The point of paragraphs

Objectives

NLS

T3: To understand how paragraphs or chapters are used to collect, order and build up ideas.

S1: To understand that some words can be changed in particular ways and others cannot.

What you need

- Photocopiable pages 165 and 166.

Shared text-level work

- Using the extract *Amul and the drum* (photocopiable page 165), ask the children to help you sketch out a summary of each paragraph. Discuss with the children the ideas that paragraphs indicate: *a change in what is happening or who is taking over the development of the story*. Explain that paragraphs order ideas and that chapters usually denote changes of scene or emphasis. *Amul and the drum* is based on a traditional folk tale, and as is often the case with these types of stories, they are economical in terms of dialogue and concentrate on events and action. In this story, each paragraph is like a new chapter. Write down the paragraph headings with summaries from the children.

Shared sentence-level work

- Display an enlarged copy of the first poem on photocopiable page 166. Ask the children what the problem is with some of the word endings. Can they help you sort it out and make it make sense? Explain to them that there may be more than one correct answer. The second poem on this page is the one that the writer intended. Don't show this to the children until they have discussed the first poem.

Guided and independent work

- Ask the children to select a poem they have written themselves or a published poem and change some word endings to make deliberate mistakes. They should then swap their altered poems with a partner and see if they can find alternative word endings that make the poems make sense.
- Encourage the children to select a short piece of prose from a class library book; or alternatively you can pre-select extracts for them. Work with the children to help them create paragraph headings for the first three to four paragraphs and make notes to summarise what is happening.
- Using the same word, but with different endings, see how many fun sentences the children can make. Remind them that the sentences have to make sense, for example, *The actors acted actorly when acting out the act.*

Plenary

- Ask the children who have been making fun sentences using the same word root to share their work with the class. Vote on the funniest phrases!
- Ask some of the children to read out their poems with deliberate mistakes in them. The class should attempt to identify the deliberate mistakes, and suggest replacement words in each poem. Can they classify them correctly and make the poem make sense?
- Then ask the child who re-wrote the poem, correcting the deliberate mistakes, to read his or her version out. Have they used the same word classification as suggested by the class?

Differentiation

Less able

- Work with these children using the grid 'Endings' to look for words in a piece of writing and to help them classify original words correctly and then add endings to re-classify them under their headings.

More able

- Ask these children to use some different word endings to generate a word-play poem. They may end up with tongue-twisters too. For example:
The builder builds to build a building.
The skater skates to skate.
The painter paints to paint a painting.
But in waiting, the waiter just waits to wait.

Punctuation cards

Objectives

NLS

T10: To describe and review own reading habits and to widen reading experience.

S2: To identify the common punctuation marks including commas, semi-colons, dashes, hyphens, speech marks, and to respond to these when reading.

What you need

- Photocopiable page 165
- a pre-selected variety of extracts from stories containing dilemmas or issues for characters
- sets of cards with individual punctuation marks: *full stop, comma, semi-colon, speech marks, exclamation mark, question mark.* (Some sets should be the punctuation marks themselves and some written as words.)

Differentiation

Less able

- Work with these children on an extract from their own reading. Can they identify punctuation marks? Help them to read so that they respond to the punctuation marks.

More able

- Ask the children to play a game with this story opening:

Mary lost her mum's purse on the way to the shop. Mary didn't know what to do. If she told her mum that she had lost it, she knew her mum would be very angry. Should she tell her that someone has stolen it? Or should she tell the truth?

They should take one of Mary's choices each, create three or four consequences that relate to that choice and compare scenarios.

Shared text-level work

- Choose an extract from a class or school library book (possibly a story you have read to the class before) and model a response to them of how you react to what is being said and done within this extract of text: *identify the issues, react as a reader, describe the choices facing the characters and look at how the characters deal with these choices.*
- Review the extract with the children and discuss their reactions to the text.

Shared sentence-level work

- Tell the children that you are going to read the first paragraph of *Amul and the drum* (photocopiable page 165) to them. Give each child a set of punctuation cards (see *What you need*).
- Now read the paragraph to the class. Ask the children to hold up a card that displays the correct punctuation mark, as you read. Discuss their choices with them as you progress through the passage.
- Discuss with the class the reasons why punctuation marks help the reader understand what has been written, how it is linked together and how phrases are spoken.

Guided and independent work

- Ask the children to read either an extract of their own choice or one you have pre-selected for them. The extract needs to contain an issue and dilemma. The children should work in pairs. Each pair should: *identify the key issue and dilemma and which characters are involved; discuss the choices confronting the characters and see if they can think of one alternative each to the situation.*
- Give the children a copy of *Amul and the drum.* Work with them to help collect punctuation marks from the text. They should take a paragraph each.
- Put a set of punctuation cards on the table - each card with a different punctuation mark in words: *full stop - comma -semi-colon - question mark - exclamation mark - speech marks.* They should write the word from the text that comes before the punctuation mark, followed by the mark, on each card. Ask them what each of these punctuation marks do within the text.

Plenary

- Ask the children who have been working in pairs on an extract to report back to the class on the issues and dilemmas they have identified.
- Have a class discussion about the particular characters facing dilemmas and encourage suggestions as to how the issues could be resolved. Compare different solutions.
- Ask the 'More able' group to share their issues and dilemmas about Mary. Ask the class to discuss the choices Mary made in each scenario and the moral dilemma involved in the series of actions that the character takes.

What are the consequences?

Objectives

NLS

T11: To explore the main issues of a story by writing a story about a dilemma and the issues it raises for a character.

S2: To identify the common punctuation marks including commas, semi-colons, dashes, hyphens, speech marks, and to respond to these when reading.

S&L

47 Drama: to create roles showing how behaviour can be interpreted from different viewpoints, for example presenting characters as they might see themselves then as others see them.

What you need

- One or two examples of texts that show consequences of actions.

Shared text-level work

- Explain that you are going to look at consequences of actions. Write a brief scenario on the board (or use the following):

> Darren is late for school again! He'll get a detention if he doesn't get there on time, and his mum has threatened to ground him for a fortnight if he gets detention! There's a shortcut through the park. If he takes it, he knows he won't be late. But his mum has told him never to go through the park on his own. What should Darren do?

- Look at *Darren's dilemma* with the class. Ask them to create a scenario for both his choices with you. Write this on the board, discussing the issues and dilemmas. Create three consequences for each choice.

Shared sentence-level work

- Remind the children that punctuation marks enhance and clarify a text. Using ideas from the class, model an opening paragraph for *Darren's dilemma*. Discuss the use of punctuation as you write and ask the children to justify their choices. Read the paragraph back to them, responding to the punctuation selected. Does anything need altering?

Guided and independent work

- Divide the class into three groups. Give the first set of children the three consequences if Darren is late for school. Ask them, in pairs or threes, to write a paragraph for each consequence. Remind them about using punctuation.
- Give the second group the three consequences if Darren goes through the park. Ask them, in pairs or threes, to write a paragraph for each. Remind them about using punctuation.
- Ask the third group to create a scenario and act-out *Darren's dilemma*.

> **Scene:** Darren at the entrance to the park talking about choices and his situation. Add two more characters: Mum, and Darren's teacher in the playground, about to ring the bell, noticing Darren's absence! Ask these characters to stand away from Darren. Children devise a spoken script: Darren talks about his choices and as he talks, they create 'pauses' where Mum and the teacher give opinions about Darren and the consequences of his actions.

Differentiation

Less able

- Ask the children to make freeze-frames for each of the alternative consequences of Darren's dilemma, and add some thoughts for Darren to speak out loud for each of these.

More able

- Ask this group to continue work on Mary's story: write paragraphs for each of the consequences, and add additional consequences in order to finish the story. Remind them to use punctuation.

Plenary

- Ask the children to share their stories for both *Darren's dilemma* and *Mary's story*. Discuss the choices made and how the children have used vocabulary, phrases and punctuation to enhance their stories.
- As *Darren's dilemma* is read, the children who have created freeze-frames can make their frames and add Darren's spoken thoughts. The group who have dramatised *Darren's dilemma* can perform their scene to the class.

Amul and the drum

Amul had always wanted a drum. Even when he was very small he would tap, tap, tap with his hands on anything he could find. His mother would say, "Amul! Amul! No more! You are turning my head into a drum!" Amul's mum was poor. She cleaned houses for the rich people in the town, but they only paid her with grain. Every week she would go to the market to sell the grain she had left, so that she could buy food and clothes for Amul. Every time she went to the market, she would say to Amul, "is there anything I can bring you?" Amul would always reply, "yes please Mother. A drum!" His mother would smile and say, "I'll do my best." Amul knew she would, but he knew that she would never have enough money to buy a drum.

One day, when Amul's mother went to the market, she found that the price of grain had risen. She sold all the grain she had and when she had bought all she needed for Amul and herself, she found that she had money left over. There was enough to buy a drum! She set off quickly to the market stall which sold musical instruments. But, as she came round the corner of the street she came across a woman with four children. They were all crying. The woman begged her for help. She had no money to feed her children. Amul's mother felt her heart fill with sorrow. She gave them the money she had saved for Amul's drum. The woman thanked her, "I have nothing I can give you in return," she said, "except these drum sticks. They belonged to my husband, but both he and the drum are long gone; please take them." Amul's mother took them thinking to herself, "if I couldn't get him a drum, I have got him the next best thing."

Amul was thrilled! He took his drumsticks everywhere, tap, tap, tapping on anything he found. As he was playing one day, he heard an old woman crying. She had no sticks to light her fire and bake bread for a wedding party. Amul loved his drumsticks but was sad to see her so upset. He gave her his drumsticks to light the fire. She was so pleased that she gave him a piece of wedding bread. Amul hated giving away his drumsticks, but did not let it show. He thanked her and went on his way.

As Amul walked slowly home by the river, he heard angry voices. It was a man and his wife, arguing about which one of them should go home and fetch food for their hungry baby, who was wailing like a cat with a thorn in its paw.

"You go! You forgot the food!" shouted the husband. "I have to wash these clothes for the wedding party this evening." Amul could not bear to hear the baby cry so gave the child the piece of bread the old woman had given him. The man and his wife were so pleased that they gave Amul a fine coat, good enough for a wedding party.

Evening came. Amul strutted over the bridge that led to his house, wearing his fine new coat. Then he saw a man shivering with cold. He had no shirt on his back. "Robbers took everything except my horse! They even took the shirt from my back," cried the man. "I was going to a wedding, but now I have nothing to wear, so I cannot go." Amul was sad to see him so upset. He gave the man his fine new coat saying, "Take this! I have no need of a fine coat. I have no wedding to go to." The man was so pleased that he gave Amul his horse. "I have no need of my horse," he said. "The wedding is but a short distance from here and you have shown me great kindness."

Amul climbed up on the horse and started for home. Then he ran into a wedding party with musicians, sitting under a tree with faces as long as a lizard's tongue. "Why so glum?" asked Amul. The bridegroom said, "the man who promised a horse for me has not arrived. I cannot walk to my wedding." Amul hated seeing them look so sad. "Here! Take my horse!" The bridegroom was overcome with joy. "You have saved my marriage! What can I give you in return?" Amul did not hesitate. "A drum! A drum! Please!" Amul rushed home to tell his Mother the whole story, beating his drum as he went. She heard him coming long before he came in through the door, and smiled.

A traditional story re-told by Campbell Perry

Endings

Noun	Verb	Adjective	Adverb	Not Sure	Doesn't Work
Drum	To Drum		Drummingly	Drummingly	
Drum(mer)	Drumming				
	Drummed	Drummingest			Drummingest

■ Choose words from different classifications e.g. drum (noun) and see if you can put appropriate endings on the word to re-classify it. If you are not sure or it doesn't work, put it in the correct column on the right.

(Version 1)
Waves, waves
Poundingly the shore.
Licks the sand
With salts watered tongue
Waves, waves
Hungrily for more
You greed eats
'Til the land is no more
And you won.

Campbell Perry

The version below is the one that the writer intended.

(Version 2)
Waves, waves,
Pounding the shore,
Licking the sand,
With salt water tongues,
Waves, waves,
Hungry for more,
You greedily eat,
'Til the land is no more,
And you've won.

Campbell Perry

Issues and dilemmas 2

In this unit the children will examine a story in detail; looking at the changes that confront characters and the decisions they make. The children will reflect on alternative endings and assess the impact that these alternatives could have on the reader. The sentence-level work, linked to Unit 31 *Grammar for Writing*, examines aspects of word order and the impact of punctuation within a text on the reader.

Hour	Shared text-level work	Shared sentence-/ word-level work	Guided work	Independent work	Plenary
1 Questions for the dreamweaver	Identifying issues and courses of action within a story.	Creating questions using the five *wh* words and creating answering statements.	Writing five questions to a character with answering statements.	Writing a letter from a character giving the reason for the decisions they made.	Discussing characters' actions and speculating about alternatives.
2 The most important words	Summarising key elements from a given text in one or two sentences.	Creating negative questions accompanied by a negative statement.	Summarising key elements in one or two sentences.	Creating negative statements and creating negative or positive statements.	Discussion of choice about which key elements to include in a text.
3 Use no punctuation!	Modelling a summary of text. Using the summary to create the 'bare bones' of a story.	Responding to the use of punctuation. Creating punctuation in a piece of text.	Using punctuation. Making decisions about what punctuation to use to clarify texts for the reader.	Creating stories through use of new summaries in words and pictures.	Discussion of key elements selected in summaries when re-creating a story.
4 Who is your favourite writer?	Modelling a response to text using some guidelines.	As in *Shared text work*.	All groups will be working on a summary of a favourite story, book or poem and writing their own critiques.	All groups will be working on a summary of a favourite story, book or poem and writing their own critiques.	Discuss the children's responses. Have they followed the guidelines?
5 Alternative endings	Modelling an alternative ending for stories through class discussions.	Reminding children about the power of punctuation in that text.	Creating an alternative ending for a well known story and discussing the impact on the reader.	Creating an alternative ending for *The Dreamweaver's child* and discussing the impact on the reader.	Discuss the impact on the children through the changing of story endings.

Key assessment opportunities

- Can the children identify issues and dilemmas in stories and how characters' decisions affect the development of the story?
- Can the children develop ideas for generating alternative changes within a story and provide an alternative ending?
- Are they able to evaluate the impact of their alternative endings on the reader?
- Are they more confident in the use of punctuation and the new word order in their stories to provoke the reader's response to speech, action, atmosphere and events?

Questions for the Dreamweaver

Objectives

NLS

T8: To write critically about an issue or dilemma raised in a story, explaining the problem, alternative courses of action and evaluating the writer's solution.

S3: To understand how the grammar of a sentence alters when the sentence type is altered, when, for example, a statement is made into a question, a question becomes an order, a positive statement is made negative.

What You need

- Photocopiable pages 173 and 174 (enlarged).

Shared text-level work

- Display an enlarged version of photocopiable pages 173 and 174, *The Dreamweaver's child*. Tell the children that you want them to listen for the issues and dilemmas raised in the story as you read it.
- When you have finished reading the story, ask the children to tell you the issues raised and note them on the board. Remember to use different 'voices' as you tell the story to sustain interest and impact.

Shared sentence-level work

- Listing the five *wh* words (*who, where, what, when, why*), ask the children to help you create some questions about the Dreamweaver, for example: *Where does the Dreamweaver live? What does the Dreamweaver do?*
- Now ask the children to create answering statements, for example, *The Dreamweaver lives in a mountain*. Explain that they can use these questions and answers to map out the characters and their actions in the story by creating a question and an answering statement.

Guided and independent work

- Work with the children and ask them to look at the story *The Dreamweaver's child* in pairs. Ask them to write five questions, using the five *wh* words, about Arlo and the dilemmas he faces in the story. They should then answer their questions in this way: *a statement saying the course of action Arlo takes*; *a statement with an alternative course of action,* which they have devised.
- Ask the children to imagine a different end to the story:
  That Arlo dreams about his mother, but does not tell his father in his dream he sees his mother and she tells him to come and search for her. He must have three things to help him on his journey; Arlo takes his harp, the Dreamweaver's ring and the prism. Before he goes, he writes his father a letter justifying his course of action.
- Ask the children to write Arlo's letter and leave it in the dome of dreams for his father.

Differentiation

Less able

- Ask the children to use the model questions from the *Shared sentence-level work* about the dreamweaver's actions. Ask them to think of some alternative decisions for him.

More able

- Ask these children to write a script for a conversation between Arlo and The Destinies as he goes across the web to rescue his mother. They must use the text to inform their decisions and the choices they make as they write the script. In this instance, they must interpret the writer's ending.

Plenary

- Discuss the alternative courses of action that the children have been writing in their statements. Which endings do they prefer?
- Ask the children to come up and act out their scripts for the ending. The children can discuss and speculate upon alternative endings.
- Ask the children who have written letters to Arlo's father to share their work with the class. Discuss how the content relates to the story *before* Arlo leaves.
- Discuss how Arlo justifies his actions to his father. Have the children used persuasive language techniques and explained their dilemma and subsequent course of action successfully?

The most important words

Objectives

NLS

T20: To summarise a sentence or paragraph by identifying the most important elements and rewording them in a limited number of words.

S3: To understand how the grammar of a sentence alters when the sentence type is altered, when, for example a statement is made into a question, a question becomes an order, a positive statement is made negative.

What you need

- Photocopiable pages 173 and 174 (enlarged).

Shared text-level work

- Display an enlarged photocopy of the story *The Dreamweaver's child.* Read the opening paragraph to the class, responding to the punctuation given. Ask the children to identify the key ideas in this paragraph and using these ideas, summarise the key elements in the sentences. This will mean that they will have to 're-word' in order to encapsulate the key elements.
- Ask for volunteers to come to the front and create a freeze-frame to picture the key elements and see if the class can agree on a caption sentence to accompany each freeze-frame.

Shared sentence-level work

- Remind the class that in Hour 1 they created positive questions with positive answering statements. Today they are going to look at making negative questions with accompanying negative statements. Explain that there may be another way of provoking speculation about decisions or choices characters make or could make. For example:

  Q: Why didn't the old man stay and help Arlo?

  A: The old man didn't want to be trapped in The Land of Lost Dreams forever.
- See if the children can create some other negative questions and answering negative statements. They can also use a combination of negative and positive, for example: *positive question - negative statement; negative question - positive statement.*

Guided and independent work

- Work with the children on two selected paragraphs from the story. Ask them to summarise the key elements in a maximum of three sentences per paragraph.
- Ask the children to work in pairs to create a series of questions and answers using the five *wh* words. Each one of the pairs can choose to write each other positive or negative questions. They can use the text of the story to help them develop questions about any of the characters. They exchange questions with their partners and they then must make a statement of the other type, that is, if the question is positive the answer should be negative.
- Ask the children to create freeze frames and caption sentences for another paragraph in the story.

Plenary

- Ask the children to read their summaries of each paragraph they have looked at. Discuss the key elements they have highlighted. Have they missed any?
- Invite some children to discuss the questions and answers they worked on and exchanged in pairs. Have they answered negative questions with positive statements and vice versa?
- Ask the children who have been creating freeze frames to come out and perform their work for the class.

Differentiation

Less able

- Work with these children to choose a paragraph from the story and read it. Can they agree on the key elements in it? Can they summarise each sentence, verbally, so that you can scribe it for them?

More able

- Ask this group to write a brief summary of the story - two or three sentences per paragraph, dividing the paragraph between them to make the task easier.

Objectives

NLS

T24: To summarise in writing the key ideas from, for example a paragraph or a chapter.

S2: To identify the common punctuation marks and to respond to them appropriately when reading.

S&L

44 Speaking: To tell stories using voice effectively, for example identifying the ways presentational features contribute to message and impact.

What you need

- Photocopiable pages 173 and 174
- examples of children's summaries from the last session.

Differentiation

Less able

- Work with these children using the previous session's work on summarising key elements into one or two sentences. Ask them to create freeze-frames and a short dialogue/narrative, using these sentences.

More able

- Using the previous session's paragraph summaries as cues, ask the children to create freeze-frames for each paragraph and a short narrative of dialogue for each section. They can split the task, concentrating on different sections.

Use no punctuation!

Shared text-level work

- Tell the children that you are going to recap summarising key elements from a story from previous hours.
- Model your own summary of the story *The Dreamweaver's child* using work from the class. Try to create key sentences or phrases that encapsulate the actions and decisions made to create a 'bare bones' account of the story.

Shared sentence-level work

- Remind the children that punctuation is very important. Explain that used effectively it guides the readers' response in the way the writer intends. As an example, read a paragraph from *The Dreamweaver's child* without using the punctuation. Discuss what problems this then creates for the reader in terms of interpretation, clarity and atmosphere.
- Now read the paragraph again observing the punctuation and discuss the difference between the two readings.

Guided and independent work

- Either ask the children to select a short paragraph from a reading book or pre-select a short extract for them (about four or five sentences long). Ask them to write this out with no punctuation. Working in pairs, they should exchange their punctuation-free texts. Ask them to put what they think is the correct punctuation into their partner's text. They can then look at their text and compare it with the original. Note particularly the use of commas, full stops and speech marks.
- Using their brief summaries of paragraphs from *The Dreamweaver's child*, ask them to write their own version of the paragraph, padding out the bare bones text with their own descriptive words and speech, adding pictures if they wish.
- Tell the children that they are going to be storytellers. They select a paragraph each from *The Dreamweaver's child* (combine some shorter ones if necessary) and write down the key points. These will act as prompts. Using these in the correct sequence, ask them to rehearse telling their paragraph in their own words. Remind them that using voices to sustain impact is important. They should aim for a 'narrative' voice and then create voices for the characters.

Plenary

- Ask the children who have been creating freeze-frames for a section of the story to show their work to the rest of the class. The other children can discuss their choices of key elements and see if these match their own decisions.
- Ask the children who have been working as storytellers to tell the story in their own words. You could combine the freeze frames with the story telling. Remind the children to remember to use different voices for each character in the story and to keep their own voice when being the narrator.

Who is your favourite writer?

Objectives

NLS

T9: To read further stories or poems by a favourite writer, making comparisons and identifying features of the writer's work.

S2: To identify the common punctuation marks and to respond to them appropriately when reading.

S&L

47 Drama: To create roles showing how behaviour can be interpreted from different viewpoints, for example presenting characters as they might see themselves, then as others see them.

What you need

- Children need to bring a couple of favourite books or poems
- a selection of extracts from class fiction books, or poems
- teacher's choice of text or texts
- photocopiable pages 173 and 174.

Differentiation

Less able

- Choose one or two stories/poems that this group like. Ask: *why do you like this writer, what do you like about the story?* Gather answers in groups of statements for each question. Scribe these or ask them to write them down.

More able

- Ask this group in addition to the main task, to choose a book they like and one they do not. They should write a summary for each, justifying their decisions using the guidelines that the teacher modelled.

Shared text and sentence-level work

- This session combines the shared text- and sentence-level work.
- The teacher should select a favourite story or a poem and display it for the class to read.
- Talk to the children about the writer and your reason for enjoying his or her work. Stress the following:

> - The use of language.
> - The way in which the writer creates choices for characters.
> - The style of writing.
> - The way punctuation is used to enhance the text.

Ask the children for their comments on your choice. Discuss with them the kinds of story they like.

Guided and independent work

- Ask all the children to write a brief summary of a book or poem by a favourite writer. Some will need guidance. They should concentrate on summarising their paragraph or paragraphs under the key headings you used in the shared work. Why does the book/poem appeal to them? Encourage them to include to the criteria listed above.
- Ask the children to use *The Dreamweaver's child*, and ask them to improvise this scene:

  Arlo in the land of Lost Dreams. He is standing on the web. He can see his mother sleeping in the centre. The Destiny of Fate appears.

- Ask them to think about the following: *How does Arlo see himself in this situation? What does The Destiny of Fate say and how does he view Arlo?*
- Ask the children to imagine that the following characters are thinking about Arlo as he enters the web in The Land of Lost Dreams:
  - The Dreamweaver
  - The old lady
  - The old man
  - Arlo's mother.
- Set the following scene: Arlo on the web, his mother asleep in the centre, and the Dreamweaver away to one side. The old man and the old lady stand around the edge of the web.
- The children should develop a script that reveals what each of these characters are saying about Arlo as he tries to save his mother (who can be talking in her sleep). Help the children by suggesting that the thoughts of the old lady and old man (spoken aloud) should be based on their meetings with Arlo in the story.

Plenary

- Ask the children to read their summaries and discuss their reasons for discussing that particular story/poem.
- Ask the children who have been creating the scene from *The Dreamweaver's child* to perform their piece. Have they successfully developed a scene showing the characters' differing viewpoints?

Alternative endings

Objectives

NLS

T12: To write an alternative ending for a known story and discuss how this would change the reader's view of the characters and events of the original story.

S2: To identify the common punctuation marks and to respond to them appropriately when reading.

What you need

- Photocopiable pages 173 and 174
- a story that is known to the class.

Shared text-level work

- Using *The Dreamweaver's child*, ask the children to suggest some alternative choices for Arlo from the point where he leaves to find his mother. For example, *when he meets The Old Lady - he gives her his dreamweaver's ring*. It could be that he decides not to - examine the choices from that point onwards and ask the children to make alternative choices. Agree these choices with the children.
- Ask them to suggest alternative endings based on these choices. Write these ideas on the board.

Shared sentence-level work

- Looking at some examples of how punctuation informs the text and the reader, tell the children that they are going to write an alternative ending to *The Dreamweaver's child* or an alternative story the children know or have written a summary about.
- Emphasise that the children should be very careful over their choice of punctuation. Remind them that varying sentence length will help sustain the reader's interest and develop atmosphere in the story.
- They should also be particularly careful with their use of commas when using adjectives or adjectival phrases.

Guided and independent work

- Ask the children to decide a series of choices to end the story of *The Dreamweaver's child* in a different way. They can either use suggestions from the shared work or use their own ideas. Ask them to write an alternative ending to the story, paying particular attention to the punctuation. They can work in pairs, firstly agreeing on the alternative ending - then one writes the ending and the other writes a brief outcome of how this ending will affect the reader's view of the characters and events.
- Work with the children on a story that is known to them. It could be a well-known folk or fairy-tale (for example, *Goldilocks*, *Cinderella* and so on). Ask them to work in pairs and to agree on an alternative ending. Again, one child will write the ending paragraph and the other will summarise the effect this will have on the reader's view of the characters and events.

Differentiation

Less able

- Ask the children to create a scenario for a different ending for *The Dreamweaver's child* or an alternative story. They should create freeze-frames of their endings and generate spoken narrative to accompany these.

More able

- Using either text, ask the group to agree an alternative sequence of events and ending. Divide the *sequences of actions, setting, choices* and *resolution* between the group. Ask them to write a brief paragraph for each component.

Plenary

- Ask the children to read some of their endings for both *The Dreamweaver's child* and the other story, and their partners to read out how they think this will affect the reader's point of view. Ask the class to comment on the choices and effect of these decisions.
- Remind the children to follow their punctuation as they read so that they create atmosphere and sustain listener interest.

The Dreamweaver's child – part 1

At the top of a very high mountain there lived a Dreamweaver and his son Arlo. All day long, Arlo would play his harp to the four winds as his father made a blanket of dreams for the world below. The Dreamweaver would say to Arlo, "remember son, when you see a star twinkling in the heavens, it means that someone somewhere is dreaming." Arlo had never had a dream.

Then, one night, something strange happened. As Arlo slept he saw a face; a face like his own but older. He heard a voice; a voice like his, but softer. He ran to tell his father that he had, for the first time ever, had a dream. His father looked troubled. "A dream is like a mirror to the heart," he said. "The face you saw, the voice you heard, was your mother." Arlo was astonished. "My mother? I never knew I had a mother!" The Dreamweaver told him the story.

"I am one of the four Destinies who rule the mortal world. But, I went against their laws and married a mortal woman. The Destinies were angry and would have taken you away. Your mother begged them to take her instead. They did, and you are here and she is in The Land of Lost Dreams, where she will stay for eternity."

"I will find her," said Arlo. The Dreamweaver said, "you are a brave boy. I cannot go for I must make dreams forever. Take these Arlo, they will help you. I made this dreamcatcher's ring. It is your mother's wedding ring. The prism was made on the day you were born. You must take a third thing with you; something of your own." "I will take my harp," said Arlo. The Dreamweaver took Arlo to the dome of dreams and told him to stand under the dancing lights from the prisms there. Suddenly, Arlo felt himself grow light.

Suddenly, he found himself in a deserted village at the bottom of the mountain. A path, wound like a fallen ribbon through the village and up into the mountains beyond. Arlo started to walk. As he came to the last house in the village, he heard the sound of sobbing. It was an old lady. She was weaving a beautiful quilt. It had villages, mountain paths and forests on it. "Why are you crying?" asked Arlo. The old lady told him that she had seen the quilt in her dreams, but every time she tried to finish it, she awoke before she saw the missing piece. Arlo took the Dreamweaver's ring from his finger. "Take this," he said. "Catch your dream! Hold it fast! Finish your quilt!" The old lady thanked him and smiled. Arlo turned and walked on up the path higher and higher into the mountains.

Story re-told by Campbell Perry

The Dreamweaver's child – part 2

The path narrowed. The rock face towered over him from all sides. There seemed no way over and no way round. The he saw a door in the rock face. But it was a door with no handle. Arlo knocked loudly on it. "Who's there?" shouted a gruff voice. "I am Arlo the Dreamweaver's son, please let me in. I have come for my mother." With that, the door creaked open. Arlo entered.

At the entrance to a large cave, sat an old man making shoes. He did not look up as Arlo entered. "Welcome to The Land of Lost Dreams. If you wish to stay, then you must change places with me. There is no way out. You must wait here until someone else knocks on the door and that could be a very long time." "I will stay," said Arlo. The old man pointed to the roof of the cave. "Give me your shoes and I will hang them with all the others. They too came to The Land of Lost Dreams." Arlo swallowed hard but tried to hide his fear. The old man smiled. "Here, I have made you a fine pair of shoes. Give me yours and take these." With these words, the old man walked out of the door. It closed silently behind him and Arlo saw that there was no handle. No escape. He put on the shoes.

Inside the cave Arlo could see a giant web. He stepped onto it. Beneath it, was just emptiness. He was afraid. He clutched his father's prism tight and heard his voice. "Remember Arlo, a dream is like a mirror to the heart." He looked up and saw, at the centre of the web, the sleeping form of his mother. It was exactly the same shape as the missing piece in the old lady's quilt. A voice, as cold as crystal cut through the silence. "I am The Destiny of Fate and your fate is in my hands." The figure glowed like a flame. Arlo said, "I have come for my mother. I am not afraid." The web shook. Arlo trembled. Taking his harp from his shoulder, he began to play. "Even the destiny of fate is not more powerful that the forces of nature," cried Arlo. He brought the ice cold winds from the East and the North. They swept round the cavern, wrapping their frosty fingers around the flickering flame of Fate. The flame went out. Arlo played again. The warm winds from the South and West sighed into the cave, raised the sleeping form of his mother on a bed of cloud. Arlo climbed up beside her.

The cloud swept out of the cave into a clear, starlit sky. The cloud caressed them through the night air until they came to the Dreamweaver's home. Arlo's mother awoke. The Dreamweaver enfolded Arlo and his mother in his arms. She looked up at them both and smiled. A star twinkled in the sky. "I think I've just had a wonderful dream," she said. The Dreamweaver smiled back. " No," he said, "your dream begins here."

Story re-told by Campbell Perry

Narrative reading and writing

These ten lesson plans are designed to form part of the three-week unit, Narrative Reading and Writing. There is scope to ensure that, before looking at tales from other cultures, children are familiar with stories within their own culture. This unit also looks at sentence word-order, punctuation, use of paragraphs and chapters, and the distinction between *it's* (it is) and *its* (possessive). Other grammatical areas include conjunctions, adverbs and adverbial phrases to link sentences, covering aspects of *Grammar for Writing* Unit 32.

Hour	Shared text-level work	Shared sentence-/ word-level work	Guided work	Independent work	Plenary
1 Once upon a time	Reading traditional stories, focussing on recurring themes.	Examining words and phrases with common roots.	Discussing recurring themes in fairy tales, and categorising thematically.	Retelling *Cinderella* in own words.	Listening to stories; evaluating thematic sets and overlaps.
2 Happy ever after	Identifying moral issues and characters' relationships; observing the effect of changing story ending.	Creating rhetorical questions, altering sentences' word order.	Discussing feelings about characters' actions.	Using paragraphs effectively in creating story endings.	Listening to children's writing and discussing its impact on views about the original characters.
3 The twelve stones	Looking at a story from another culture, its characters, setting and theme.	Distinguishing between *its* and *it's;* revising months of the year; looking at names' diminutives.	Writing an episode to form part of the shared text, in the same style and voice.	Researching names, their meanings and diminutives, especially from other cultures.	Evaluating the effectiveness of content and style of children's writing.
4 Working magic	Reading a story from another culture.	Looking at various uses and functions of paragraphs and punctuation, including *it's.*	Writing an alternative ending to a story from another culture.	Cloze procedure worksheet to practise when to use *its* and *it's.*	Reviewing function of paragraphs.
5 Rich rewards	Identifying dilemmas in stories from other cultures, comparing themes, moral values and our responses.	Using visual skills to learn spellings and build up words with similar patterns; punctuation of direct speech.	Using direct speech within narrative with correct punctuation.	Practise spellings, especially *knight; sword; wander(ed); wonder(ed).*	Reinforcing how changing sentences, can change reader's response.

UNIT 4

Hour	Shared text-level work	Shared sentence-/ word-level work	Guided work	Independent work	Plenary
6 Exploring issues	Exploring dilemmas and implicit issues in stories.	Investigating grammar related to sentences' word-order.	Writing a background story to shared narrative, to become the first chapter of a longer story.	Developing individual spelling strategies.	Discuss plausibility of proposed plots and if and how they affect reader-sympathy.
7 Weaving threads	Examining characters and how their actions reveal their values and relationships, influencing the reader's reaction.	Looking at sentences, paragraphs and chapters and their form and purpose.	Developing a plan for a longer story and brief chapter contents.	Writing about main issues and dilemmas in a story.	Listening to plans and discussing plausibility of plots.
8 Another chapter	Looking at use of direct speech; its ratio to narrative and usefulness.	Examining punctuation and its use as an aid to reading for understanding and effectiveness.	Writing a new ending to a known story, seeing how it changes reader's response.	Identifying and learning mis-spellings in own writing; using joined writing with even letters and spacing.	Hearing children read their work aloud, checking on punctuation.
9 Making connections	Considering how chapters and paragraphs demarcate stages of a story.	Identifying adverbial phrases including those that indicate a passage of time and conjunctions.	Continuing stories begun in earlier sessions.	Using conjunctions and adverbial phrases in writing.	Reinforcing how word order and grammar is changed when conjunctions are added.
10 Stems and branches	Locating and classifying words with a common stem and abstract nouns.	Creating verbs, adverbs and adjectives from nouns, recognising common stem.	Writing a synopsis of each chapter for longer story plan.	Adding suffixes to stem words.	Reinforcing classifications of words and common suffixes.

Key assessment opportunities

- Are children demarcating their narrative with appropriate use of paragraphs and chapters?
- Do they use *its* and *it's* with increased confidence and accuracy, identifying and correcting errors in their own writing?
- Are children able to identify themes and issues common to several stories, and justify their opinions by direct reference to the text?
- Do they recognise and react to punctuation correctly when reading aloud?

Once upon a time

Objectives

NLS
T2: To read stories from a variety of cultures, focusing on recurring themes and language.
S3: To understand how the grammar of a sentence alters when the sentence type is altered.
W14: To build up speed and ensure consistency in size and proportions of letters and spacing between letters and words.

S&L
44 Speaking: To tell stories using voice effectively for enhanced impact.

What you need

- A selection of familiar fairy tales from Britain and/or across Europe such as *Cinderella, The Golden Goose, Goldilocks, Red Riding Hood, Beauty and the Beast, Puss in Boots, Hansel & Gretel, Jack and the Beanstalk, The Frog Prince, Snow White*
- photocopiable page 187 (top half, enlarged).

Shared text-level work

- Write *Once upon a time, They lived happily ever after, Long ago in a far off land, And they never wanted for anything again,* on separate cards. Invite the children to read these aloud. Ask in what sort of writing they would expect such phrases. Which are openings; which endings?
- Demonstrate saying *Once upon a time* in a monotonous and then in an expressive voice. Read extracts to demonstrate how the language of folk tales encourages reading aloud. Emphasise refrains, such as, *Mirror Mirror on the wall...* .
- Ask the children to name their favourite fairy tale, recall the basic storyline and determine its theme, such as *rags to riches, kindness rewarded, greed punished, love conquering obstacles, impossible tasks achieved, wishes fulfilled, tricks and treachery punished, true beauty being within.*
- Explain that many familiar fairy tales originate outside the UK, such as Grimm's (German), Andersen's (Danish), Aesop's (Greek), while others are traditional English, Welsh, Scottish and Irish.
- Point out how characters' names and settings can indicate foreign origins, such as *Hansel* and *Gretel,* large forests, deep snow and hard winters.

Shared word-level work

- Discuss traditional folk story-language. Examine specific words and phrases and modern variations. Compare *Once/Once upon a time; ever after/afterwards/evermore/for ever; wanted/in want/wanting* in the sense of *lacked/went without.*

Guided and independent work

- Ask children, in groups, to discuss recurring themes in familiar fairy tales, listing titles in sets that may overlap. Headings might include: *Wishes, Tasks, Greed, Love, Kindness, Poverty.*
- Use the top half of the worksheet on photocopiable page 187 to help the children retell *Cinderella* in their own words. Encourage them to use traditional language and neat handwriting for increased legibility.
- Ask the children to read their stories aloud to each other, with appropriate expression and changes of voice, pace and emphasis.

Plenary

- Hear some of the children's retellings. Identify use of language appropriate to the genre. Praise effective use of voice.
- Look at the thematic lists and discuss if stories are allotted appropriately. Do some overlap across several issues?

Differentiation

Less able
- Provide opening sentences for each stage of story retelling for the children to sequence, copy and expand; tape oral retellings.

More able
- Ask the children to organise their text into distinct paragraphs.

Happy ever after

Objectives

NLS

T2: To read stories from other cultures, discussing place and cultural context, identifying relationships.
T1: To identify social, moral and cultural issues in stories, e.g. the dilemmas faced by characters.
T12: To write an alternative ending for a known story, and discuss how this would change the reader's perceptions.
T3: To understand how paragraphs or chapters are used to collect, order and build up ideas.
S3: To understand how word-order affects meaning, grammar and punctuation.

What you need

- Photocopiable page 187 (bottom half)
- a version of the story *The Frog Prince*.

Shared text-level work

- Distribute copies of *The Frog Prince* in pictures (photocopiable page 187). Ask the children to follow the pictures as you read. Encourage them to tell you when the story moves beyond the illustrations, and to listen extra carefully to the closing paragraphs.
- Explain that each picture represents one episode or one paragraph in a retelling of the story. Write key words for each picture, based on class discussion and recall. For example, *1. Princess with favourite toy – golden ball. Ball sinks.*
- Discuss the ending of the story. Explain that there are no pictures because the children are to create a different ending.

Shared sentence-level work

- Read aloud the notes relating to the first picture/paragraph. Discuss what needs to be added to turn these sentences into prose. Experiment with word order: *The princess was happy. Was the princess happy?* Expand on how rhetorical questions can be used in stories.
- Discuss the characters' actions and their feelings towards one another. Ask: *Was the frog reasonable to demand a reward? Was the king right to make the princess honour her promise? Why did the princess change her feelings towards the frog? Were the children satisfied with the ending and why?*

Guided and independent work

- Organise the children into pairs or groups to discuss alternative endings to the story. Remind them how they felt about the characters and the original outcome of their actions. Ask them to create an ending that will make the reader feel differently towards characters. For example, *what if the king refused to let the frog into the palace?* Compare the children's feelings towards the king.
- Ask individuals to draw pictures in the two empty *Frog Prince* story boxes and write one paragraph per picture to change the story ending.
- Challenge the children to write sentences to sum up the characters' feelings at the beginning and end. From these, create rhetorical questions, using appropriate changes of word-order and punctuation.
- Provide some jumbled sentences from an original version of *The Frog Prince* for the children to re-order and sequence.

Plenary

- Listen to new story endings and discuss their impact on the children's views of the original story and the characters' relationships. Discuss if any new version of the story needs a fresh title to reflect the new ending.

Differentiation

Less able

- Suggest possible endings for the children to develop, such as the princess turning into a frog.

More able

- Challenge the children to rewrite the opening of the story in their own words.

The twelve stones

Objectives

NLS

T2: To read stories from other cultures, looking at place, time, customs, relationships and recurring themes.
W12: To research names and understand how diminutives are formed.
W1: To revise months of the year (High Frequency List 1).

What you need

- Photocopiable pages 188 and 189 (enlarged)
- books of forenames and their meanings; internet access.

Shared text-level work

- Write the story's first two sentences, leaving a space for the character's name. Ask if it sounds familiar. Although *Cinderella* had two step-sisters, the characters' relationships are similar in this story.
- Insert the name, *Zelenka*.
- Display the title and first page of the story to read together.

Shared word- and sentence-level work

- Discuss the name *Cinderella* and the literal meaning of *Cinders* – a diminutive often applied to the character. Explain that in *The twelve stones* the central character's name varies in different retellings. *Zelenka*, the name used here, means *little innocent one*.
- Identify rhetorical questions. Write *Pick violets when it's snowing.* How does it read without the question mark? Write *Her stepmother did thank her!* Ask children to read it and the original sentence expressively. Highlight verb positions.
- Write the story title and the stone-men's names. Work out the names of all 12 men, applying the three adjectives, *early/mid/late*, across the four seasons. Elicit that these might equate to months, comparing the gardening calendar. Allocate alternative month names to each stone.
- Discuss how universal the month names are? How does place affect their *characters*? Does January bring snow in, say, Africa? Across Europe? How does our climatic experience affect our understanding?
- Based on the story so far, ask how the next paragraph might begin. Explore seasonal sequence and respective harvests.

Guided and independent work

- Write the following sentence for the children to copy: *The following day, Zelenka's stepmother decided she'd like some apples.* Ask the children to complete the next episode in similar style and tone to the first two.
- Ask the children to read each other's paragraphs and compare language style and story development.
- Encourage the children to list common forenames and their diminutives. Start them off with traditional examples such as *John/Jack; William/Billy; Sarah/Sally.* Encourage them to explore names from different languages and cultures, their meanings and diminutives, using websites and books. Observe how the diminutive of *Hans* is *Hansel* – it is longer as with *John/Johnny.*
- List the names of the months in order, checking spellings.

Plenary

- Read aloud the first part of photocopiable page 189 up to *No, she did not!* Ask the children how their paragraphs compared. How did the content vary? The wording? Listen to examples.
- Discuss if and why versions were similar. Ask the children to explain why they wrote as they did.

Differentiation

Less able

- Invite the children to tape-record their next episode of the story.

More able

- Suggest that the children add more atmospheric adjectives and dialogue to their story to flesh out the characters.

Working magic

Objectives

NLS
T2: To read stories from other cultures by focusing on, for example differences in place, time, customs, relationships and recurring themes.
T3: To understand how paragraphs are used to build up a story.
T12: To write an alternative ending for a known story, and discuss how this would change the reader's view of the characters and events of the original story.
S2: To identify and use the common punctuation marks.
W10: To recognise the function of the apostrophe in *it's* (*it is*).

What you need

- Photocopiable pages 188, 189 and 190.

Shared text-level work

- Distribute copies of the whole story, *The twelve stones.* Invite confident readers to re-read the first page, as others follow, and read on to the end.
- Discuss the ending with the children. Point out that different versions' endings vary. In some, each month waves the mace in turn – grass springs from the woman's head, flowers from the sister's nose, and so on, before December's snow finally sees the greedy pair off. Do they think that this ending fundamentally alters the story's outcome or characters' experience?
- Compare differences in retellings of, say, *Cinderella*. In some, the ugly sisters' feet simply do not fit the shoes; in other more graphic versions they cut their feet till they bleed, trying to make the shoes fit. Again, does this difference alter the outcome or our feelings towards it?
- Discuss what determines where new paragraphs are needed. What changes between paragraphs in terms of language – such as different adjectives to describe the fire. Ask what remains unchanged.

Shared word- and sentence-level work

- Draw attention to the small asterisks in the margins. These are aligned with sentences that contain either *its* (*possessive*) or *it's* (*contraction*). Ask the children to read these sentences aloud, observing the difference in spelling and function in the sentence.
- Highlight the use of direct speech marks. Point out how other punctuation marks sit within these. Identify rhetorical questions. Ask how we know that Zelenka isn't speaking aloud. Ask where speech marks would go if she were.

Guided and independent work

- Use the worksheet on photocopiable page 190 for children to practise using *its* and *it's* correctly. If required, the speech marks may be obscured for children to position as well.
- Ask the children to retell the story in their own words writing for a target audience of five-year-olds and under. Remind them to use paragraphs appropriately.
- Invite the children to write a new ending for the story that will alter the feelings of one or more of the characters, and the reader's feelings towards the outcome.

Differentiation

Less able
- Provide the bare bones of the story for the children to complete as a cloze procedure, by reference to the original story.

More able
- Challenge the children to investigate *it's*: *it has*, for example *It's been snowing.*

Plenary

- Review the use of *its* and *it's* with reference to the worksheet.
- Listen to opening sentences of new paragraphs in the children's own stories, reinforcing their function.

Rich rewards

Objectives

NLS

T1: To identify dilemmas in stories and how characters deal with them.
T2: To read stories from other cultures, by focusing on, for example, differences in place, time, customs, relationships and recurring themes.
S2: To recognise and use speech marks.
W6: To spell words with common letter strings but different pronunciations.

What you need

- Photocopiable page 191.

Shared text-level work

- Find the locations of story sources on the globe, including Britain, Germany, Denmark, the Czech Republic and Japan.
- Read the story from Japan (photocopiable page 191) together. Consider the appearance of a Japanese knight and his sword compared to an English medieval knight. Ask the children which English knight fought a dragon. Why did the knight in this Japanese story put his sword away? How did the monster repay his compassion?
- What made the dragon go in search of the knight? How do we know it was not simply hunger or curiosity? Ask the children to support their responses by direct reference to the story.
- Ask if the children can think of any tasks that were driven by love rather than greed in stories from their own culture.
- Consider the level of detail in the story. How much do we know of the relationship between the knight and the monster; the knight and his would-be bride; the monster and the Dragon King? Which relationship most concerns the reader?
- Examine the values held by the knight and the monster - love of home; of a woman; care and loyalty towards each other. Compare the woman's values.

Shared word- and sentence-level work

- Write the words *knight* and *sword* and locate them in the text. Identify the silent letter in each word. Help the children to recognise that these spellings can only be memorised.
- Locate the word *wandered* in the text. Compare with the often-confused *wondered* and establish their respective pronunciations and meanings. Compare spellings and pronunciation of the words *wan, wand, wander, squander; won, wonder, son, done, Monday*.
- Identify the use of direct speech in the story. What proportion of the story is direct speech compared with narrative? (The ratio is around 3:4 - or nearly half.) Consider how direct speech breaks up the narrative but can still carry the plot forward.

Guided and independent work

- Ask the children to practise the spellings identified above by (a) *copying the sentences in which they appear* and by (b) the *Look>Read>Cover>Write>Check* methods.
- Challenge the children to select sentences from the story's narrative to express in direct speech and vice versa. For example: *The knight challenged the monster; "I pity you," he whispered.*

Differentiation

Less able

- Ask the children to illustrate each stage of the story, identifying direct speech to put in characters' speech bubbles.

More able

- Ask the children to find words containing *ea* with different pronunciations, such as *tears, head, search, beautiful* and practise spellings.

Plenary

- Compare the children's sentences with the original. Ask how the changes affect the meaning and how they affect the reader's response.
- Share examples of correct speech punctuation.

Exploring issues

Objectives

NLS

T1: To identify and explore issues and dilemmas implied, rather than explicit, in a story.

T11: To explore the main issues of a story by writing a story about a dilemma and the issues it raises for the character.

S3: To investigate word-order and grammar when verbs are changed.

W3: To develop strategies to learn and practise spellings.

What you need

- Photocopiable page 191
- writing materials.

Shared text-level work

- Re-read the story. Identify characters of which we learn little. Ask which characters have no name? Does Samébito having a name indicate his level of importance?
- Explain that it is easy to discover what *is in* a story but that what is *not explicit* is open to interpretation. Ask which areas are glossed over.
- Pose questions about the background situation. *What do they think happened before this story begins? Do we know why the Dragon King of the Sea banished the monster and why, at the end, he decides to pardon him? Can we insert any clues as to why, later, he will weep rubies?*
- Ask them to consider the monster's future – *do his looks change with his fortunes? Or do we learn that we cannot judge by looks alone but by how characters behave? Does Samébito's expulsion change his nature; looks; attitude?* Reveal how, in creating a plot, we must also flesh out the characters, so that readers can identify with them or relate to their motives and feelings.

Shared word-level work

- Look at the words describing Samébito: *hideous monster. What expectations do they give the knight? How about the reader? Are these justified?*
- Identify verbs ending in *ing* and *ed*. Experiment changing these around, and altering word-order such as, *Visiting the monster every day, he fed him fresh fish.*

Guided and independent work

- Ask the children in groups to explore inexplicit threads and plan a background story developing the character and situation of Samébito. Remind the children that their plot must address unanswered questions and that it will end with Samébito's banishment from the sea.
- Suggest that, to develop the whole story, all characters would need names. Ask the children to research names with a Japanese origin. Suggest, where possible, noting the meaning of the names to suit characters.
- As the children expand the story, words will recur frequently. Ask them to identify which they will need to practise for increased writing speed and accuracy. Offer strategies such as finding small words within longer ones (*same bit o; thou sand),* and spelling by analogy (*night with a k).*
- Highlight sentences in the story for the children to rewrite, changing word order and verb endings.

Plenary

- Listen to opening chapter plans. Examine whether ideas are contextually plausible and consistent with our knowledge of the characters.
- Invite the children to spell words that they have been practising.

Differentiation

Less able

- Help the children to imagine possible scenarios for their opening chapter through discussion of undersea environments.

More able

- Ask the children to experiment with attention-grabbing opening lines.

Weaving threads

Objectives

NLS

T11: To explore the main issues of a story by writing a story about a dilemma and the issues it raises for the character.

T13: To plan own longer stories in chapters.

S3: To understand how the grammar of a sentence alters when the sentence type is altered.

What you need

- Photocopiable page 191
- writing materials.

Shared text-level work

- Following on from the previous hour, suggest to the children that other untold stories are implied in the text. Discuss another character's motivations and actions. *Does the knight's lady marry him on receipt of the jewels?* Why do they think she demanded them – *was she beholden to someone? Simply materialistic? Under a spell?*
- Pursue further story threads: *What did the knight love about her? Do the jewels satisfy her or does she make fresh demands? Does the knight rescue her from a threatening situation or discover her to be greedy and selfish?*
- Return to story-plans prepared in the previous lesson. Ask the children to consider these stories as an opening chapter of a longer story that will eventually incorporate the original text. Write chapter numbers in a column. Alongside, begin to note what each chapter should cover, such as, *Chapters 1/2: Introducing setting, Dragon King and Samébito and events that cause King's anger, Chapters 2/3: Samébito's expulsion and meeting with the knight*, and so on.
- Look at the original story and decide if this will form one or more chapters, justifying decisions by reference to plot development. How far do paragraphs help create chapters?
- Remind the children that, until they have made their full story plan, including the knight's love interest and the ending, they cannot finalise the number of chapters.

Shared sentence-level work

- Copy the first sentence of the original story. Examine why this works as an opening sentence. Look at the indefinite articles – *a knight; a monster*. Ask how these will change when the reader gets to the beginning of Chapter 2. *Will it begin with the knight or the monster, bearing in mind continuity?*
- Experiment with the sentence's construction while preserving the essential facts. Ask if they think the word *hideous* would still apply? How could this perception be made to belong to the knight rather than the reader? Would it require a separate sentence?

Guided and independent work

- Ask the children to write their opening chapter, leading on to the shared text. Encourage use of dialogue that reveals the characters' feelings and motivations. Remind the children to use speech marks.
- Ask the children to develop their whole story plan, using chapter numbers to plan and pace their story.
- Invite them to create chapter titles as *handles* to each chapter's content.

Plenary

- Listen to the children's opening chapters. Determine how far they succeed in progressing a plausible plot – do the listeners feel sympathy with the monster?

Differentiation

Less able

- Act as scribe for children. Present their sentences out of order for them to read, sequence and copy.

More able

- Ask children to add detail as they incorporate the original story.

Another chapter

Objectives

NLS

T3: To understand how paragraphs and chapters are used to collect, order and build up ideas.

T12: To note how changing aspects of a story may change the reader's view of the events and issues in the original story.

S2: To identify, use and respond to common punctuation marks.

W2, W13: To identify and learn mis-spelt words in own, joined, writing.

S&L

44 Speaking: To tell stories using voice effectively.

What you need

- Word-processed, large-font copies of good examples of children's opening chapters.

Shared text-level work

- Invite the authors of the chosen chapters to read their story of the *Dragon King and Samébito* aloud to the class, with the shared text displayed. Encourage expressive use of voice, pace, stresses and pauses.
- Look at the proportion of narrative to dialogue - does it reflect that of the original story. How, if at all, could it be improved?
- Consider their use of paragraphs. Are they arbitrary or logical in terms of story phases?

Shared sentence-level work

- Point out examples of effective use of punctuation and how this determines how we read the story. Examine how each child has used speech marks. Discuss how this helps the reader adopt changes of voice when reading aloud.
- Ask the children to read others' work aloud, demonstrating their response to punctuation. Invite comments from others as to the efficacy of its positioning.

Guided and independent work

- Ask the children to return to their own story so far, amending punctuation, checking spellings - especially watching for words that do not look the right length or shape.
- Ask them to read their stories so far, aloud to a partner, to highlight areas for improvement and to practise reading with expression.
- Add repeated mis-spellings to their spelling logs and practise them.
- Encourage the children to continue writing their stories, building chapters from their story plans, and concentrating on the closing chapter. Remind them to use joined-up handwriting throughout.
- Ask the children to decide on a title for their story that reflects the whole (new and original) narrative.
- Ask them to write some observations about the characters in the original story, compared to how they have changed or developed them in their new story. They should begin, *In my new ending of the story the reader may feel differently about...* .
- Ask the children to copy and complete this sentence, writing a paragraph about the effect on the reader of their new ending and the reasons.

Plenary

- Hear less confident children read parts of their story aloud, pointing to punctuation as required - praise effective use of voice.
- Invite the children to read in threes, one as narrator and two adopting character roles, reading direct speech.

Differentiation

Less able

- Create a brief storyboard in sketches to help the children retain sequence and continuity in their own stories.

More able

- Ask the children to write a paragraph of concise, appealing blurb for a back cover-style introduction.

Making connections

Objectives

NLS

T13: To plan own longer stories in chapters from story plans.

S3, S4: To identify adverbial phrases and connectives, varying punctuation and word order in sentences.

W13: to use joined handwriting.

What you need

- Photocopiable page 191 (enlarged).

Shared text-level work

- Share the text without annotation. Remind the children of the use and purpose of paragraphs - demarcating stages and developments in the plot.
- Compare paragraphs to the use of chapters in longer stories, used as divisions and sub-divisions of the whole text.

Shared sentence-level work

- On the displayed text, underline the following *adverbs/adverbial phrases* that link ideas, but are in two separate sentences: *Every day, In time, Soon, In the lake, At last, As he cried, Gently, Immediately.* Then underline conjunctions that join clauses within one sentence (*when, and*). Also, underline *bidding* in the last sentence, a non-connective.
- Display the annotated text, asking the children to identify time-related adverbial phrases and connectives, discussing their differing functions. One underlined word is *not* a connective; can they tell which?
- Demonstrate how the underlined words help cohesion, by re-reading the narrative but omitting them - clauses become shorter sentences and sentences that relate to previous sentences lose continuity.

Guided and independent work

- Write the following conjunctions: *because, when, but, so, as, although.* Remind children that these are used in single sentences. Ask them, using joined-up handwriting, to find one or more ways of joining the following pairs of sentences. Remind the children that they will need to add commas, remove some full stops and change some capitals. Sometimes the conjunction may start the new sentence.
  - *The knight was not rich. He felt very sad.*
  - *The knight visited the lake. He fed fresh fish to the monster.*
  - *The knight lay dying. Samébito worried where he was.*
  - *The monster wept rubies. There were not enough.*
  - *You are pardoned. You may return home.*
- Compile a class list of adverbial phrases from the shared text, adding others, such as, *However, Meanwhile, Suddenly, Later.* Include some from *The Twelve Stones: Long ago, The next morning, The following day.*
- Encourage the children to complete their longer stories, based on *The knight's ten-thousand jewels*, revising the text to incorporate connectives.
- Ask the children to plan their own new story, in chapters, choosing:

- a recurring theme (as in Hour 1 – kindness rewarded, and so on)
- a setting
- main characters – with or without disguise
- a problem or task and magical help
- a happy solution.

Differentiation

Less able

- Offer suggestions for children to develop: *a talking sheep; an enchanted gate; a princess who cannot smile.*

More able

- Ask the children to write a brief explanation of their choice of theme.

Plenary

- Examine the children's use of connectives. Suggest nonsensical examples for children to correct, such as *The knight lay dying* because *Samébito worried where he was.*

Stems and branches

Objectives

NLS

T13: To write own longer stories in chapters from story plans.

W8: To practise extending and compounding words through adding parts.

W14: To build up speed and ensure consistency of letter size and spacing in handwriting.

What you need

- Copies of photocopiable pages 188, 189 and 191.
- ruled writing paper.

Shared text- and word-level work

- Re-read the story of Samébito. Ask the children to note any words that relate to mood, emotions or appearance; intangible things such as *hideous; angry*.
- List the following words: *beauty, instance, anger, banishment, gentleness, mourning, warmth, greed, decision, freedom, care*. Establish that they are abstract nouns.
- Demonstrate how verbs, adjectives and adverbs relate to them – for example *beautify, beautiful(ly)*.
- Highlight suffixes that appear in other similar nouns *ment, ness, sion*. Explain how these endings indicate that the words are nouns. Examine how other suffixes suggest types of word, such as *ful, ly*.
- Draw attention to common stems of related words and links between meaning and spelling.
- Examine how the suffix *-ing* can be both a present participle of a verb and a noun, according to context. Write: *Samébito was mourning the loss of his home. His mourning made him cry. He was mournful. He spoke mournfully.* With the class, classify each word with the common stem and determine its function in the sentence.
- Find examples of words related to abstract nouns in the shared texts, again determining the type of word and grammatical function.

Guided and independent work

- Ask the children to write a synopsis of the main events of each chapter in their new story plan.
- Remind them to make use of adverbial phrases as they begin writing their opening chapter. Encourage them to build up speed as they write, while keeping their handwriting evenly spaced and proportioned. Challenge the children to legibly complete a number of paragraphs so that they can each read their partner's opening narrative.
- Ask the children to look at stories, including the shared texts, and to write sentences containing words related to the list of nouns.
- Challenge the children to use dictionaries to investigate other words related to the abstract nouns, such as *beau, carefree, decisive,* and comparatives, such as *warmer, warmest.* Examine how some words require *more, most, less, least* to create comparatives. Ask them to listen to hear if words sound right – *decisiv*er*?* – and to use dictionaries to check validity.

Plenary

- Hear and discuss story plans, discerning themes, traditions and sources.
- Offer examples of adjectives and adverbs and ask the children to work out the related noun, such as *joyful/joy; happily/happiness; brave/bravery*.
- Share examples of even handwriting and lengthy extent, pointing out how even letter size and spacing facilitates reading.

Differentiation

Less able

- Highlight the required words in shared texts for children to copy sentences.

More able

- Challenge the children to create a word table: *noun, verb, adjective, adverb,* including further abstract nouns.

Once upon a time/Happy ever after

Cinderella

The Frog Prince

The twelve stones – part 1

A Czech folk tale

Long ago, there lived a young girl called Zelenka. Her stepmother and sister made her work all day while they did nothing. One winter's day, just as Zelenka had lit the fire, her stepmother said,
'Violets would sweeten the room. Go and pick some!'

Pick violets when it's snowing? But her stepmother pushed Zelenka out into the biting wind and snow. She searched hopelessly until, at last, she came upon a circle of twelve stones around a blazing fire. As she approached to warm herself, the stones turned into twelve men, some young, some middle-aged, some old. The oldest, named Late-Winter, held a gold mace. *
'What brings you here, little one?'
'I need violets for my stepmother,' she shivered.

Late-Winter handed his mace to a young man, named Early-Spring, who whirled it around. Its warmth melted the snow and violets appeared. *
Zelenka picked some eagerly. She thanked the twelve men and ran home.
Did her stepmother thank Zelenka? No, she did not!

The next morning, when Zelenka finished sweeping, her stepmother said,
'Strawberries would be tasty. Go and pick some!'

Pick strawberries when it's snowing? But, fearing a beating, she stepped out into the snow. Poor Zelenka trembled with cold but, at last, she found the circle of twelve stones around a roaring fire. Again, the stones turned into twelve men, some young, some middle-aged, some old. Late-Winter spoke through his snowy white beard. *
'What brings you back, little one?'
'I need strawberries for my stepmother,' she sighed.
Late-Winter handed his mace to a middle-aged man, called Mid-Summer.
He swirled it around until strawberries grew under the melting snow.
Zelenka picked some swiftly. She thanked the twelve men and ran home.
Did her stepmother thank her? No, she did not!

Retold by Celia Warren

Narrative Unit 1 phase 1

The twelve stones – part 2

The following day, Zelenka's stepmother decided she'd like some apples.
'Go and pick some,' she said, pushing Zelenka into the blizzard.

Zelenka thought of the twelve kind men and set off to find the circle of stones and its glowing fire. As before, Late-Winter greeted her. *

'Back again, little one? What now?'

'My stepmother wants apples,' she said, through chattering teeth.

Late-Winter handed his mace to an old man called Late-Autumn. Soon the mace was a whirl of gold, its warmth melting the snow, for an apple tree to grow. *

'Shake the tree,' Mid-Winter told the girl.

Zelenka did so and caught two ripe apples. She thanked the twelve men and ran home. Did her stepmother thank her? No, she did not!

'Only TWO?' cried the greedy woman. ' Did YOU eat the rest?'

'There *were* only two,' sobbed Zelenka.

Her stepmother and sister snatched them, pushing Zelenka aside. The apples were so delicious, they wanted more. In their greed, they decided to search for themselves. The air was so bitter, not even a bird sang, but soon Zelenka's stepmother and sister saw flames light the sky. They pushed carelessly past the stones, not even noticing them turn into twelve men, some young, some middle-aged, some old.

'What brings you here in such a rush?' asked Late-Winter.

'Give us apples or get out of our way,' the rude pair demanded.

Late-Winter shook snow from his long white beard. He whirled his mace. The fire died away, the sky darkened, and an icy wind stung their greedy faces. Soon, their blood froze as cold as their hearts. Zelenka's stepmother and sister sank silently into the snow.

At home Zelenka waited and waited but her cruel stepmother and sister never returned. At last the young girl knew she was free. She would never slave for anyone again.

Retold by Celia Warren

Narrative Unit 1
Phase 1

Working magic

It's = It is, a contraction indicated by an apostrophe

Its = possessive; belonging.

For example: **It's** the fire. **Its** heat is sweltering.

It is the fire. **The fire's heat** is sweltering.

■ Write **it's** or **its** in each space so that the sentences make sense.

1. Look at the dragon. ______ limping because ______ leg is broken.
2. The troll shook ______ ugly head. "Look! ______ not dead!" they said.
3. A pot that cooks ______ own porridge? ______ magic!
4. We have an apple tree, but no apples will grow on ______ branches now that ______ winter.
5. The poor frog looked at the princess, ______ eyes big and hopeful. "You must keep your promise," said the king, "______ only right!"
6. One minute ______ a pumpkin, and the next ______ a gold coach!
7. Look at the coach and ______six horses. They were six mice just now!
8. The clock struck midnight. "______ time for me to go!" said Cinderella.
9. "______ a magic bean," said Jack. "The stalk is so high ______ top is in the sky.
10. Hansel and Gretel came upon a little house. ______ walls were made of gingerbread.

The knight's ten-thousand jewels

A traditional story from Japan

A knight was walking by the sea when a hideous monster heaved itself ashore.

'What are you?' he cried, drawing his sword.

'My name is Samébito,' the monster said, his head drooping. 'The Dragon King of the Sea is angry with me. He's banished me from my home. Kill me if you will. I shall die anyway on land.'

The knight was moved with pity.

'Come with me,' he said, and led the monster to a lake, graced with lilies. Every day the knight visited the monster, feeding him fresh fish.

In time, the knight met a beautiful woman and instantly fell in love.

'If you wish to marry me,' she said, 'you must bring me ten-thousand jewels.'

The knight was not rich. He wandered home sadly and took to his bed, eating nothing. Soon he became ill.

In the lake, Samébito grew lonely. At last he went in search of his friend. When he found him ill in bed, Samébito was moved to tears.

'You could die,' he sobbed.

As he cried his tears became sparkling rubies. The knight fell from his bed, gathering the jewels. Soon he had hundreds – but not enough!

'Weep again!' he said. 'I need ten-thousand jewels.'

'I cannot weep at will,' declared the monster. 'When I thought you lay dying tears came easily, but now you are well.'

The knight sighed and explained his anguish. Samébito listened with pity.

'Perhaps if I returned to gaze at my old home, I should grow mournful and weep again.'

Gently, the knight led him to the seashore. Immediately, Samébito burst into tears. The knight soon collected ten-thousand jewels. Just then a voice roared from the sea.

'Samébito! You are pardoned. You may return home.'

The monster splashed gladly into the sea, bidding farewell to the happy knight who set off to claim his bride.

Retold by Celia Warren

Narrative Unit 1 – Phase 1

UNIT 5

Note-taking and discussion

The emphasis in this unit is on note-taking to support discussion and promote reasoned arguments to support a viewpoint, even though it may not be one that the children support. The unit is closely linked to principles contained in Unit 32 of *Grammar for Writing*, which is designed to help the children use appropriate connectives in their prose.

Hour	Shared text-level work	Shared sentence-/ word-level work	Guided work	Independent work	Plenary
1 For and against	Identifying key elements in an article. Sequencing them logically.	Using 'for' and 'against' boxes to help clarify the point of view you support, using connectives.	Collecting key points from a letter.	Using 'for' and 'against' boxes to help them make a decision statement.	Sharing of decision statements and key elements to support an argument.
2 Summarising an argument	Summarising key arguments 'for' and 'against' in a text.	Working with a 'skeleton letter' to select suitable connectives to fill out the prose.	Summarise arguments 'for' and 'against' a point of view in an article.	Summarise an argument in their own words.	Children report back on their summaries. Discuss the points made. Discuss connectives.
3 Points of view	Using key elements as a 'prompt' for developing a logical argument.	Looking for and listing connectives in a text.	Isolating key elements in an argument from a text. Summarising main points.	Sequencing points of view. Using connectives to link them together.	Presentation of arguments in a logical sequence. 'Oral' presentation of points of view.
4 School rules	Modelling the beginning of an article in support of an argument.	Using boxes 'for' and 'against' or creating a decision statement.	Summarising arguments using the three sentence structure and connectives.	Generating a writing frame to use in supporting an argument.	Sharing of summarising and writing frames.
5 Making a case	As above.	As above.	Writing a letter in support of an argument.	Writing a letter opposing an argument.	Sharing of work 'for' and 'against'. Discuss the persuasiveness of the argument.

Key assessment opportunities

- Can the children identify the key elements of an argument within a text?
- Can they summarise the key points of the argument in their own words?
- Are the children able to write prose for or against certain viewpoints?
- Can they use connectives in an appropriate way to clarify and enhance their prose?

For and against

Objectives

NLS

T16: To read, compare and evaluate examples of arguments and discussions.
T17: How arguments are presented, for example ordering points to link them together so that one follows from another.
S4: The use of connectives, for example adverbs, adverbial phrases, conjunctions, to structure an argument.

What you need

- Photocopiable pages 198 and 199.

Shared text-level work

- Display photocopiable page 198 (enlarged) of arguments for and against fox hunting. Read the article 'for' to the children. Now ask them to identify key elements in the argument. Write these down in the correct order. Emphasise that the sequence of elements is important when writing a letter or article supporting a point of view. These extracts are the presentation of an argument.

Shared sentence-level work

- Using the foxhunting extracts, read the counter case – the argument against. Tell the children that you are going to model the way to put your point over as strongly as possible.
- Create three boxes on the whiteboard, one for arguments 'for', one for arguments 'against' and one for your 'decision'.
- Ask the children to help you put the arguments for and against in each of the boxes. Tell them that if you want to make the argument strongly then put two statements together, for example, *Foxes often kill new-born lambs. This costs farmers a great deal of money in lost income.*
- Now you tell them you need a connective to add the alternative point of view, so you add, *On the other hand many new-born lambs are too weak to survive and foxes do farmers a favour by taking them away!*
- Ask the children to suggest one or two more elements that can be connected and then argued against by using an opposing statement starting with a connective.

Differentiation

Less able

- Photocopy and give the children an extract with good use of connectives. Tell them they are going to be 'connective detectives'. Ask them to highlight each connective. Write or type these in large-print and display on the wall for children to make use of.

More able

- Give this group an extract from a library book, written in short simple sentences, which do not use many connectives. Ask them to re-write this passage, linking the simple sentences together with connectives. Restrict them to a maximum of three connectives before they use a full stop.

Guided and independent work

- Using the article about fox hunting, ask the children to continue the work begun in the shared sessions. They should:

- Pick out the key statements 'for' and 'against'
- Make a decision on which argument they support
- Summarise the argument for and against (one sentence each)
- Put their decision in a third sentence beginning it with a suitable connective.

- Work with these children and using the letter about 'litter' (photocopiable page 199), ask them to collect the key points from the letter and sequence the key elements in the correct order.

Plenary

- Ask the children to report back with their three sentence statements on fox hunting.
- Ask the children to state the arguments about the key elements of the letter on litter in the correct order. Ask the rest of the class to make counter points as each point of the letter is raised.

Summarising an argument

Objectives

NLS

T20: To summarise a sentence or paragraph by identifying the most important elements and rewording them in a limited number of words.

T21: To assemble and sequence points in order to plan the presentation of a point of view.

S4: The use of connectives, for example adverbs, adverbial phrases, conjunctions, to structure an argument.

S&L

46 Group discussion and interaction: To identify the main points of each speaker, compare their arguments and how they are presented, for example developing an oral presentation from previous written work and identifying some presentational differences.

What you need

- Photocopiable pages 198 and 199.

Differentiation

Less able

- Ask the children to develop an argument in favour of 'animal rights'. They agree a sequence of key elements, divide these and write a brief paragraph each. They should use one statement against, one in favour and their decision.

More able

- Ask these children to make notes on arguments for and against fox hunting, deciding on the sequence. Taking one side of the argument each, they write a brief summary in support of it and rehearse an oral presentation using their notes as prompts.

Shared text-level work

- Using photocopiable page 198 about fox hunting from the previous hour, ask the children to use their knowledge to help you summarise the key points from the argument for and against.
- Then look at the 'Litter louts' letter on photocopiable page 199 and use the arguments identified in Hour 1 to build-up some key elements for a counter argument.
- Get the children to help you summarise the points for the counter argument regarding litter and to put them into a sequence.
- Then between you and the class use the sequence to create a skeleton letter in the shared sentence-level session.

Shared sentence-level work

- Using the skeleton letter, ask the children to help you write a reply in the form of a writing frame, using suitable connectives as you work.
- Remind the children of the connectives that have already been modelled and used in previous sessions and how they can add to the effectiveness of their writing.

Guided and independent work

- Give the children a copy of the 'Litter louts' letter and ask them to summarise it in their own words. They should write no more than two sentences per paragraph.
- Work with the children to help them summarise the arguments 'for' and 'against' fox hunting. They should sequence the points of view and use connectives. They can work in pairs to do this, one of the pair supporting 'for' and one supporting 'against'. The work from the previous session will help them in their task, as will the shared work from this session.
- Using the skeleton letter as an example, develop counter arguments to the 'Litter louts' letter. Ask the children (in pairs) to write a full letter in reply; they should identify key elements from the skeleton letter and write at least a paragraph each to make a collective response.

Plenary

- Children can make their oral presentations of their arguments 'for' and 'against' fox hunting. They should work in pairs and deliver their speeches 'for' and 'against.'
- Ask the rest of the class to tell you which connectives the pairs have used and whether they think that the sequence of the arguments is in a logical order. Now the whole class can vote on the issue. Which side wins?
- Ask the children who have written letters in response to the litter complaint to read their replies aloud for the class. Remind them to make sure that they sequence their paragraphs in the most effective order. Have they used persuasive language?

Points of view

Objectives

NLS

T16: To read, compare and evaluate examples of arguments and discussions.
T17: How arguments are presented, for example ordering points to link them together so that one follows from another.
S4: The use of connectives e.g adverbs, adverbial phrases, conjunctions, to structure an argument.

What you need

- A teacher-prepared text on climate change (useful websites include www.greenpeace.org.uk/gp_pollution/climate_change.cfm and www.greenphase.com/climatechange.html
- photocopiable page 199.

Shared text- level work

- Collect information on climate change and make an enlarged display sheet. The text should include information on greenhouse gases, climate and fossil fuels.
- Ask the children to help you summarise the key ideas from your text.
- Underline the key ideas and write them down in sequential order.
- Ask for volunteers to come out and, using the key words as a prompt, summarise the key elements listed. You could write these on cards to help them, for example, *greenhouse gases, fossil fuels, climate.*
- Explain that these key elements will act as a prompt for presenting an argument.

Shared sentence-level work

- Using your text from the *Shared text-level* session, ask the children to help you list the connectives used. Underline these and write them on the board.
- Remind them that connectives will help them to order their argument logically and add fluency to the text they write.

Guided and independent work

- Ask the children to read the teacher-prepared text on climate change, isolate the key elements and put them in the correct sequence. Once they have done this, they should write a brief summary in one or two sentences for each paragraph using their own words. Have they all used the same sequence for the key elements? If some are different, ask these children to justify their selection.
- Work with the children and help them to word-process a letter addressed to the Prime Minister voicing their concerns about climate change. They should remember to:

> - agree the key elements of their argument
> - put these in an agreed order
> - think about a sequence of connectives for each paragraph
> - write a paragraph each. Check it then email each paragraph to one computer
> - assemble the letter in the correct order
> - check and correct errors
> - Print it out. Send it!

- Ask the children to look through any of their own writing on fox hunting. They should work in pairs and help each other to look for mis-spelt words. They should collect these words in a spelling bank or log, and learn them using the *Look>Say>Cover>Write>Check* strategy.

Plenary

- Ask the children to give a brief oral presentation of their counter argument on climate change. The children who have made captions in support can then come out and hold up their work to show the case in favour.

Differentiation

Less able

- Work with these children to make a list of key captions from the climate change text. They should put these on cards and put them in logical order.

More able

- Ask these children to write down key elements in defence of the school children accused in the 'Litter louts' letter on photocopiable page 199. They should write key elements first and sequence the elements in a logical order using connectives before writing a response.

School rules

Objectives

NLS

T20: To summarise a sentence or paragraph by identifying the most important elements and rewording them in a limited number of words.

T21: To assemble and sequence points in order to plan the presentation of a point of view.

S4: The use of connectives, for example adverbs, adverbial phrases, conjunctions, to structure an argument.

S&L

46 Group discussion and interaction: To identify the main points of each speaker, compare their arguments and how they are presented, for example developing an oral presentation from previous written work and identifying some presentational differences.

What you need

- Photocopiable pages 198 and 199
- a copy of school or class rules.

Differentiation

Less able

- Read the school rules to the group. As you read these, ask them to think of arguments 'against' school rules. Write these down on separate pieces of paper. Ask the children to agree the order.

More able

- In pairs, ask the children to do the opposite of the modelled sentence-level work. They take one or two elements in favour of school rules and add a third - the decision statement opposing them. Divide the rules equally among the group.

Shared text-level work

- Display an enlarged copy of the school or class rules.
- Ask the children to help you identify the key elements from each rule. Write these down on the board.
- Now tell the children that you are going to write an article in support of school rules.
- Ask the children to help you sequence the key elements in a logical order. This might not be the same order as on the list.
- Ask them to help you write an opening statement in support of school rules. For example, *School rules are important because...*

Shared sentence-level work

- Remind the children about the three boxes they used to collect arguments 'for' and 'against' fox hunting. Have they used them to support their argument?
- Draw three boxes on the board - one for school rules, one against school rules, one for the decision.
- Model an example of how you would use these statements. For example, two statements for and against, the third your decision in favour.

Guided and independent work

- Ask the children to summarise the key points in favour of school rules and using the three box approach, make arguments to support school rules. They should take one or two key elements each. Help them create counter arguments to use in sentence one or two before adding a decision sentence in favour.
- Ask the children to generate a writing frame to use in support of the argument for school rules. They use the key elements as a prompt and write the first few words after the sentence following that connective. They can use the collection of connectives on the chart to help them.
- Help the children, in pairs, to make a formal presentation to the class on *School uniform is unnecessary in the 21st century*. One of each pair will be 'for' and one 'against'. Before splitting into pairs they should discuss and agree their key points and put them in the order they wish to present them. Then each pair takes their chosen key points 'for' and 'against' and prepares a written statement. Remind them that how they speak and phrase their arguments is important. These will be presented in the plenary.

Plenary

- The great school uniform debate! Ask the group who prepared the presentation to come and deliver it to the class in the agreed sequence. The class then discuss the issues and give their opinion on the style and delivery of each side's presentation. Ask the class to vote.

Making a case

Objectives

NLS

T23: To present a point of view in writing, for example in the form of a letter, a report or a script, linking points persuasively and selecting style and vocabulary appropriate to the reader.

S4: The use of connectives, for example adverbs, adverbial phrases, conjunctions, to structure an argument.

What you need

- An opening statement and an introduction for an article in support of opening a school sweet and snack bar to raise money for a new digital projector.

Shared text- and sentence-level work

- Display an enlarged photocopy of your opening statement and introduction to the article about the school sweet and snack bar.
- Ask the children to think about the advantages of having the sweet and snack bar and to help you write down key elements in support of this.
- Invite them to help you to put these in a logical order.
- Now ask them to think of key elements to counter the argument and sequence these. What might the disadvantages of the sweet and snack bar be?
- You are going to model writing a paragraph using boxes 'for' and 'against'. Remind the children that you want to present all the information to show that you are well informed, so you want to put the two opposing arguments in two paragraphs first, and then add a decision paragraph that is in favour.
- Remind them about the use of good connectives as you write, to make the arguments flow effectively.

Guided and independent work

- Ask the children to write a letter to the school's Chair of Governors in support of the sweet and snack bar. Remind them that they must use a logical sequence, good connectives and vocabulary that suits the task.
- Remind them to use the three-sentence approach practised in the shared work where possible.
- Work with the children to write a letter opposed to the opening of a sweet and snack bar. Help them collect their thoughts on 'for' and 'against' boxes and to use the three-sentence approach, for example, two in favour followed by a decision statement 'against'.

Plenary

- Select examples from each group's work on the sweet and snack bar and discuss their statement sequence and use of connectives.
- Which group presented their arguments most effectively? Which group would they vote for?
- Ask the children in the class to pretend that they are parents and governors of the school and select a child to be Chair of Governors. The children who have been writing about school uniform should present their arguments 'for' and 'against' wearing it.
- The child playing the role of Chair of Governors must run and control the meeting. After the arguments have been presented, the Chair invites comments from the parents and school governors.
- When the parents and governors have expressed their opinions, a vote should be held by a show of hands. If there is a draw, the Chair has the casting vote.

Differentiation

Less able

- Help this group to write captions against the opening of a sweet and snack bar using the writing frame below as a starting point, adding their statement after each phrase. They can add a picture if they wish.
If... Then... On the other hand... But... So... Finally...

More able

- Ask half the group to write a letter to the School Governors in support of school uniform. The other half write a letter 'against'. Remind them to collect their statements in boxes 'for' and 'against' and to use the three-sentence approach to select connectives to present their arguments.

Fox hunting 'for' and 'against'

Argument 'For'
Fox hunting has been a necessary countryside activity since the fifteenth century.

If you think fox hunting is cruel you should know the following facts. Firstly, foxes kill 2% of all new born lambs, this can cost farmers about £1000 per year in lost income. It is likely that this number will increase now fox hunting is banned. As a result, farmers will lose more and more income. Furthermore, the number of foxes will increase year on year, quite dramatically.

Secondly, there is the impact on the rural community. Now fox hunting is banned, many people who live in the countryside will lose their livelihoods. In addition, many innocent foxhounds will have to be destroyed because there will be no use for them. Finally, fox hunting is a kinder way of controlling foxes than any of the alternatives such as gassing or trapping.

Argument 'Against'
Every year some 16,000 foxes are hunted and killed by foxhounds. First of all, I would like to say that the majority of people in this country are in favour of a ban. So, in a democratic society the will of the majority shouldn't be ignored. Furthermore, vets have proved that foxes do not die instantly when they are attacked by hounds. And in addition, studies of foxes have shown that long chases and being hunted down cause terrible distress for the fox. Furthermore, the argument that foxes kill newborn lambs and deprive farmers of income is nonsense. It is a well-known fact that some lambs are too weak to survive. So, foxes are doing farmers a favour by removing them. Finally, I should like to say that there are other methods of controlling the fox population, such as gassing, shooting or trapping.

The number of foxes will increase now fox hunting is banned, so farmers will lose more lambs. We will have less meat to eat. Hunting is not as cruel as shooting or trapping. These methods will mean an even more painful death for the fox. Lots of people will lose their jobs. Hunting is a way of life in the countryside. Therefore, fox hunting is the best method of controlling the fox population.

By Campbell Perry

Non fiction Unit 1 Phase 2

Litter louts

Dear Sir

I live in one of the houses across from the school. As a long-time resident, I had worries about the building of a new school and I have to say my worries have been confirmed.

Since the school was opened five years ago, I have noticed a tremendous increase in the amount of litter in the streets. Furthermore, most of the litter is crisp packets and sweet papers. This fact leads me to conclude that your pupils are responsible. The streets are full of shouting and screaming kids every morning and afternoon. I know that they are always in the shop before and after school, buying sweets and crisps.

In addition, I have to say that I have seen children dropping litter in the street and I am sure that they go to your school. Almost certainly the blame lies with your pupils and although there is a new youth club in the estate, I am sure these young people are not responsible. After all, these children only go there in the evenings and my son, who attends the club, is sure that neither he nor his friends are littering the streets.

Finally I have to ask you to do something about this state of affairs. You must punish the children responsible and send children out at lunchtime and playtime, with a supervisor, to collect up the litter they have dropped.

Consequently, I expect an apology from every child in your school and an undertaking that you will not allow children to bring sweets and crisps into school.

Yours faithfully

Mr R.U.B. Bish (a neighbour)

Non fiction Unit 1 Phase 2

UNIT 6

Persuasion

This unit concentrates on the use of persuasive language and advertisements. The children will encounter linguistic devices such as jingles, poems, alliteration and sentence compositions; all of which are designed to persuade either the reader or the audience to believe what is being said to them. The unit bases much of the work on Unit 31 of *Grammar for Writing* to give children opportunities to arrange and rearrange sentence statements into questions and imperatives.

Hour	Shared text-level work	Shared sentence-/ word-level work	Guided work	Independent work	Plenary
1 Persuasive letter	Looking for key words, phrases and vocabulary in persuasive text.	Looking at word order. Converting statements to questions, use of tense, nouns, verbs.	Re-ordering words in a sentence into questions.	Writing a persuasive letter.	Sharing the persuasive letters and discussing use of language.
2 Persuasive language	Experimenting with persuasive language styles.	Changing positive statements into negative ones.	Writing a concise website home page letter/ advertisement.	Using diminutives, changing positive statements to negative ones.	Discussing the use of persuasive language in advertisements.
3 Adverts with impact	The language of advertisements, linguistic devices.	Changing statements to imperatives.	Designing an advertisement for a magazine using linguistic devices.	Changing statements to imperatives.	Discussing the advertisements' design, looking at the use of language and the use of imperatives.
4 Compose a jingle	Comparing sound advertisements, 'jingles', and visual advertisements in terms of language used.	Using *Why? Where? When? What? Who?* in sentences that are turned into questions.	Using positive and negative statements or imperatives in an advertisement.	Composing a radio jingle or TV advertisement.	Listen to the jingle, looking at the designed advertisments and discussing the use of persuasive language in each.
5 Promote a school event	Looking for linguistic impact in a variety of advertisements.	Looking for the use of statements, imperatives and questions in advertisements.	Writing a commissioned advertisement using a writer's brief for a school event.	As before, writing a commissioned advertisement using a writer's brief for a school event.	A review of examples. Ask children to talk about what they choose and why they used particular linguistic devices.

Key assessment opportunities

- Can the children recognise the use of linguistic devices, vocabulary and phrases used in persuasive language?
- Are they able to create their own advertisements to demonstrate their knowledge of persuasive techniques?
- Can they order and re-order sentence statements into questions and imperatives?

Persuasive letter

Objectives

NLS

T18: From examples of persuasive writing, to investigate how style and vocabulary are used to convince the intended reader.

S3: To understand how the grammar of a sentence alters when the sentence type is altered.

What you need

- A collection of advertisements and letters of persuasion
- photocopiable page 206 (enlarged).

Shared text-level work

- Using photocopiable page 206 (enlarged), explain to the class that this is a typical example of 'scam' emails sent to persuade people to part with money.
- Read the extract and ask the children to listen for persuasive vocabulary, phrases or styles of writing.
- Read it again, and with the children's help, highlight the persuasive language and note these on the board.

Shared sentence-level work

- Explain that the grammar of a sentence alters when the sentence type is changed. A sentence that is a statement can be made positive or negative, a question or an order. Changing the order of words, tenses of verbs, adding or removing words, or changing punctuation can achieve this.
- Use this sentence as an example, *Mrs Booth is going to the shops.* Give children a word each on separate pieces of card and give one child a full stop.
- Ask them to arrange themselves to give the sentence meaning. Point out that 'going' is the main verb and 'is' is an auxiliary verb.
- Now give another child a question mark. Ask the class to re-order the words into a question.
- Now try this with a change of tense, *Mrs Booth has been to the shops.* Explain that *has* is the auxiliary verb and *been* is the main verb – both in the past tense.
- Discuss which types of sentence can be re-ordered into a question without using any other words. Ask for examples.

Guided and independent work

- In pairs, ask each child to write a maximum of ten sentence statements using a main verb, an auxiliary verb and the present tense. They then exchange their sentences and try to change their partner's statements into questions, re-ordering the same words.
- Give the children the following information and ask them to write a persuasive letter:

> - You are desperate to go to the school disco on Friday night
> - Mum and Dad want you to go with them to visit friends for the evening
> - You do not get on with the friends' children
> - A school friend's parents have offered to take you to the disco, collect you and allow you to stay the night
> - What can you write to persuade your parents? Should you mention the relationship you have with the friends' children?

Plenary

- Ask the children to share some of their persuasive letters with the class. Can the class spot the use of persuasive language in the letters?

Differentiation

Less able

- Ask the children to make simple sentence statements using the present tense, a main verb and auxiliary verb. Cut each sentence into separate words and a full stop. Jumble these up and ask the children to stand with a word each and order themselves.

More able

- In pairs, ask the children to write ten statements each for their partner, using a main verb, an auxiliary verb and a range of tenses. They then swap sentences, re-ordering exactly the same words into questions.

Persuasive language

Objectives

NLS

T18: From examples of persuasive writing, to investigate how style and vocabulary are used to convince the intended reader.

S3: To understand how the grammar of a sentence alters when the sentence type is altered.

W12: To understand how diminutives are formed.

What you need

- Photocopiable pages 206 and 207.

Shared text-level work

- Using photocopiable page 206, discuss with the children in detail the key words, vocabulary and word order that the writer has used. For example, the letter starts respectfully with *Dear Sir/ Madam.*
- Now show them an enlarged copy of the short mobile phone advertisement (photocopiable page 207), which could be on a website homepage.
- Discuss the differences in the two styles and the use of language: one over-written and the other with much economy of style.

Shared sentence-level work

- Using the example sentence from Hour 1, *Mrs Booth is going to the shops*, remind the children about the key facts when we re-order words.
- Ask the children who re-ordered their statements in Hour 1 to come out and stand with their separate words for the sentence and show the correct order. Now give a child the question mark card and ask him/her to re-order sentences into questions, with advice from the class.
- Using examples from children who re-ordered statements into sentences using different tenses, and sometimes only a main verb, to share their examples with the class. This will help remind everyone about key facts in re-ordering.
- Using the example, *Mrs Booth is going to the shops*, change the positive to negative, *is not going*. Explain what happens when you use only a main verb. The same conventions apply when you have to add words, *Mrs Booth goes to the shops* has to have the addition of *does* and *not*.

Guided and independent work

- Ask the children to write a persuasive letter to advertise something on a website homepage or in a magazine. They can use a maximum of 50 words.
- Work with the children and ask them to pair-up and for each child to write ten positive statements using either a main verb or a main and auxiliary in each one. They should exchange sentences with their partner and change their partner's statements from positive to negative.
- Ask the children to work in pairs to collect diminutives using:

Group 1 – suffixes such as *-ette* – *ladette*
Group 2 – a prefix such as *mini-* – *mini-mart*
Group 3 – an adjective such as *little* – *little horrors*
Group 4 – a noun such as *pig* – *piglet*
Group 5 – a nickname such as *Darren* – *Daz.*

Differentiation

Less able

- Work with these children to produce an 'oral' advertisement for an object in the classroom. Guide them in the use of words and economy of style, using the mobile phone example.

More able

- Ask the children to create imperatives from statements. Give them the examples, *Mrs Booth is going to the library.* (*statement*) *Go to the library!*(*imperative*). Explain that an imperative always begins with the verb in the present tense, for example, *Come and play, Mind the doors, Go to bed.*

Plenary

- Ask the children to share their persuasive letters for a website homepage.
- Ask the children to share their oral advertisements. Discuss the use of persuasive language.

Adverts with impact

Objectives

NLS

T19: To evaluate advertisements for their impact, appeal and honesty, focusing in particular on how information about the product is presented: exaggerated claims, techniques for grabbing attention, linguistic devices such as puns, jingles, alliteration, invented words.

S3: To understand how the grammar of a sentence alters when the sentence type is altered.

What you need

- Two examples of food advertisements from newspapers or magazines, for example for a type of ice cream. These should include persuasive language, imperatives, alliteration and a play on words.

Differentiation

Less able

- Ask this group, as a whole or in pairs, to create an advertisement for a favourite sport, hobby or leisure activity. Their advertisements should have an imperative and alliteration included in the text.

More able

- Ask this group to create an advertisement in pictures and words about a new style of trainers. Their advertisement should include alliteration, imperatives and, if possible, a pun.

Shared text-level work

- Display an example of a newspaper or magazine advertisement for food. Discuss with the class the language of the advertisement. Is it persuasive? Is it honest? What techniques does it use to get its message across? (Perhaps *alliteration, a pun, imperatives.*) Collect the words and phrases on the board.
- Ask for a volunteer from the class to help you play the 'imperatives game'. Give the volunteer a statement, for example, *I would like you to put your hand on your head.* The volunteer picks a child in the class and turns the statement into an imperative, for example, *Put your hand on your head!* If the volunteer gets the imperative right and the child in the class also thinks that it is correct, the child then obeys the command. This is a variation on 'Simon Says', and could equally be played with the whole class.

Shared sentence-level work

- Start by using advertisements that contain imperatives and some examples of imperatives written by the more able group in Hour 2. Tell the children that imperatives are always in the present tense, they are the same whether they are singular or plural and they only use a main verb at the beginning of the sentence.
- Ask the children to offer examples of imperatives.

Guided and independent work

- Ask the children to work in pairs. Each of the pairs should write up to ten statements. When they have finished they can swap their statements with their partners and see if they can turn each of the statements into imperatives.
- Using the example of a food advertisement from the shared text-level session, ask the children to design, in pictures and words, an advertisement of their own for a food they enjoy eating. They should include alliteration, a pun (if possible) and one or two imperatives.

Plenary

- In this session remind the children about the techniques of advertising. They are going to look at advertisements that have been created by children in the class. Ask them to look out for any persuasive language used.
- Ask some of the children to display their advertisements for the rest of the class and to stand up and talk about the techniques that they used (*alliteration, puns, imperatives*). Can the other children pick out these techniques, and how effectively do they think they have been used?
- Ask children to come out to the front and play the variation on 'Simon Says' with the class, and explain how they converted statements to imperatives. The class only do what they are commanded if they think that the imperative they are being given is written and spoken correctly.

Compose a jingle

Objectives

NLS
T19: To evaluate advertisements for their impact.
S3: To understand how the grammar of a sentence alters when the sentence type is altered.

What you need

- Advertisements selected by you or the class to demonstrate use of language, exaggerated claims and so on
- examples of children's advertisements from Hour 3; radio jingles; TV advertisements
- two advertisements advertising the same product but to a different target audience, for example, mobile phone advertisements.

Differentiation

Less able
- Compare the two advertisements from the shared session. In two groups, ask the children to decide on a product. Each group designs the same advertisement but for different target age ranges: one at young people, the other at people of their parents' age.

More able
- Ask the group to decide on a product, then split the group into two. Group 1 design an advertisement using visual images, questions, statements, alliteration, etc which are persuasive; Group 2 create a radio advertisement – they only have the power of persuasive language. How does their advertisement vary from Group 1's?

Shared text-level work

- Using a selection of advertisements which cover key points, such as exaggerated claims, linguistic devices and invented words, discuss with the class how these advertisements target different ages and types of consumer. Look at the two advertisements and compare them.
- Listen to a radio jingle and ask the children why radio stations use them – look for answers that concentrate on the power of language, rhyme and music, when there is no visual stimulus.

Shared sentence-level work

- Using *Why? Who? Where? When? What?* put a different *wh* on each finger of your hand (or give out cards with each of these words written on). Then ask a question, such as: *Does your cat scratch fleas?*
- Ask the children to offer ideas for adding wh words at the beginning of the questions. Discuss what they have to do with the words in order to retain the sense of the question:

> - Why does your cat scratch fleas?
> - When does your cat scratch fleas?
> - Where does your cat scratch fleas?
> - Who does your cat scratch fleas?
> - What does your cat scratch fleas?
> - (Note what happens with 'who' and 'what'.)

- Now ask if they can add a *persuasive* statement after each question and then an imperative:

> - Question – Why does your cat scratch fleas?
> - Statement – Flea-free cats purr all day.
> - Imperative – Give your cat 'Flea away'!

Guided and independent work

- Ask the children to compose a jingle they can sing to the class advertising a favourite radio station or television programme.
- Work with the children to create an advertisement that uses: *a question – a positive statement – an imperative*. These should accompany a visual image.
- Give the children a selection of questions similar to the example in *Shared sentence-level work*. (*Does your cat scratch fleas?*) Ask them to put *Why* in front of the questions and to then add a statement followed by an imperative, as in the above example, *Flea-free cats... ; Give your cat...* .

Plenary

- Listen to some of the jingles the children have created and discuss use of language and rhyme. Discuss the impact of this on the listener.
- Look at some examples of advertisements that use question – statement – imperative in their blurb.

Promote a school event

Objectives

NLS

T25: To design an advertisement, such as a poster or radio jingle on paper or screen for example, for a school fete or an imaginary product, making use of linguistic and other features learned from reading examples.

S4: The use of connectives eg. adverbs, adverbial phrases, conjunctions, to structure an argument.

W15: To use a range of presentational skills.

What you need

- Children's collection of favourite advertisements and one from the teacher/ teachings assistant. Ensure different types of advertisement - jingle, posters (or newspaper), television.

Differentiation

Less able

- Work with this group to generate persuasive captions for this school event on the computer. They can experiment with four styles and sizes to make their captions look attractive and grab attention.

More able

- Ask this group to generate a short television advert. If you have cameras that link into your computer system, or to and from a digital projector, the group can combine moving and still images for the advertisement.

Shared text-level work

- Bring one example of each type of collected advertisement. Choose children or the teaching assistant to justify their choice in terms of linguistic impact, style, use of devices, and discuss them (imperatives, statement, question and so on).
- Ensure that you bring the following presentational skills used in advertisements to the children's notice. Tell them that unless an advertisement is presented skilfully, it will lose its impact, no matter how clever it may be in its creation.

> - Always print scripts for captions, sub-headings and labels
> - Use capital letters for posters and headings
> - Use a range of computer-generated fonts and point sizes, if creating an advertisement using ICT.

Shared sentence-level work

- Explain that advertisements can be made even more persuasive by using connectives to structure the argument, for example, by using some of the following – *if, then, on the other hand, so, finally*.
- Display the following example: You should remember to brush your teeth every day. They will get dull and yellow if don't and your breath might smell bad. You should use this toothpaste. It is called Ultratect and we make it. Explain that all the essential information is there, but ask if it grabs the reader's attention?
- Now display this example: If you want bad breath and dull, yellow teeth, don't brush them! On the other hand, you may want the confidence of all day protection. Use ULTRATECT! Then you can smile with confidence. So brush your teeth with ULTRATECT! Discuss the difference. Which one has the most impact?
- Ask the children to suggest more statements. Then see if they can use good connectives, as in the second example, to sharpen these up.
- Remind them to use this technique in their own blurbs.

Guided and independent work

- Each group will be given the same 'commission' and writing brief for the same product. Commission the class to devise and design an advertisement for a forthcoming school event. The method used in the advertising campaign will vary but the message will be the same.
- Ask one group to produce a poster advertising the event. It can be hand-designed or computer-generated.
- Ask another group to produce a radio jingle to advertise the event. The jingle can be preceded by some spoken persuasion.

Plenary

- This is an opportunity to share and discuss examples of each other's work and how the groups have used various techniques to persuade their audience.

Scam email

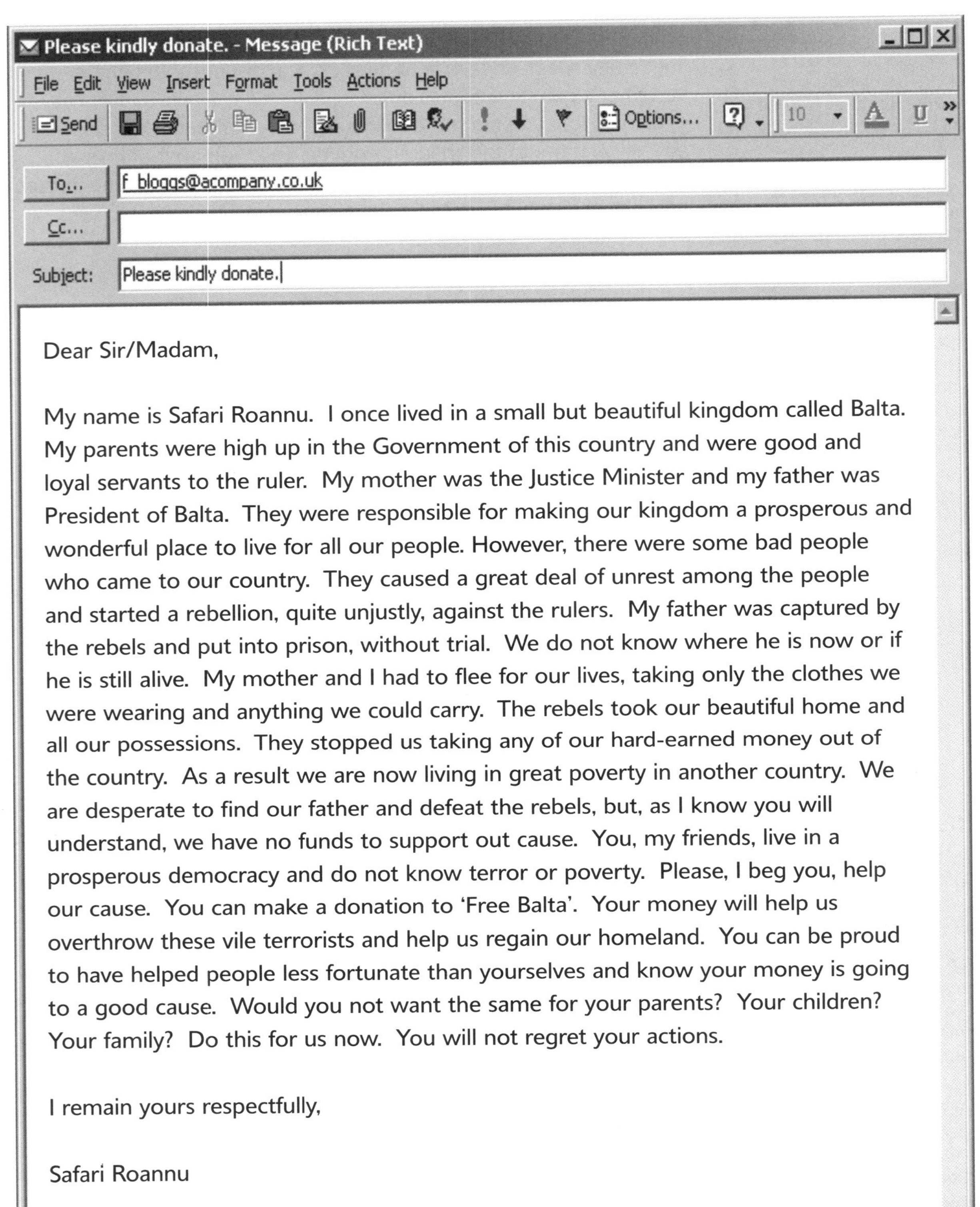

Dear Sir/Madam,

My name is Safari Roannu. I once lived in a small but beautiful kingdom called Balta. My parents were high up in the Government of this country and were good and loyal servants to the ruler. My mother was the Justice Minister and my father was President of Balta. They were responsible for making our kingdom a prosperous and wonderful place to live for all our people. However, there were some bad people who came to our country. They caused a great deal of unrest among the people and started a rebellion, quite unjustly, against the rulers. My father was captured by the rebels and put into prison, without trial. We do not know where he is now or if he is still alive. My mother and I had to flee for our lives, taking only the clothes we were wearing and anything we could carry. The rebels took our beautiful home and all our possessions. They stopped us taking any of our hard-earned money out of the country. As a result we are now living in great poverty in another country. We are desperate to find our father and defeat the rebels, but, as I know you will understand, we have no funds to support out cause. You, my friends, live in a prosperous democracy and do not know terror or poverty. Please, I beg you, help our cause. You can make a donation to 'Free Balta'. Your money will help us overthrow these vile terrorists and help us regain our homeland. You can be proud to have helped people less fortunate than yourselves and know your money is going to a good cause. Would you not want the same for your parents? Your children? Your family? Do this for us now. You will not regret your actions.

I remain yours respectfully,

Safari Roannu

Mobiles Calling!

SCHOLASTIC

In this series:

ISBN 0-439-97164-0
ISBN 978-0439-97164-5

ISBN 0-439-97165-9
ISBN 978-0439-97165-2

ISBN 0-439-97166-7
ISBN 978-0439-97166-9

ISBN 0-439-97167-5
ISBN 978-0439-97167-6

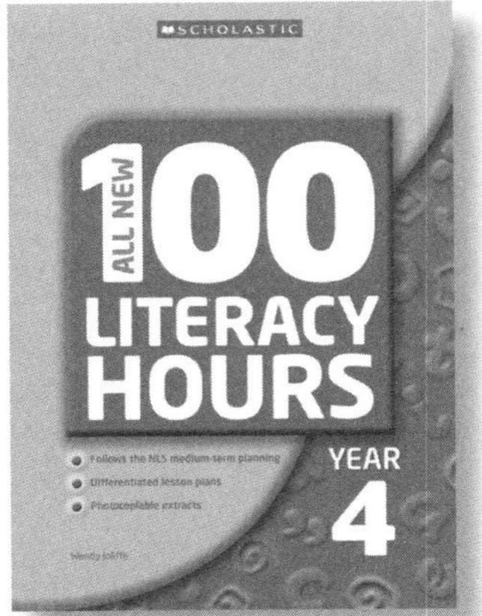

ISBN 0-439-97168-3
ISBN 978-0439-97168-3

ISBN 0-439-97169-1
ISBN 978-0439-97169-0

ISBN 0-439-97170-5
ISBN 978-0439-97170-6

To find out more, call: 0845 603 9091
or visit our website www.scholastic.co.uk